THE LEGAL CONTEXT
OF SOCIAL WORK

BY

J. D. McCLEAN, B.C.L., M.A.

of Gray's Inn, Barrister
Professor of Law in the University
of Sheffield

LONDON
BUTTERWORTHS
1975

ENGLAND: BUTTERWORTH & CO. (PUBLISHERS) LTD.
London: 88 Kingsway, WC2B 6AB

AUSTRALIA: BUTTERWORTHS PTY. LTD.
Sydney: 586 Pacific Highway, Chatswood, NSW 2067
Melbourne: 343 Little Collins Street, 3000
Brisbane: 240 Queen Street, 4000

CANADA: BUTTERWORTH & CO. (CANADA) LTD.
Toronto: 2265 Midland Avenue, Scarborough
M1P 4S1

NEW ZEALAND: BUTTERWORTHS OF NEW ZEALAND LTD.
Wellington: 26–28 Waring Taylor Street, 1

SOUTH AFRICA: BUTTERWORTH & CO. (SOUTH AFRICA) (PTY.)
LTD.
Durban: 152–154 Gale Street

ISBN Casebound: 0 406 62121 7
Limp: 0 406 62122 5

727938
6000801639

PREFACE

There is a growing awareness of the relevance and significance of the legal context in which social workers use their professional skills. This has been stimulated by changes in patterns of social work, by the re-organisation of many social work agencies, and, not least, by the rapid growth in the volume of social legislation which affects the social worker and his client. The needs of the practising social worker must be reflected in the education of social work students, and the first curriculum study commissioned by the Central Council for Education and Training in Social Work was entitled *Legal Studies in Social Work Education*. I was fortunate enough to be a member of the Study Group charged with preparing that report, published in August 1974.

The report identified a number of components in a basic programme of legal studies for social work students. These include areas of law, such as housing law, on which clients may seek advice; information about the legal system and the administration of law; and wider questions as to the role of law in society. But central to the whole exercise is "professional law", the law which empowers the social worker to act, and which sets limits to and provides guidelines for much of his work. Although this book was first planned before the C.C.E.T.S.W. group was established, it will, I hope, meet the need for a short but readable textbook on this crucial area, the professional law of social workers. In particular, it examines aspects of child care law, adoption law and practice, the mental health legislation, and the role of the social worker in his professional dealings with the courts. I have resisted the temptation to go beyond this area; within it I have not avoided technical legal difficulties where they are of practical importance and I have tried to indicate, so far as a mere lawyer can, some of the implications for social work practice. I have tried to reveal something of the attitudes and assumptions of lawyers, and this may provide teachers with a starting-point for a discussion of the role of law and of lawyers.

I have provided in footnotes the usual apparatus of legal references, for I hope that some lawyers, whether in private practice, local authorities, the courts or in universities and colleges, will find this a helpful introduction to an area in which they are increasingly asked to advise, but which is neglected in legal education.

The text was completed in September 1974, but some more recent developments have been noted. In particular the Children Bill, which appeared in December 1974 and will, if it becomes law, implement many of the recommendations of the Departmental Committee on the Adoption of Children and make other related changes in the law, is summarised in an Appendix.

There can be few books as short as this which have had so many contributors. It grew out of my teaching in the University of Sheffield and I acknowledge my indebtedness to past and present colleagues in the Faculties of Law and of Social Sciences and in the Sheffield Social Services Department who have shared in that teaching at various times. A similar debt of thanks is due to my friends on the C.C.E.T.S.W. study group, whose wisdom and practical commonsense helped me much; and to several generations of students (many of whom had an awesome amount of professional experience) who taught me with kindly tolerance as I explored unfamiliar legal territory. To all those who have helped in producing this book, my grateful thanks. The mistakes are all my own work.

Sheffield   DAVID MCCLEAN
February 1975

CONTENTS

Chapter 1

SOCIAL WORKERS AND LAWYERS

In 1967, the American Bar Foundation conducted an intriguing experiment amongst lawyers and social workers who were working together in the Chicago Legal Aid Bureau. The object of the exercise was to discover what image the two professional groups had of their own and of the other group. The participants were asked to score the two groups on an attitude scale with matched pairs of adjectives such as "rigid–flexible" and "cautious–reckless".

The lawyers were seen by both groups as assertive, intelligent, articulate, responsible, professional, practical and confident; the social workers, again by both groups, as honest, sympathetic, sensitive, concerned, responsible, intelligent and thoughtful. These gratifying findings contain one slightly sour note: the social workers rated lawyers almost as highly as themselves, but lawyers proved sadly ungenerous in their overall rating of social workers.[1]

These findings could provide an excuse for much speculation, but the most important point about the study is the very fact that it took place at all. Not many decades ago, social workers and lawyers would never be found working side by side; indeed they would have very few points of contact. Their clienteles were, literally, streets apart. The growing together of the two professions has been a striking feature of recent years.

It is always tempting to suppose that developments are of more recent origin than is actually the case. On the legal side the search for ways of providing legal services available at a reasonable charge in every locality is not new: the county court system was established in 1846 with just these objectives in mind, though the beneficiaries were local businessmen rather than their working-class customers. Similarly the origins of Legal Aid, free or subsidised legal services for the indigent,

---

[1] A. D. Smith and B. A. Curren, *A Study of the Lawyer–Social Worker Professional Relationship* (American Bar Foundation 1968).

can be traced back even further than the Poor Prisoners' Defence Act of 1903.

The rapid development of official legal aid and advice facilities in more recent years, and of unofficial advisory centres in some areas, has brought to the lawyers a new sort of client with a new range of problems. Increased State activity has spawned a whole new area of administrative law with its attendant regulations and tribunals. Subjects like Poverty Law and Welfare Rights have appeared in curricula for law students.

Social workers have been caught up in a similar development. Concern for the whole situation in which a client finds himself leads to a growing awareness of the uses of law and of legal agencies. The financial problems of a deserted wife and the housing problems of tenants may well have legal remedies. Even the most radical types of community work, which may sometimes involve extra-legal battles with bureaucrats and others, and resort to self-help such as squatting, must also use the law and legal machinery to protect rights in appropriate cases.

Most important of all has been the development and elaboration of legal rules directed specifically at the social worker, spelling out the powers and duties he possesses and prescribing the conditions and procedures for certain types of intervention. This, the professional law of social workers, is the subject-matter of this book. Not only is this body of law of growing complexity, but it also affects a growing number of social workers as the profession increases in size and its "generic" pattern becomes established. All this must bring a greater awareness of the legal context of much social work, and increasing contacts between social workers and members of the legal profession.

DIFFERING ATTITUDES

Increasing contacts do not necessarily produce greater mutual understanding; they can lead instead to feelings of irritation that the other professional group does not share the same assumptions, attitudes and concerns. It is certainly the case that social workers and lawyers come to a situation with different professional approaches. They will see the same set of facts in different terms, and ask themselves different questions about it.

There are many types of lawyer: the academic view is not necessarily that of the practising solicitor; the "common law" man (whose daily work concerns accidents at work, and contract disputes) has a subtly different mind from his conveyancer colleague; working environment and political opinions exert their influence. Similarly, of course, there are many differences of emphasis within the social work profession, and varying "schools" of social work. If a generalisation can be risked, the lawyer can be said to think more in terms of rights, duties and remedies; the social worker of needs and relationships.

An illustration is provided by this extract from an introductory book for intending social work students,[1] describing part of the daily work of a psychiatric social worker:

"The doctor wanted to meet me at the home of Mr G. Mrs G had called him to see her husband who was acting very strangely: he had not been at work for a week, spent most of the day pacing up and down the garden talking to imaginary people. On two occasions he had been violent with her in the night. The doctor thought it sounded as if admission to a mental hospital would be required and he would be glad of my opinion. . . . Mr G seemed very wild and distraught. The doctor said he should go to hospital. I telephoned for the ambulance. Helped Mrs G to get Mr G ready. I had to spend quite a lot of time explaining to her what would happen and outline to Mr G what would occur within the next few hours. He was at first very resistant to the idea of going into a mental hospital, but as I talked quietly with him he calmed down. The fact that his wife would be coming in the ambulance with him seemed to reassure him."

The social worker will see in that account many things: the needs of Mr G for treatment, but also information and reassurance; the importance of the relationship between Mr G and his wife; the differing contributions to the resolution of the situation of the doctor and the social worker. The lawyer, reading the same account, is itching to ask what is actually happening: is this a voluntary admission of an informal patient or is use being made of the compulsory procedures under the Mental Health Act 1959? It could be either; we are not told, and the lawyer wants to know.

He will no doubt be told (quite rightly) that in this practical situation, the last thing the patient should be bothered with is an account of that alarming piece of legislation. The social worker seeing a difficult situation focusses on the needs of those concerned, their relationships one to another, and works to resolve the problem. What has the law got to do with it?

One answer—and the question could be answered at many levels— is to say that the lawyer, while one hopes he would be sensitive to the needs of all those involved, uses his professional training to examine the rights and duties of the parties by applying to this particular set of facts the general rules and principles of the relevant body of law. He would analyse the situation at a particular moment in time in some such terms as these. If a man wants to talk to imaginary people in his back garden instead of going to work he has a perfect right to do so (though he cannot complain if his employer objects). Equally, if a man is mentally disordered, the law gives other people the right, and some other people the duty, to ensure that he receives proper treatment, even against his will. This intrusion upon his private rights is hedged about by safeguards and conditions; the lawyer will look closely

---

[1] N. Timms, *Social Work*, pp. 28–9.

to see that they are observed. If they are not, and a man's rights are improperly infringed, the law will provide some remedy, some procedure for protecting the rights or obtaining compensation for the wrong done.

There is an element of caricature in this description of a lawyer's attitude. He is not so blinkered, or so pessimistic, that he spends his day applying legal rules to ordinary situations: he buys his can of baked beans without meditating upon the Supply of Goods (Implied Terms) Act and the various procedures in the courts or the local authority offices which could be invoked if the baked beans were contaminated by some foreign matter. But if such a calamity overtakes him, the framework of legal rules will provide an answer.

Social work, in everyday practice, can at any moment produce the difficulty, the conflict, the man who unexpectedly "stands up for his rights". The mentally disordered man, or his wife, unexpectedly refuses to cooperate. The foster-parent refuses admission to the visiting social worker, or announces that she is going to keep the child. To know the rights and wrongs of the situation, in legal terms, is as much a part of the social worker's equipment as are his powers of reasoned persuasion.

LAW AS A BLUNT INSTRUMENT

Lawyers, like other professionals, are tempted to overstate the importance of their own specialism. Constitutional lawyers like to quote the saying that Parliament through the law can do anything except make a woman a man or a man a woman;[1] and some even deny that qualification, for Parliament could give a woman the legal rights and duties of a man.[2] The truth is that there are many things that the law cannot do, and in which the skills of the social worker stand more or less alone.

An obvious example is in marriage guidance work. A marriage becomes unhappy; the husband and wife are living together but the relationship is stormy, perhaps violent, and there are arguments about money and how the children should be brought up. In that immediate situation the law has little to contribute. In its general approach it reflects social policy as to marriage and divorce, but that merely provides a background to the present troubles. If the difficulties in the marriage reach a certain level of gravity, if for example the wife leaves home or the husband refuses to maintain her or the children, then legal machinery and remedies are provided; the domestic jurisdiction of the magistrates' court is available. Yet in the type of case described there is nothing for the court to do: the law can protect a wife's right to maintenance but not her hope and expectation of a reasonably happy

---

[1] De Lolme, *Constitution of England* (1770).
[2] See Hood Phillips, *Constitutional Law* (2nd Edn 1957), p. 23.

marriage. No one would want to hasten the parties to the court-house; all would rather seek to achieve a reconciliation and greater understanding.

The law can protect an individual from certain types of injury, loss and hardship, provided the individual concerned can and will operate the legal machinery; but the law cannot give happiness, prosperity or health except by establishing agencies which can employ people to make their own contribution to the well-being of others.

LAW AS REPRESSION

It has to be admitted that some social workers have an almost instinctive revulsion to the idea of law, which naturally hinders pro-ductive dialogue with lawyers. What seems to happen is that these social workers emphasise one particular facet of law and its function, and lawyers another.

One observer will highlight the repressive function of law. Weber wrote that "an order will be called law if it is externally guaranteed by the probability that coercion (physical or psychological), to bring about conformity or avenge violation, will be applied by a staff of people holding themselves specially ready for that purpose".[1] Similarly, an official Soviet definition of law is "a set of rules for social relation-ships, which corresponds to the interests of the dominant class and is safeguarded by the organised force of that class".[2] Law is thus seen as an expression, or even *the* expression, of governmental power; though it follows that in a revolutionary situation it will become a vehicle for the revolutionary will.

Some lawyers will perhaps share that view, but most will be much happier, paradoxically, with the views of Karl Marx, at least with the views he expressed as a young man in 1842:[3]

> "Legally recognised freedom exists in the state as law. Laws are as little repressive measures directed against freedom as the law of gravity is a repressive measure directed against movement because although it keeps the heavenly bodies in perpetual motion yet it can also kill me if I wish to violate it and dance in the air. Laws are rather positive, bright and general norms in which freedom has attained to an existence that is impersonal, theoretical, and independent of the arbitrariness of individuals. A people's statute book is its Bible of freedom."

So the lawyer tends to speak of "the Rule of Law"—to which govern-ments must be subject as are the governed, of "freedom under the law",

[1] *Max Weber on Law in Economy and Society* (translated by Shils and Rheinstein) (Har-vard 1954), p. 5.
[2] Decree of the People's Commissariat of Justice of December 12th 1919; see *Soviet Legal Philosophy* (Harvard 1951).
[3] Article in *Rheinische Zeitung*, May 1842; see McLellan, *Karl Marx, Early Texts* (Blackwell 1971), p. 36.

and of law as guaranteeing justice to the individual, the oppressed "little man", as against State bureaucracy.

Both positions are valid. Law is about the rights of individuals and of organized groups. Giving a right, or a freedom, to one person will often entail a limitation on the rights or freedoms of another.[1] In criminal law, a branch of law which has always fascinated sociologists and political theorists, the emphasis is on restricting the freedom of some for what is thought to be the benefit of the whole; and the model of law as consisting of prohibitions and sanctions is not inappropriate. That model is less clearly applicable to the legal rules specifying the form of a civil marriage ceremony, or entitling the wife to maternity allowance under the system of social security, or providing for the granting of a divorce decree if the marriage is shown to have irretrievably broken down.

Similarly, the lawyer cannot entirely share the view that the law is rigid and static. Quite apart from formal legislative changes, the law is capable of continuous development and growth. The law contains general rules and principles which can be applied to the particular facts as they arise. The fact that the rules are only general and have constantly to be tailored to meet new fact-situations gives the law a flexibility and a capacity for change. The later chapters of this book will bear this out. There are numerous situations mentioned in which the law is uncertain: it is not clear how the general rule will apply to that set of facts; or no appeal court,[2] in which questions of law as opposed to disputes of fact are more likely to arise, has pronounced upon the matter; or two principles are potentially relevant, and no court has yet decided which is to prevail. Even when the law is stated with confidence, the reader must beware of changes; law books lead the field in built-in obsolescence.

PROCEDURAL FORMALITY

Yet another source of irritation to the non-lawyer is the legal delight in formal procedures. It sometimes seems that the lawyer sets out to construct an obstacle course which has to be negotiated, with all its delays and technicalities, by anyone who seeks to get something actually done.

This complaint does in fact include a number of separate points. Some of them may become clearer from an examination of what happened when a lawyer deserted his normal practices for a more relaxed, informal style.

In February 1971, a seventeen-year-old girl living in Kent gave birth to a baby boy. He was placed for adoption and in August the mother

---

[1] Cf. Schur, *Law and Society, a Sociological View* (Random House 1968), p. 12.
[2] I.e. the Court of Appeal, one of the several Divisional Courts, or the House of Lords. For an account of the legal system, law reporting, etc. see books such as Walker and Walker, *The English Legal System* (Butterworths, 3rd Edn 1972).

signed the necessary form consenting to the adoption. In accordance with the usual procedure she was interviewed a couple of months later by a senior social worker from the county council's social services department,[1] and at that interview the mother withdrew her consent. The social worker reported that the mother "was crying and obviously has never, until recently, quite realised what she had done and now she wants the child". The legal position was that the adoption could not proceed unless the county court judge to whom the adoption application had been made decided to dispense with the mother's consent. Subsequent events are best described by quoting verbatim from the judgment of the Court of Appeal:[2]

> "On 8th November the judge at Tonbridge saw the mother and the grandmother in his chambers and asked them to reconsider the withdrawal of consent. On 10th November notice was served on the mother that on 15th November an application would be heard at 2.00 pm to dispense with her consent. Then in the morning of 15th November the proposed adopters, who were also not legally represented, were seen for the first time by the learned judge in his chambers at Sevenoaks. In the afternoon he saw the mother and grandmother. The guardian *ad litem*, as represented by Mrs Watts, another social worker, was present at the morning interview and, having arrived a little late, for about 15 minutes of the afternoon interview. On none of the above occasions was sworn evidence taken, nor were either the adopters or the mother shown any extract from any report.
>
> "The complete note of the learned judge reads:
>
> " 'I took no evidence, but I made a few notes, as follows:—[the mother] I want the baby back. I would stop work. The baby's father . . . is willing to help. He lives around Kilburn way. It's a long time ago since we were in touch—3 months. ([Grandmother] says more). He saw baby once. Never made any contribution. Promised to come back with money, but he did not. There is no question of our marrying. [Grandmother] I feel awful about this. I explained to them that the applicants were an entirely satisfactory couple, who had no children of their own but had already adopted a child: and that [the baby] was well looked after and happy with them. I dispensed with the mother's consent on the ground that it was unreasonably withheld.'
>
> "According to Mrs Watts he had before announcing his decision addressed certain questions to the mother and then made some comments as to the interests of the child. At the conclusion of what Mrs Watts described as 'the interview' the judge, according to the mother, announced his decision as follows: 'It is better for the child to be adopted. I dispense with your consent. You are young and you will soon get over it.' "

This procedure was described by counsel as that of "a benign judge dispensing with care and tact a Solomon type of justice". The judge, taking an active interest in the case, and putting the welfare of the

---

[1] The director of which was the formal guardian *ad litem*. For details of adoption procedure, see chap. 8.
[2] *Re M. (an infant)*, [1972] 3 All E.R. 321, at p. 324.

child first, had spared the mother (who was only eighteen at the time of the hearing) the ordeal of a formal hearing with sworn evidence, cross-examination, and lawyers' probings. He accepted the advice of the professionals who thought the adoption should go ahead, and the prospective adopters had been caring for the baby for several months, and expressed the natural and proper hope that the emotional wounds would heal with the passing of time.

After a full hearing the Court of Appeal quashed the adoption order, and ordered that another county court judge should consider the matter afresh. The first judge had in effect ignored the basic rules of procedure, what lawyers like to call "the rules of natural justice". The reasons which the Court of Appeal gives are full of instruction as to lawyers' attitudes.

Stripped of rhetoric, the basic proposition is that the parties to a dispute should be able to argue their case fully before an impartial judge who will then decide in favour of one or the other.

The judge must be impartial. He must, of course, be free from obvious bias; he must have no financial or other interest in the outcome; he must not "be judge in his own cause". But also the judge must take care that he does not fall into the trap of assuming that the professionals with whom he deals each day are necessarily and always right. The magistrate listens each day to the same police officers, and will come to know and respect them; but the police can make mistakes, and the magistrate must not become "prosecution minded". The Court of Appeal in *Re M.* had to point out that "neither well intentioned but busy directors of social services nor their staff are necessarily infallible".

The parties must present their cases in full. The one who is seeking some favourable ruling must explain his reasons and support his assertions. It is often a salutary experience to try to explain to a layman why he should accept what you know from professional experience to be the case: the actual supporting argument and evidence can turn out to be painfully thin. If a party's case is to be fully explored, it must be tested by the other party's questions and counter-assertions. If he is to be able to do that, the other party must know in advance something of the case he has to meet; and, so far as may be, all the case should be open for challenge, with no parts of the case sent privately to the judge by one party and kept hidden from the other. (Here the whole business of "confidential reports to court" gives rise to some very real practical and theoretical difficulties.)[1] Lord Devlin, speaking in a wardship case of the secrecy which professional social work practice sometimes tends to encourage especially in children's cases, said

"It must be remembered that the object of disclosure . . . is not merely to remove a sense of injury that might otherwise result from secrecy, but

[1] See pp. 21–35.

because secrecy may of itself prevent the point from being fully canvassed and so possibly prevent that course being taken which, if the full facts were known, would truly be in the interests of the ward."[1]

In *Re M.*, the mother was given no indication of the arguments which might be advanced by the prospective adopters. They never gave evidence in any formal sense; the mother was not present when they spoke to the judge, and could not question or challenge them in any way.

Finally, the parties must, so far as possible, be given an equal chance. The ordinary man may feel he has little chance against the professionals, especially in the extraordinary setting of a court-room. He must have legal advice and assistance in presenting his case. A judge, however well meaning, cannot properly act as friend and comforter of one party while maintaining his impartiality. In *Re M.*, there was no legal representation, and the unsatisfactory result was that the judge himself had to advise the mother how she should react to the decision he had taken, and which had led to his own premature intervention in the case before the facts were properly presented to him.

THE SAFEGUARDS OF LEGAL PROCEDURE

It is possible to spell out some of the characteristic legal ideas which *Re M.* helps to illustrate.

The first is the idea of a third-party monitoring system for all decisions. The administrator is not to be trusted to be infallible; he must be liable to be called upon to justify his actions before an impartial third party. So tax inspectors are subject to appeals to tax commissioners; civil servants may be rebuked by the Ombudsman; lower court judges may have their decisions taken on appeal to a higher court; and social workers, in the sensitive areas in which they are in potential conflict with the client, may find that the local magistrates' court provides that reviewing, monitoring agency.

The second is based on similar thinking. The courts themselves can err, especially if the judge is drawn into the arena. To minimise the risk the English courts adopt an "adversary" system: the parties to the dispute produce the evidence and arguments, leaving the judge to act solely as umpire. The use of this system has a number of consequences: if the parties are allowed to decide what material is to be put before the court, there must be guidelines as to what is and is not permissible; and, as the two sides will usually be putting forward opposing contentions, there must be rules as to who must prove what, and with what degree of cogency. The former guidelines constitute the law of evidence, and some aspects of it, those which may affect the social worker directly, are examined in chapter two. The latter rules are those as to "burden of proof" and "standard of proof". In general terms, the

[1] *Official Solicitor* v. *K.*, [1965] A.C. 201, at p. 242; cited in *Re M.*, *supra*.

party asking the court for help bears the burden of proving his case: if he fails to establish his case, he loses. In most cases it is enough if he does establish that, "on the balance of probabilities", his contentions are true; in criminal cases the higher standard, "beyond reasonable doubt" is required.

The third idea is the need for openness and publicity. Some legal rules are designed to give public recognition and authority to what would otherwise be private arrangements—marriage, adoption, divorce. It is socially convenient and valuable for those transactions to have a certain formality and publicity, despite the admitted value of confidentiality and the need to save the parties needless embarrassment. Similarly the proper administration of justice is thought to require publicity; justice must be seen to be done. So the details of a divorce case may be printed in the Law Reports, and there are public galleries and press seats in the local courts. Some exceptions are made to ensure privacy for the domestic and juvenile courts, and in some cases where reports are published (as in many children's cases, or nullity of marriage matters) the parties are allowed the anonymity of initial letters rather than their full names.

These ideas are alien to the professional administrator. He prefers to establish the facts for himself, to exercise and rely upon his own professional judgment, and to place clear curbs on the dissemination of information to those not directly concerned. Working in this way he can achieve maximum efficiency in pursuing the objectives of his organisation. But he will sometimes make mistakes, and the lesson that the law has learned over the years is that in some areas mistakes cause such harm and distress that procedures of admitted inefficiency should be insisted upon because it has been found that mistakes are reduced in number and public confidence in the decisions reached is enhanced.

LAW AND THE SOCIAL WORKER

There are differences in decision-making styles between lawyer and social worker which go deeper than matters of procedure. In actual cases the lawyer may seem to take a harder and less flexible attitude. One reason may be that the relationship between a lawyer and his client is very seldom as close, and as long-lasting, as that in social work; the lawyer exacts fees from his client and that fact has a marked "distancing" effect. But there is also something in the nature of law which can make it seem impersonal.

So, the law has to use a broad typology of situations and of people. If a legal rule requires the demolition of dangerous premises, this rule must apply whoever owns the premises. It will apply to property bought by a company for speculative purposes and also to the cottage which is the last remaining substantial esset of the elderly widow. To make exceptions would create injustices; "hard cases make bad law".

The lawyer owes a certain allegiance to the consistency of the principles which go to make up the framework of legal rules. He may, as a result, seem on occasion to put law before justice, to neglect the individual in favour of some abstract idea. In fact the social worker is not unaware of the same sort of pressures: his concern for the individual may have to be checked by the need to preserve objectivity, to protect the client's "self-determination", or by the need for an even-handed application of agency policy or a fair distribution of scarce resources. The setting is different, but the dilemma is much the same.

This chapter has concentrated upon the differences in outlook between two professions and by taking them out of context has inevitably exaggerated them. In some later chapters the subject-matter is the social worker's powers and the ways in which the law imposes conditions and creates safeguards against his errors and abuses of power. Again the social worker reader may feel that the law is against him, restricting the exercise of his professional skills. It must be kept in mind that the powers he wishes to use are as much a creation of the law as the conditions set upon their use, and that in areas which fall outside the scope of this book, when for example a client turns to his social worker for advice about trouble with the landlord or the hire purchase company, the law can be an ally indeed.

Chapter 2

SOCIAL WORKERS AND
THE COURTS

There are many social workers who have distinctly negative attitudes towards courts of law. It may be useful to begin by identifying some of the underlying reasons.

One basic reason is unfamiliarity with and dislike for the intimidating ritual mumbo-jumbo of the courts, or, as the lawyer might prefer to phrase it, the elegant refinements of legal procedure. It is always alarming to have to perform in public; in the court-room there are added hazards, such as the difficulty of recalling the correct form of address for His Lordship, or His Honour, and the extraordinary furniture which always seems to have been designed for someone of an altogether different build. Even an experienced officer can be badly disconcerted by the procedural oddities inflicted upon him by a strange judge or a remote court, and it is not much consolation to know that neither the police nor the bar are immune from such anxieties.

At a deeper level, the court may symbolise for some social workers the restricting and dehumanising features they see in the law itself. Or, in some contexts, a court hearing is a symbol of failure, where casework has failed to remedy an unhappy situation.

Perhaps the major reason is that the court is the setting for potential conflict between the social worker and those who do not necessarily share his values or seek to advance the same interests. The legal representatives of the parties, acting their partisan role, may try through cross-examination to recruit the social worker to their side by leading questions or selective quotation of reports. The sentencer may feel obliged to reject a soundly-based professional recommendation to serve what he sees to be the public interest. Above all the rules of evidence as they are applied in a contested case may seem calculated to suppress relevant information and harass those who are trying to establish the truth.

EVIDENCE

The law of evidence is a complicated and highly technical subject.

More than in most branches of law, the rules are invariably accompanied by exceptions and qualifications. Some of the complexity is the result of historical development. Major reforms of the rules applicable in civil cases have been made, and the reform of criminal evidence has been the subject of a highly controversial report by the Criminal Law Revision Committee. But equally the nature of the rules of evidence is governed in part by the special problems which have to be solved.

In a contested case, the first task of a court is to establish the facts. Unless the facts are self-evident, as in contempt of court cases where disappointed litigants throw tomatoes at the judge or members of the public sing Welsh songs as a political demonstration, the facts must be established by evidence, usually the testimony of witnesses. From that obvious statement all sorts of difficulties flow.

Psychological studies amply document the unreliability of testimony.[1] The initial perception of an event by a witness can never be complete or wholly accurate. The later operations of recall and verbalisation introduce fresh distortions. .The resulting testimony with much other information is then subjected to the mental processes of a judge, or to the group decision-making of magistrates or jurors. At best this is a very suspect way of discovering objective truth, assuming that such a thing is discoverable. Rules of evidence cannot remove psychological facts, but they can try to reduce the risk of further distortions from other sources.

For example there is the problem of the dishonest witness. The oath and the penalties for perjury may have some effect despite the daily evidence of their ineffectiveness. The affirmation is the equivalent of the oath and the disapproving attitude which some magistrates display when social workers or other regular witnesses choose to affirm[2] is to be deplored. Cross-examination is also designed to expose dishonesty as well as to check innocent mistakes. It is for this reason that the cross-examiner is allowed to use leading questions, tempting the witness into inconsistencies or admissions; counsel may not "lead" his own witness (except in areas free from dispute) because of the danger of suggesting an answer.

This problem of suggestion does not only apply to questioning in court. Police interrogation is hedged about with legal rules because of the risk of false confessions as a result of pressures, often quite subtle, being brought to bear. The danger does of course exist in any interview situation, especially where one party to the conversation is an articulate professional and the other uncertain and unhappy; social workers and their clients may fit this description no less than police officers and those "helping their enquiries". Once a statement has

---

[1] For a recent and readable review, see Trankell, *Reliability of Evidence* (1973).
[2] Perhaps for scriptural reasons: Matthew 5, vv. 33–4.

been made in an interview or in writing the maker of the statement may become committed to it, and be reluctant to change his views; the interpretation of events advanced in the interview may in fact operate as a psychological barrier to more accurate recall of the original situation.

Experience teaches that there are a number of situations in which witnesses' statements are particularly unreliable. A young child may happily mix fact and fantasy, and may be "rehearsed" by a parent. This can make the assessment of the child's view of a custody dispute or of a proposed adoption particularly difficult. Similarly complaints of sexual assault and statements by accomplices anxious to minimise their part in a crime are especially suspect. In these cases the lawyers look for "corroboration", supporting independent evidence, before giving weight to the statement. This principle is especially important in affiliation proceedings.

There is a more general point or series of related points arising from these considerations. If a witness is challenged by cross-examination or by other witnesses, the challenge can take two principal forms: that he is mistaken or wrong, and that he is unreliable through bias or dishonesty. So the issues in dispute include not only questions of fact but also questions as to the "credit" of a witness. A particular piece of evidence may be treated as admissible on one issue, credit, but inadmissible in so far as it goes directly to the factual disputes; the resulting metal gynmastics can bewilder.

The basic test for the admissibility of evidence is "relevance", but the law has its own restricted view of what is relevant. A trained social worker is expected to make assessments of character, looking at the whole history of a person and of his relationships with others. The courts are more usually concerned with the question whether an event occurred, or whether a condition existed at a particular point in time. So if a man is accused of burglary on a certain date, it is generally irrelevant that he has sixteen previous convictions for burglary; the question is whether he committed the offence charged and it is dangerous to assume guilt from past guilt, however realistic the assumption might be.

Even relevance in the lawyer's sense is subject to other considerations, including the practical one of the need to complete trials in a reasonable time. If one witness asserts that another is unreliable and not to be trusted on oath he is not allowed (except in cross-examination) to give details of all the incidents and circumstances which caused him to form that view. They may be highly relevant to the issue of credibility, but the scope of the enquiry must be circumscribed in the interests of speed and clarity.

Fortunately a social worker does not need to master the rules of evidence, but there is one area which needs some further consideration, the rules as to "hearsay".

HEARSAY

One of the best-known rules of evidence is "the rule against hearsay". One formulation of the rule is that "a statement other than one made by a person while giving oral evidence in the proceedings is inadmissible as evidence of any fact stated".[1] There are an inordinate number of exceptions both as to oral statements and documents, and statutory reform has tempered the operation of the rule in some cases, but the principle behind the rule is of great importance, and particularly for social workers because of their traditional methods of working.

If a social worker is asked about the character of a named person, he may want to say, "I have no personal knowledge of that, but X, a colleague of mine, knows him well and thinks this of him." This is hearsay, because the source of the statement is not the witness but X. Unless one of the exceptions applies, the rule against hearsay will render it inadmissible, and the witness who embarks upon such an answer may well find himself rudely interrupted.

The reason is that all the causes of inaccuracy in testimony—the difficulties in the way of accurate perception and recall, for example—apply with redoubled force when information is passed from one person to another. None of the procedural checks on accuracy, the oath, cross-examination, or just the visibility of the witness to the court are available, and the evidence in the absence of special circumstances is unreliable.

The importance of this rule to social work practice will be obvious. Asked to prepare a social enquiry report, a social worker will not rely solely on his own knowledge. He will consult files prepared by others, he will go and talk to head teachers, police officers, and others with information. All this is hearsay and within the exclusionary rule.

As we shall see, the rule against hearsay appears not to operate in the particular case of reports to court. In some circumstances, reports are expressly exempted from the rules of evidence; in others the rules seem in practice to be set aside at least provisionally, so that hearsay can be received. But the rationale of the rule against hearsay still holds good; information gained via others must be less reliable than information obtained in person, and a good report will clearly distinguish between the two, just as it will between assertions of fact and opinion.

Outside the area of reports to court, the rule against hearsay is much affected by the Civil Evdence Act 1968 which relaxes the rule to make "first-hand hearsay" (where the witness obtains the information from the original source and not through one or more intermediaries) admissible in some circumstances, and also relaxes the rule to make it easier to rely on records kept by persons under a duty to compile them. This last phrase applies not only to records required by law, as are

---

[1] *Cross on Evidence* (Butterworths, 4th Edn 1974), p. 6.

records of visits under the Boarding-Out of Children Regulations 1955, but also records kept as part of the duties of one's employment, which will clearly include all records kept in social work agencies. The Act contains important procedural safeguards which limit its practical effect, and it only applies to civil cases in the High Court and county courts, and not to cases before magistrates.

THE SOCIAL WORKER'S ROLE IN COURT

A social worker can appear in court in a number of different roles. He may be called as a witness in support of an application made by the agency for which he works, or in some other case of which he has special knowledge. In these situations he is bound by all the normal rules of evidence. The special factors which are relevant when he is asked to give evidence against his own agency, or in other circumstances where he feels the information should not be revealed, are discussed below.[1]

He is more likely to appear as an officer of the local authority or other agency which has brought the proceedings, or against which proceedings are taken,[2] or which is otherwise a party to the proceedings.[3] Where he is conducting the case, rather as does a prosecutor, the social worker must be aware of a dual responsibility. He owes a duty not only to the agency he represents but also to the court, and this may involve drawing the attention of the court to matters which tell against his own case if they are not otherwise brought out into the open.

Finally the social worker may appear as the expert agent of the court in the preparation of social enquiry and similar reports. This area is governed by a large number of special rules which are examined below.[8]

A RELUCTANT WITNESS

A social worker may find himself called as a witness not on behalf of his agency but in an action brought against it. Or he may be called as a witness in some dispute between private individuals with whom he may have had professional dealings. He may have good reasons for wishing not to give evidence, which might be against the interests of his agency or (in his view) of the person calling him as a witness. The facts of an American case[5] illustrate one possible situation.

A social worker was attached to a Mental Health Clinic in Wisconsin. He conducted interviews with clients which were always described as

---

[1] See pp. 16–9, below.
[2] E.g. applications in "beyond control" cases under Children and Young Persons Act 1963, s. 3 (as to which, see p. 65, below).
[3] E.g. cases in which an authority has a right to make representations before a child is committed to its care, such as Matrimonial Causes Act 1973, s. 43 (2) (as to which, see p. 72, below).
[4] See pp. 21–35, below.
[5] *State* v. *Driscoll* 53 Wisc. 2d 699, 193 N.W. 2d 851, 50 A.L.R. 3d 554 (1972).

"confidential conferences". One series of such conferences was with a Mr Driscoll; Mrs Driscoll came to some of the interviews. Mr Driscoll's sexual problems were fully discussed, and he admitted various indecencies with his young step-daughter, and to having had sexual intercourse with her. From the point of view of the psychiatric and social work staff of the Clinic, these interviews were an essential part of the treatment process, and complete confidentiality was crucial to their success. None the less, when Mr Driscoll was charged in the criminal courts with gross indecency and unlawful sexual intercourse with his step-daughter, the social worker was called as a prosecution witness and was required to give evidence as to the statements made by the accused in the confidential conferences. The State Supreme Court held that the social worker was properly compelled to give the evidence despite the breach of confidentiality which was entailed.

To the lawyer this type of case concerns the proper relationship of two legal principles. The first is that justice requires full disclosure of the facts to the court, and the court will therefore assist parties to litigation by enforcing the attendance of witnesses. As a general principle everyone is a "compellable" witness and the court will issue a witness summons or subpoena requiring his attendance; disobedience can lead to arrest. The second principle is that certain types of discussion must be guaranteed confidentiality as a matter of policy. This principle is applied to discussions between a person and his legal professional advisers. The discussion is "privileged", that is to say that evidence may not be given about what was said unless the client agrees. A leading commentator justified legal professional privilege in these terms:

> "Candour is essential, and the subject-matter with regard to which legal advice is sought, as well as the circumstances in which it has to be given, often renders it improbable that the fullest confidences would be exchanged if communications between the client and his adviser had to be disclosed."[1]

The social worker's reaction is probably, "But that applies just as well to discussions which I have with my clients." He may react similarly to the following more detailed analysis in a leading American treatise on the law of evidence:

> "[F]our fundamental conditions are recognised as necessary to the establishment of a privilege against the disclosure of communications:
> (1) The communications must originate in a *confidence* that they will not be disclosed.
> (2) This element of *confidentiality must be essential* to the full and satisfactory maintenance of the relation between the parties.
> (3) The *relation* must be one which in the opinion of the community ought to be sedulously *fostered*.

---

[1] *Cross on Evidence* (Butterworths, 3rd Edn 1967), p. 243.

(4) The injury that would inure to the relation by the disclosure of the communications must be *greater than the benefit* thereby gained for the correct disposal of litigation."[1]

That analysis has been much cited but the courts of different countries have almost always refused to extend the area of privilege to include communications between social workers and clients. The argument seems to be that the exception for lawyers is well established and is intimately related to the administration of justice; go beyond that relationship and social workers, the clergy, physicians, bankers, journalists, schoolmasters, college tutors, blood relations, fiancés, could all put forward some sort of plausible case for special treatment. In some countries, the social work profession has received special protection via legislation;[2] but a system of case-law would find it difficult to distinguish social workers from at least some of the other categories listed.

The English position was made clear in *R.* v. *Nottingham Justices, ex parte Bostock*[3] in 1970. The mother of an illegitimate child approached an adoption society. She named a man as the father of her child, and he was later visited by one of the society's agents, no doubt to see whether he would make any objection to the proposed adoption and to explore his medical history. The mother later began affiliation proceedings against the man, and sought to call the social worker, presumably so that the social worker could give evidence as to statements admitting paternity. The Divisional Court held that the evidence should be received. It had been argued that public policy required the preservation of confidentiality as between the man and the adoption agency, but the Lord Chief Justice (Lord Parker) dismissed that argument shortly: "For my part the real aspect of public policy that is involved in this case is that no man should evade his responsibility if he has one."[4]

The resulting legal position is that as a general rule discussions between social workers and clients are not privileged. Confidentiality does not prevail over the interests of justice requiring disclosure. To this general principle there are some exceptions. One set of exceptions applies in certain cases concerning children; the other (the rule as to "without prejudice" statements) applies more generally.

Considerable confidentiality in adoption negotiations is ensured by regulation 7 of the Adoption Agencies Regulations 1959. This provides:

---

[1] 8 *Wigmore on Evidence* 527, para. 2285. Italics in original.
[2] The Morton Commission, reporting in 1956, recommended that marriage guidance counsellors be given a privileged position by statute; this was not implemented.
[3] [1970] 2 All E.R. 641; [1970] 1 W.L.R. 1117.
[4] A Canadian decision in which similar communications were held to be privileged is often cited, but is only a decision of a Police Magistrate and of little authority: *Re Kryschuk and Zulynik* (1958), 14 D.L.R. (2d) 676.

"Any information obtained by any member, officer or representative of a registered adoption society or of the society's case committee[1] in the course of negotiations entered into by or on behalf of the society with a person proposing to place an infant at the disposition of the society with a view to his being adopted, or with a person proposing to adopt him, shall be treated as confidential and shall not be disclosed except so far as may be necessary for the purpose of proceedings under the Adoption Act, 1958, or for the proper execution of his duty or to a person who is authorised in writing by or on behalf of the Secretary of State to obtain the information for the purposes of research."

This protects the parent placing the child and the prospective adopters, but does not apply to interviews with other people, such as the putative father in the *Nottingham Justices* case.[2]

Once adoption proceedings have been set in motion, further protection is given by the rules of court[3] which direct that any information obtained by any person "in the course of, or relating to, proceedings" shall be treated as confidential. Again this did not apply in the *Nottingham Justices* case[2] where the relevant interviews were some four months before the birth of the child, so that adoption proceedings were many months in the future.

These provisions only apply in adoption cases, but the same policy issues arise in other cases concerned with children. This was recognised in a *Practice Direction*[4] relating to wardship and guardianship of minors cases. If a local authority or adoption society is asked to give evidence or produce its records[5] in such a case, application may be made to the court which may order that information which it would be harmful to the infant to disclose to the parties may be produced in the form of a confidential report to court. In this way the court obtains the information it needs, but the parties are denied the right to cross-examine; like all compromise solutions, this fails to satisfy all the competing interests. The *Practice Direction* only applies in the High Court; it is open to other courts to adopt the same procedure if they so desire.

WITHOUT PREJUDICE STATEMENTS

It is obviously desirable that disputing parties should be reconciled, that they should settle their dispute without going to court. Litigation adds bitterness to a dispute and is expensive to the parties and to the State (especially where the parties have Legal Aid). So the law seeks to encourage negotiation and compromise. If the negotiations are to

---

[1] The regulation also applies to local authorities: see Adoption Agencies Regulations 1959, reg. 9.
[2] *R. v. Nottingham Justices, ex parte Bostock*, [1970] 2 All E.R. 641; [1970] 1 W.L.R. 1117.
[3] Adoption (High Court) Rules, r. 25; Adoption (County Court) Rules, r. 27; Adoption (Juvenile Court) Rules, r. 30.
[4] [1968] 1 All E.R. 762; [1968] 1 W.L.R. 373.
[5] As to records, see further p. 21, below.

succeed, the parties must abandon set positions and be prepared to concede particular points in exchange for a corresponding concession by the other side. They are more likely to do this is they are sure that they can take back all proffered concessions if the negotiations break down. The result is that statements made without prejudice to the maker's original position are privileged and cannot be put in evidence. The phrase "without prejudice" does not have to be used; the test is whether there is a real negotiation towards a settlement of a dispute.

The principal application of this rule for social workers is in marriage guidance work. Where spouses are estranged and call in a probation officer to help them, and so hope to avert separation or divorce proceedings, their conversations with him will be "without prejudice" and immune from disclosure. As Denning, L.J. put it in *McTaggart* v. *McTaggart*,[1]

> "If a probation officer should be compelled to give evidence as to what was said in the course of negotiations, it would mean that he would not be told the truth, or, at all events, not the whole truth. The parties would have at the back of their minds, the thought that whatever they said might be given in evidence against them or for them and would colour their statement accordingly. There is no chance of reconciliation unless the parties are able to talk with frankness to the probation officer and with complete confidence that what they say will not be disclosed. If they are genuinely seeking his assistance, they must be taken to negotiate on that understanding, even though nothing is expressly said."

This rule applies whoever is acting as conciliator. It does not have to be a probation officer or any specially qualified person. The rule has been applied when the conciliator was a solicitor,[2] a barrister who became a High Court judge shortly afterwords,[3] a vicar[4] and a neighbour.[5] It will also apply outside the area of matrimonial disputes, for example to negotiations between the father and mother of an illegitimate child as to maintenance in an attempt to avoid embarrassing affiliation proceedings.[6]

The "without prejudice" rule is designed to protect the parties to the dispute, and they can waive its protection if they so wish. If that happens, the social worker or other conciliator must give evidence; he has no independent right of refusal. So in *Pais* v. *Pais*,[7] a husband and wife asked a priest to act as a marriage guidance counsellor. He was later served with a subpoena to give evidence. Both parties were willing

---

[1] [1949] P. 94, at pp. 97–8.
[2] *Mole* v. *Mole*, [1951] P. 21; [1950] 2 All E.R. 328.
[3] *Pool* v. *Pool*, [1951] P. 470; [1951] 2 All E.R. 563.
[4] *Henley* v. *Henley*, [1955] P. 202; [1955] 1 All E.R. 590.
[5] *Theodoropoulas* v. *Theodoropoulas*, [1964] P. 311; [1963] 2 All E.R. 772.
[6] See *R.* v. *Nottingham Justices, ex parte Bostock*, [1970] 2 All E.R. 641; [1970] 1 W.L.R. 1117; the interviews in that case were not designed to settle any dispute, so the rule was not applied.
[7] [1971] P. 119; [1970] 3 All E.R. 491.

that he should give certain limited evidence, as to the dates on which the parties saw him. It was held that, despite his objections, the priest could be required to answer questions on those matters.

DOCUMENTS

The principle that the court will aid the parties to obtain full disclosure of the facts applies to documents as well as oral evidence. There are various procedures known as "discovery" or "disclosure of documents" under which a party to a civil dispute can obtain documents in the possession of the other side. If fully applied, these procedures could lead to the full dislcosure of case-notes and records, an appalling prospect. In fact there are important qualifications affecting the social work area, though their precise scope is not entirely clear.

The provisions already examined[1] give a measure of protection in adoption, wardship and Guardianship of Minors cases, and some documents will be protected by the "without prejudice" rule. In addition case records kept under the Boarding Out of Children Regulations 1955 are privileged from disclosure. This was established by a Court of Appeal decision, *Re D. (infants)*,[2] which was based in part on the interpretation of a regulation[3] that permitted case records to be inspected by specially authorised persons, and, by implication, by no-one else. The Court of Appeal also based itself on general principles, that it was contrary to public policy to order the disclosure of records in this type of case. Unfortunately it is not clear what type of case the Lord Justices had in mind. Harman, L.J. emphasises the wardship jurisdiction which was being invoked, but also remarks that he had never heard of any order for discovery of documents in the "domestic jurisdiction"; Karminski, L.J. spoke of the undesirability of records kept under statutory authority being disclosed in "infant cases".

The result seems to be that case records will be given some protection by the courts, but that this is not an absolute rule applying in all cases. And there is one important procedural pitfall to be avoided: a witness may take notes with him into the witness-box to refresh his memory, but if he does so the notes must be shown to the opposing party for inspection and possible use in cross-examination. The social worker witness must take care to leave confidential records in his office; if he carries them into the witness-box, he throws away all protection.

REPORTS TO COURT

When a social worker is called as a witness he is bound by the rules of evidence and the requirements of the adversary mode of procedure. He is there to answer questions put to him, and to answer them with

---

[1] I.e. those discussed at pp. 18–19, above.
[2] [1970] 1 All E.R. 1088; [1970] 1 W.L.R. 599.
[3] Boarding Out of Children Regulations 1959, reg. 10.

statements of fact; expressions of opinion and of professional interpretation may not be wanted, and in some contexts will be positively discouraged. The subjects covered and the tone of the exchanges are determined by the questioner; the witness cannot say, "Those questions are all very well, but what is much more interesting and important is . . ."

As the author of a report requested by and addressed to the court, the social worker's position is very different. He acts as the agent of the court, as an investigator and interpreter. Subject to particular statutory rules or the instructions of the court itself, he has wide discretion as to the contents of his report,[1] and he is often expected to draw conclusions and to make recommendations as to the appropriate decision to be made by the court. Where a point of real legal difficulty arises, a court may invite counsel to provide additional legal argument as *amicus curiae*; in a similar way, the social worker acts as the privileged friend of the court. This puts him in a position of considerable power or influence, with correspondingly heavy responsibilities.

One aspect of the situation is that the social worker has to bear in mind the needs both of the court and of the individuals on whom he reports, and with whom he has, or may come to have, a continuing professional relationship. When he is gathering information for a report, the social worker may find that he is expected by those he interviews to act principally as their spokesman; the fact that his first duty is to the court may not be immediately acceptable. When the report is written it will often be seen by those whose history and problems it describes; while the court must be given the whole picture, its presentation has to take into account the possible reactions of the subject.[2]

The lawyer's attention is caught by another aspect of the subject, one which is more likely to arise when the report is *not* seen by anyone but the judge. If this is the case, there is no way in which the contents of the report can be challenged by the parties or by their legal representatives. Any errors of fact or false interpretations or emphases will pass uncorrected. Even if a report is seen or heard by the parties it may be difficult for them to pick up and correct any and every mistake. There may be no time, or, particularly for an unrepresented party, the social constraints of the court setting may be too great to be overcome.

An example is *R.* v. *Elley*.[3] Like many of the cases to be examined in this section, this involved a police "antecedents statement" rather than a social enquiry report, but the principles apply to reports by

---

[1] Research studies suggest that in practice the personal characteristics of the authors of the report are as influential in determining the contents as the nature of the available information: see Hood and Sparks, *Key Issues in Criminology*, pp. 163 *et seq.*

[2] See King (ed.), *The Probation and After-Care Service*, pp. 110–13, 184–93 (written with the criminal court situation in mind).

[3] (1921), 85 J.P. 144.

social workers as well as by the police, and to civil as well as criminal contexts. Elley was convicted of stealing a motor-cycle and sidecar. He had previous convictions, the most recent being five years before the current trial. In making the antecedents statement, the police officer made a number of allegations as to Elley's conduct during that time: that he had twice been dismissed "for dishonesty and untruthfulness and threats of violence"; that he was "a very dangerous and persistent thief"; and that he associated with known receivers of stolen cars. Elley protested from the dock that this was all untrue, but received a sentence of three years, the judge describing him as "a dangerous rascal". In fact these additional allegations were untrue. Elley was able to establish this by going to the Court of Criminal Appeal and obtaining permission to call further evidence; his sentence was more than halved.

The need for scrupulous care before including any statement in a report to court is apparent. Not every litigant is persistent enough to take a case on appeal; even if he does, there are some areas of law, for example those involving the custody of children, where the appeal courts are notably reluctant to disturb a decision once it has been made.

In a later, similar, case,[1] the then Lord Chief Justice said that in the criminal trial situation it is the duty of prosecuting counsel to keep police witnesses in hand, and to ensure that they do not make allegations which are incapable of proof and which counsel thinks may be denied by the prisoner. This is practicable in the Crown Court where there will always be prosecuting counsel, but not in the magistrates' courts where the prosecution may well be handled by the police officer whose duty it is to put in the antecedents statement. The situations in which a social worker finds himself are likely to be of the latter sort, with no guiding hand of counsel.

Police antecedents statements are increasingly factual in nature. If a conviction is included in error it is relatively easy to challenge it and for the point to be checked. It is much harder for a more general statement as to character, reputation or disposition to be challenged; a social enquiry report contains a good deal of that "soft" information. If someone feels that the report is unfair he may have an almost impossible task of proving a negative or of correcting a false overall impression. In the antecedents context the courts have repeatedly deplored the practice of including general derogatory remarks.[2] A well-known example is *R. v. Robinson*.[3]

Robinson was convicted of possessing cannabis. Two police officers then gave evidence to the effect that he was one of the leading distributors of drugs in the Midlands, supplying a network of other "pushers"; that he seemed to have large amounts of money which could not have

---

[1] *R. v. Van Pelz*, [1943] 1 K.B. 157; [1943] 1 All E.R. 36; 29 Cr. App. Rep. 10. See also *R. v. Burton* (1941), 28 Cr. App. Rep. 89.
[2] E.g. *R. v. Bibby*, [1972] Crim. L.R. 513.
[3] (1969), 53 Cr. App. Rep. 314.

been earned legitimately; and that he associated with criminals. This evidence amounted to an accusation of a further offence, and a more serious offence, for distributors of drugs are much more heavily punished than possessors; Robinson had no notice of this additional allegation and had no real opportunity to deny it. The statements about his criminal associates were even harder to rebut; they amounted to a form of generalised "mud-slinging". The court said that information should only be put before the court at the sentencing stage if it was sufficiently particularised for the accused to be able to challenge it.

SOCIAL ENQUIRY REPORTS IN THE CRIMINAL COURTS

The best-known form of report to court is the pre-sentence report prepared by probation officers for the criminal courts. It received extended consideration from the Streatfeild Committee on the Business of the Criminal Courts[1] and has also attracted the attention of commentators and researchers.[2]

The Home Secretary has power to make it compulsory for the courts to ask for such reports, from a probation officer or other authorised person, before passing a custodial sentence,[3] but he has chosen not to exercise this power but rather to issue exhortations in the form of Circulars, which have no binding force in law. In this way he has urged the use of reports before a court imposes a sentence of borstal training, detention in a detention centre, a sentence of imprisonment (including a suspended sentence) for two years or less where the offender has not prevously received a sentence of imprisonment or of borstal training, or a sentence of imprisonment on a woman.[4] It is also urged that probation reports be asked for before a probation order is made and before an offender is committed by magistrates to the Crown Court for sentence.[5] Specific provision is made, by the Powers of the Criminal Courts Act 1973,[6] that a probation officer's report must be obtained before a community service order is made; and any available report must be considered before a person aged under twenty-one is sentenced to imprisonment[7] and before a person over that age is sentenced to imprisonment for the first time.[8]

Whenever a magistrates' court receives a report from a probation officer as part of the sentencing process a copy must be given to the defendant, or his counsel or solicitor, or (if he is under seventeen and

---

[1] Cmnd. 1289, esp. ch. 11.
[2] The literature is voluminous. See D. A. Mathieson and A. J. Walker, *Social Enquiry Reports* (Probation Paper No. 7); M. Davies and A. Knopf, *Social Enquiry Reports and the Probation Service* (Home Office Research Studies No. 18); and see the bibliography at (1973), 137 J.P. 275.
[3] Powers of the Criminal Courts Act 1973, s. 45; the power was first given in 1967.
[4] See Circular 59/1971.
[5] I.e. under Magistrates' Courts Act 1952, ss. 28 (borstal) and 29.
[6] S. 14 (2) (*b*) (i).
[7] Powers of the Criminal Courts Act 1973, s. 19 (2).
[8] *Ibid.*, s. 20 (1).

not legally represented) to his parent or guardian if present in court.[1] One of the reasons for this rule is to enable the defence to use their copy of the report as a basis for cross-examination, but there is some research evidence[2] suggesting that unrepresented defendants, while they are given an opportunity to see the report, and may well be able to discuss it with the probation officer concerned before the hearing, do not actually have a copy in court. Local practice seems to vary greatly, and the procedures to be followed in connection with pre-sentence reports are in fact left surprisingly vague by the legal provisions. Guidance can be gleaned from various sources, but there is room for much variation in practice.

One example is the time at which the reports should be prepared. Since the Streatfeild Report of 1961 it has been accepted that there is no objection in principle to pre-trial reports, the relevant interviews and enquiries taking place before the trial so that an adjournment for reports is unnecessary. There continues to be a difference of opinion about the desirability of this procedure, and there are special problems when a "not guilty" plea is likely. Where the accused objects to enquiries before his trial, his wish should be respected.

The Streatfeild Committee also considered the contents of reports,[3] and laid to rest the question whether a recommendation as to sentence could properly be included. It is clear that it can be, but some courts still seem to wish their decision-making powers to be vindicated by confining the probation services to hints and dreadful euphemisms such as "a prolonged period of training in a different environment".[4] The statutory duty of the probation officer is "to inquire, in accordance with any directions of the court, into the circumstances or home surroundings of any person with a view to assisting the court in determining the most suitable method of dealing with his case".[5] There is no doubt that the court is entirely free to decide in what form it prefers this assistance to be given.

The position as to the inclusion of hearsay remains rather obscure. In *R. v. Robinson*,[6] the "antecedents statement" case already cited, the court said that police officers should only give information upon which they could speak "from first-hand knowledge without reliance on hearsay or records". That suggests that the strict rules of evidence apply to antecedent statements, and perhaps by analogy to social enquiry reports. The everyday practice of the courts is certainly otherwise,

---

[1] *Ibid.*, s. 46. Literally this applies to oral "stand-down" reports, but is treated in practice as applying only to reports already prepared in writing.

[2] See White, "The Presentation in Court of Social Inquiry Reports", [1971] Crim. L.R. 629.

[3] Para. 336 *et seq.*

[4] See generally, Ford, *Advising Sentencers* (Oxford University Penal Research Unit, Occasional Paper No. 5, 1972).

[5] Powers of Criminal Courts Act 1973, Sched. 3, para. 8 (1).

[6] (1969), 53 Cr. App. Rep. 314.

with hearsay received in almost every report. In an earlier case the Court of Criminal Appeal upheld the reception of information which was of assistance to the court even if not strictly proved.[1] The prevailing practice seems to be to treat the strict rules of evidence as suspended in the absence of challenge. If there is objection, then it may be that matters must be strictly proved or the court must attempt the impossible and ignore the evidence it has improperly heard.[2]

There is little to be found in the legislative provisions as to the procedure to be followed in court. An example is the question of the appearance of the report's author in the witness-box. As we shall see, it is expressly provided in connection with some of the other types of report to court that the officer responsible for the report must give evidence and be available for cross-examination in any case in which any objection is made to the contents of the report. No such rule exists in the present context, and the result, highly convenient for the probation service, is that reports are presented by liaison officers or other colleagues of the original author. This leads to the daily absurdity of officers taking the oath to give their name and indicate that there is a report, neither matter being exactly controversial nor a likely subject for perjury. All the officer can add is that he did not write the report, knows nothing about the defendant and is therefore unable to answer any questions; this plainly precludes any cross-examination and makes his appearance a useless and probably unnecessary ritual.

The precise point in the proceedings at which the report is considered also varies from court to court, as does the practice as to whether the report is made available to the prosecution, and whether it is read out aloud in open court. Judicial guidance on some of these points, that the report should be received before the defence makes its plea in mitigation,[3] so that the defence has the last word, and that the practice of reading the reports aloud was undesirable[4] is not universally known or followed. It is important for the probation officer to know the local practice.

JUVENILE COURT PROCEEDINGS

The legal provisions as to reports in care proceedings or criminal proceedings in juvenile courts[5] are much more detailed, but this has not eliminated a remarkable variety of local practice.

---

[1] *R.* v. *Marquis* (1951), 115 J.P. 329; 35 Cr. App. Rep. 33; cf. *Flewitt* v. *Horvath*, [1972] Crim. L.R. 103, where the evidence, though directed to the question of penalty, was introduced during the actual trial; as hearsay it was inadmissible at that stage.

[2] See *R.* v. *Campbell* (1911), 75 J.P. 216; 6 Cr. App. Rep. 131.

[3] *R.* v. *Kirkham*, [1968] Crim. L.R. 210; (1968) 112 Sol. Jo. 151.

[4] *R.* v. *Smith*, [1968] Crim. L.R. 33; (1967), 111 Sol. Jo. 850.

[5] As to these proceedings generally, see chap. 5.

Reports are now obligatory in every juvenile court case. Reports as to the home surroundings, school record, health and character of the juvenile must be provided either by the local authority or the probation service. The Children and Young Persons Act 1969[1] places the primary responsibility on the local authority. It must prepare reports whenever proceedings are brought by the authority itself[2] and whenever the authority is notified (as they must be[3]) that proceedings are being brought by someone else. In the case of children aged between thirteen[4] and seventeen, notice must also be given to the probation service, and local arrangements approved by the justices or the probation and after-care committee may provide for the duty of preparing reports on children in this age-group to be discharged by the probation service rather than the social services department of the local authority.[5] Much depends upon the relative staffing position of the two services.

In addition the court may ask either the local authority or the probation service to make further enquiries or produce further reports. The court can address such a request to either service, and presumably to both, at its complete discretion.[6]

No report can be presented until the case against the child has been made out, that is the criminal charge is proved or, in care proceedings, the requirements in section 1 of the 1969 Act are met. The procedural rules[7] direct the court to take the report into consideration, and it would seem that the strict rules of evidence are inapplicable. There is no need for the report to be read aloud, or shown to the child or his parents, and the court may require either the child or his parents to withdraw if this is thought to be in the interests of the child while, for example, the report is discussed with the officer who has presented it. Natural justice clearly requires that some opportunity be given for challenge. As the procedure on this point is often misunderstood, the relevant rules are set out:

"Where . . . a report has been considered without being read aloud or where the child or young person, his parent or guardian has been required to withdraw from the court . . . then—

---

[1] S. 9 (1).
[2] In school attendance cases, proceedings are brought and reports prepared by the local education authority: see *ibid.*, s. 2 (8).
[3] *Ibid.*, ss. 2 (3), 5 (8). The latter refers to "young persons" but is extended to all juveniles by S.I. 1970 No. 1882.
[4] This lower age-limit is subject to variation by the Secretary of State. It was fixed at 13 by S.I. 1974 No. 1083.
[5] Children and Young Persons Act 1969, s. 34 (2), (3); for the ages, see last note.
[6] See Children and Young Persons Act 1969, s. 9 (2) (duty of local authority to comply); Powers of the Criminal Courts Act 1973, Sched. 3, para. 8 (1) (duty of probation officers; quoted above, and not limited to criminal proceedings).
[7] Magistrates' Courts (Children and Young Persons) Rules 1970, r. 10 (criminal proceedings); r. 20 (care proceedings).

(a) the child or young person shall be told the substance of any part of the information given to the court bearing on his character or conduct which the court considers to be material to the manner in which the case should be dealt with unless it appears to it impracticable so to do having regard to his age and understanding, and

(b) the parent or guardian of the child or young person, if present, shall be told the substance of any part of such information which the court considers to be material as aforesaid and which has references to his [i.e. the parent's or guardian's] character or conduct or to the character, conduct, home surroundings or health of the child or young person."[1]

and evidence may be called to challenge a statement, and the person who made the report may be required to attend (if necessary, after an adjournment).

In some courts it is the practice for almost every case to be considered on two separate occasions. The case against the child is proved at the first hearing, and reports are prepared during an adjournment. The justices, and in particular the chairman, are then able to read the reports before the second hearing and the passages which may have to be summarised for the parties' benefit can be identified. In other courts where the reports are ready to hand when the case is proved, the justices can have no advance sight of the reports, and the chairman's task is much harder. It is very important to know local practice: it is sometimes the custom to indicate by a marginal line the most important passages containing matters which may have to be put to the parties, but in other courts the same marginal indication may have a different meaning, identifying a particularly delicate matter (references to the parents' alcoholism, for example) which presents a hazard to the chairman as he tries to put over the gist of the report. In some courts, reports appear to be handed to the parents (though this is not a legal requirement); in others the parents are given little or no information, despite the rules of procedure.

DOMESTIC PROCEEDINGS BEFORE THE MAGISTRATES' COURTS

The magistrates sitting in the domestic court to deal with matrimonial proceedings have three distinct powers to ask for reports, in respect of attempts at conciliation, the future of the children, and the means of the parties. A principle which applies throughout is that the report must not be used as a form of enquiry into the merits of the case, that is the grounds on which the husband or wife seeks a separation or maintenance order. The decision on the merits must be based on the evidence presented by the disputing parties, not on the findings of a probation officer acting as a roving investigator on behalf of the

---

[1] Magistrates' Courts (Children and Young Persons) Rules 1970, r. 10 (2) (criminal proceedings); r. 20 (2) makes substantially the same provision for care proceedings with a drafting difference, the child or young person being referred to as "the relevant infant".

court. The statutory provisions owe some of their complexity to the determination of Parliament to safeguard that principle.[1]

Conciliation

The magistrates may ask a probation officer (or, indeed, any other person) to attempt to effect a conciliation between the parties.[2] If the attempt succeeds then the whole proceedings naturally come to an end. If it fails, then the conciliator may, if he thinks fit, prepare a report for the court. This is not an account of the conciliation attempt, but a summary of the allegations made by each party, and the answers to those allegations given by the other party, with a list of those who may be able to give useful evidence: a particular form is prescribed.

This report is in effect a small dossier on the case, and a good report is an admirable introductory summary for the bench. The magistrates are entitled to "make use of the report for the purpose of putting or causing to be put questions to any witness".[3] The danger is that they will be tempted to judge the case on the report rather than the evidence: the Act adds "so, however, that nothing contained in the report shall be received by the court as evidence".

There are two further safeguards. No allegation made by either party may be included in a report unless the maker of the allegation consents in writing;[4] by withholding consent, the parties can effectively prevent the making of a report. This protects the "without prejudice" principle. A copy of the report must be sent to each party, and if that step is omitted the magistrates may not make use of the report.[5]

In any event, the power of the magistrates or their clerk to question witnesses on the basis of the report is limited. They have a duty to put questions on behalf of a party to domestic proceedings who is unrepresented and finds it difficult to conduct his own case,[6] but in all other cases interventions from the bench are, or should be, strictly limited.

Reports relating to children

Once a decision has been reached on separation and maintenance issues as between husband and wife, the court may decide to call for a report concerning the future of the children. The report may be prepared by a probation officer or a local authority social worker; there is no prescribed form, but the court must specify the matters on which

---

[1] See *Higgs* v. *Higgs*, [1941] P. 27, especially *per* Sir Boyd Merriman, P. at pp. 30–1.
[2] The Law Commission has expressed the view that the court should be placed under a duty to consider reconciliation prospects in every case: Working Paper No. 53 (1973), para. 82. If this is translated into legislation, the volume of conciliation work would of course tend to increase.
[3] Magistrates' Courts Act 1952, s. 59 (3).
[4] *Ibid.*, s. 59 (1) proviso.
[5] *Ibid.*, s. 59 (2), (3).
[6] *Ibid.*, s. 61.

it requires a report, presumably indicating the nature of the access or custody question raised in the case.[1]

In a sense, the social worker *is* here being asked to report on the merits of the case, and will often include a firm recommendation. Of course the decision is for the magistrates, but the High Court has made it clear that they should differ from the view taken by the social worker only for clear reasons, which they should take care to explain.[2]

The procedure is laid down in detail in the Matrimonial Proceedings (Magistrates' Courts) Act 1960. This expressly reinforces the privilege which attaches to statements made "without prejudice"; nothing said in the course of attempted reconciliation may be included in the report unless both parties consent.[3] The report must either be made orally, or if it is in writing, as it usually will be, must be read aloud in full in court. The parties or their legal representatives are then asked if they object to anything in the report; if they do the officer who made the report gives sworn evidence and can be cross-examined, and the parties may call witnesses or give evidence themselves on any matter dealt with in the report.[4]

It is expressly provided that the report and any evidence given after an objection may be taken into account by the court even if they do not comply with the strict rules of evidence.[5] This means, for example, that hearsay, general statements as to reputation, and other material frowned on by the rules of evidence are permitted.

There are sometimes practical difficulties in producing a report, particularly when the parties live at opposite ends of the country. This problem was foreseen when the procedure was first devised in 1959,[6] but was the subject of more detailed judicial guidance in 1973.[7] The President of the Family Division emphasised that one report by one officer was almost invariably more satisfactory than two reports by two different officers. Whenever possible a single officer should see both parties and report his own observations; the court would sometimes be able to identify special features of the case which made a single report absolutely essential, and solicitors could help by prompting the court on occasion. Where distance or other factors would lead to unacceptable delay or expense, two separate reports could be tendered.

---

[1] Matrimonial Proceedings (Magistrates' Courts) Act 1960, s. 4 (2), as amended by the Guardianship Act 1973, s. 8.
[2] *Clark* v. *Clark* (1970), 114 Sol. Jo. 318.
[3] Matrimonial Proceedings (Magistrates' Courts) Act 1960, s. 4 (5).
[4] *Ibid.*, s. 4 (3). The Law Commission has expressed the view that the law should be changed so as to allow the court to dispense with the reporting officer's giving evidence where the point in issue is of little importance, and to remove the requirement that reports must always be read aloud: Working Paper No. 53 (1973), para. 140.
[5] *Ibid.*, s. 4 (4).
[6] The Act speaks of "the officer by whom the statement was or purported to be" made, and this was intended to avoid the necessity of producing the actual author of the report on every occasion: Report of the Departmental Committee on Matrimonial Proceedings in Magistrates' Courts (1959), Cmnd. 638, p. 34.
[7] *B.* v. *B.* (1973), 117 Sol. Jo. 165.

Means enquiries

Similar rules govern reports as to means. In domestic cases, including here affiliation proceedings, the magistrates, once they have resolved all other issues, may ask a probation officer to investigate the means of the parties. This course should only be taken if the magistrates find that it is the only reasonable way of discovering the facts.[1] The resulting report does not have to be sent to the parties, but it must be given orally in court, or read aloud in full, the parties must be given the opportunity to object, and if they do the probation officer must give evidence and be cross-examined. Here again the strict rules of evidence are expressly waived.[2]

The need to follow the various procedural rules to the letter was emphasised in *Higgs* v. *Higgs*,[3] a case in which the magistrates provided a neat illustration of almost the entire range of possible errors. A single report was received by the magistrates before any of the issues had been resolved. It dealt with the prospects of reconciliation, expressed an opinion as to whether the husband intended to make proper provision for the wife, and gave an account of the husband's means. Both conciliation and means would have been proper subjects for reports, but means could not be investigated until all other issues had been cleared up. In any event, as no copies were given to the parties and nothing was read aloud, so that the parties did not know of and could not object to the contents, the procedural code was ignored. As to the expression of opinion as to the merits, that was wholly inexcusable. The whole adjudication was set aside for a new start to be made.

DIVORCE PROCEEDINGS

Courts exercising the divorce jurisdiction, that is the High Court and certain county courts, have welfare officers, usually probation officers, appointed to serve them. They can be asked to help the parties when there seems a prospect of reconciliation,[4] but this is very seldom the case once matters have reached the divorce court. The major part of the welfare officer's work concerns the children affected by the proceedings.

The court can ask the welfare officer to investigate and report upon any matter arising in matrimonial proceedings which concerns the welfare of a child.[5] The court may ask for a full report, or indicate particular aspects as requiring special attention. The decision to ask for a report may be made by the judge himself, but will usually be

---

[1] *Kershaw* v. *Kershaw*, [1966] P. 13; [1964] 3 All E.R. 635.
[2] Magistrates' Courts Act 1952, s. 60.
[3] [1941] P. 27.
[4] Matrimonial Causes Act 1973, s. 6 (2) gives the court power to adjourn proceedings for this purpose.
[5] Matrimonial Causes Rules 1973, r. 95. See the Home Office *Memorandum of Guidance for Divorce Court Welfare Officers* (1968). Similar procedures are applied in any case in which a parent applies for *habeas corpus* in respect of a child.

taken by the registrar in advance of the hearing. The registrar may be asked to order a report by the parties themselves, and it is not improper for the welfare officer himself to tell the registrar of special circumstances already known to him which suggest that a reference for a report would be useful. Similarly the welfare officer may seek the guidance of the registrar during his investigations, if for example he discovers matters which might prejudice the case of either party to the divorce proceedings.[1]

In compiling his report the welfare officer is allowed access to the court file on the case, which contains the petition and other documents and is normally only open to inspection by the parties and their solicitors.[2] He will consult the various agencies which may be able to assist, local officials of the NSPCC, clergy, doctors and so on, and include an account of their views in his report. Some of this will necessarily be hearsay, but this is acceptable. As the official *Memorandum of Guidance*[3] puts it,

> "the matter is in the court's discretion, but courts have usually been willing to accept in a welfare officer's report information as to the opinion of other social workers, general impressions of character, and statements made by a child in the absence of his parents".

The parties and the children will of course be seen; the guidance given to probation officers reporting to magistrates' courts about the desirability of a single officer seeing all parties is equally relevant here.[4] The official *Memorandum of Guidance*[5] makes it clear that the report should *not* contain advice as to the decision the court should reach.

When the report is completed it is added to the court file and may be seen by the parties and their legal advisers. The welfare officer is present at the hearing and may be questioned upon it by the judge and in disputed cases cross-examined. This practice was approved in *Fowler* v. *Fowler and Sine*,[6] where the Court of Appeal strongly disapproved of the action of the trial judge in having a private discussion with the welfare officer in the absence of the parties and their representatives. There might be exceptional cases, perhaps where reconciliation was possible, for private communication between the welfare officer and the judge, but in all other cases the parties must know what information the welfare officer provides, so that they can challenge it.

---

[1] *Memorandum of Guidance*, para. 31.
[2] Matrimonial Causes Rules 1973, rr . 95 (3) (*a*), 130.
[3] Para. 34.
[4] See p. 30, above; cf. *Memorandum of Guidance*, paras. 15–17.
[5] Para. 32.
[6] [1963] P. 311; [1963] 1 All E.R. 119. The Court of Appeal followed dicta in an earlier Court of Appeal decision, *Re K. (infants)*, [1963] Ch. 381; [1962] 3 All E.R. 1000, whch was later reversed by the House of Lords, but in a way which seems to leave the divorce court practice untouched. See below.

WARDSHIP PROCEEDINGS

When a child is made a ward of court, the court may appoint a guardian *ad litem* to represent the child's interests; he reports to court in much the same way as a divorce court welfare officer. The guardian *ad litem* is usually the Official Solicitor, so this area is unlikely to be of direct concern to most social workers. It is referred to because of the leading case of *Official Solicitor* v. *K.* (entitled in the lower courts *Re K. (infants)*) which exposed a major clash of principles as to the confidentiality of reports.

The Official Solicitor was appointed guardian *ad litem* for a child who was the centre of a custody dispute. He twice submitted statements of facts to the court, which were made available to the parties; but he also submitted confidential reports which the trial judge refused to make available, though he would have allowed the parties' legal representatives to see them. Was this a proper procedure?

One view, taken by the Court of Appeal,[1] was that natural justice required full disclosure. Upjohn, L.J. stated a clear principle:

> "It seems to me fundamental to any judicial inquiry that a person or other properly interested party must have the right to see all the information put before the judge, to comment on it, to challenge it and if needs be to combat it, and to try to establish by contrary evidence that it is wrong. It cannot be withheld from him in whole or in part. If it is so withheld and yet the judge takes such information into account in reaching his conclusion . . . the preceedings cannot be described as judicial."[2]

It will be seen that this principle lies behind many of the statutory provisions examined above. But in the particular context of wardship the principle did not prevail. The House of Lords reversed the Court of Appeal decision.[3] The practice of submitting confidential reports was to be continued, but sparingly; the special paternal nature of wardship proceedings[4] made it appropriate for the decision about the disclosure of confidential reports to be within the discretion of the judge, who would usually allow the legal representatives (if any) of the parties to see the reports when the parties themselves were denied access to them. As the trial judge had said, "where the paramount purpose is the welfare of the infant, the procedure and rules of evidence should serve and certainly not thwart that purpose".[5]

One further matter was discussed in the case but not resolved. If the judge does disclose the contents of the confidential report, must he allow the parties to cross-examine its author? As we have seen, this can be done in the case of divorce court welfare reports, though it is

---

[1] [1963] Ch. 381, at p. 390.
[2] *Ibid.*, at pp. 405–6.
[3] *Official Solicitor* v. *K.*, [1965] A.C. 201; [1963] 2 All E.R. 191.
[4] As to this, see further pp. 39–41.
[5] [1963] Ch. 381, at p. 387.

more usual for the welfare officer to answer questions without giving formal evidence on oath. The point arose in a mental health context in *Re W.L.W.*,[1] a decision of the Court of Protection whose judge receives reports from officials known as the Lord Chancellor's Visitors. These reports are confidential and are only disclosed if the judge so orders.[2] It was held that once a report was disclosed the judge would normally permit cross-examination, but that he had a discretion and might refuse to allow it where on the facts of a particular case it would be injurious to the patient involved.

ADOPTION CASES

Another type of case raising these issues is adoption applications, in connection with which the child's guardian *ad litem*[3] submits a "confidential report".[4] The practice is similar to that which has emerged in the wardship cases: the judge has a discretion whether or not to let the parties know the contents of the report. In practice he will indicate to the parties any allegations made against them in the report so that they have an opportunity to challenge what is said.[5]

GUARDIANSHIP OF MINORS APPLICATIONS

The Guardianship Act 1973[6] provides for the preparation of reports to assist the court in considering an application for custody or access under section 9 of the Guardianship of Minors Act 1971. The provisions are closely modelled on those governing reports as to children affected by matrimonial proceedings before the magistrates' courts and much of what has been said about these provisions is again relevant.[7]

The court may request a report (either oral or written) on any relevant matter from either the local authority or a probation officer. The report has to be made orally or read aloud in full at the hearing, and if any challenge is raised the officer preparing the report must give evidence and may be cross-examined. The parties may call evidence on their own account. It is expressly provided that the normal rules of evidence do not apply to the reports or the evidence given by the officer in support of his report.[8]

---

[1] [1972] Ch. 456; [1972] 2 All E.R. 433.
[2] Mental Health Act 1959, s. 109 (5).
[3] See generally pp. 119–122.
[4] Adoption (High Court) Rules, r. 15; Adoption (County Court) Rules, r. 9; Adoption (Juvenile Court) Rules, r. 9.
[5] *Re P.A. (an infant)*, [1971] 3 All E.R. 522; [1971] 1 W.L.R. 1530; *Re G. (infant)*, [1963] 2 Q.B. 73; [1963] 1 All E.R. 20 (approving *Re J.S. (an infant)*, [1959] 3 All E.R. 856; [1959] 1 W.L.R. 1218; *Re E. (an infant)* (1960), *Times*, March 24th; *Re B. (an infant)* (1960), *Times*, March 25th).
[6] S. 6; see also Appendix, p. 161 *et seq*.
[7] I.e. Matrimonial Proceedings (Magistrates' Courts) Act 1960, s. 4, as to which see pp. 29–30, above
[8] Guardianship Act 1973, s. 6 (3).

OTHER CASES

The Probation Rules 1965, rule 31, places probation officers under a duty to report to the magistrates on request in connection with an application for consent to marriage.[1] The procedure to be adopted in respect of these reports, their precise status, and the application of the rules of evidence is nowhere made clear; it may be that objection by one or both parties would effectively bar the reception of such reports.

The local authority is under a duty to prepare reports when a complaint is made against them by a parent or guardian who alleges that a child is beyond control, and seeks a court order directing the local authority to institute care proceedings.[2] Here the authority is a party to the case as well as the source of reports, and the two roles must in the nature of things become entangled. This breach of principle can be excused in view of the preliminary nature of the order sought.

It would be pleasant to end this chapter with a clear statement of the principles which emerge from this review of the law governing reports to court. Alas, the principles are unclear. Amongst the relevant policy considerations are the need to ensure full disclosure of facts to the court, the need to give a party notice of the allegations made against him, the desirability of encouraging frankness amongst writers of reports and those they interview by affording some confidentiality, and the need to protect the interests of those who might be harmed by the publication of information. The balance between these competing considerations is struck in different ways depending on the type of case under consideration. And it must be added that practicalities of staffing, time spent waiting in court, travelling time and so on, though they are not discussed here, cannot be altogether forgotten in applying legal ideals to the real situation.

---

[1] Marriage Act 1949, s. 3.
[2] Children and Young Persons Act 1963, s. 3 (2).

Chapter 3

CHILDREN—CARE AND SUPERVISION

This chapter and the three which follow are concerned with the relationship between, on the one hand, children who are in a sense "at risk" and their families, and, on the other hand, public agencies such as the social services department of a local authority and the police. The phrase "at risk" covers a wide variety of situations: the child may be the victim of cruelty or neglect, he may be part of a homeless family or be an orphan, he may play truant or commit criminal offences, or he may be living with someone who is a prostitute or is mentally disordered. What these situations have in common is that they create the expectation of some sort of public intervention, with some agency offering advice or care or control.

Some social workers are concerned more with the community than with the individual family, seeking social or political change. The law imposes few specific restraints on such action; this is partly because the political philosophy of a democratic state would not permit the stifling of such activity, but also because the effects of social and political activity are diffused, and no particular individual is so particularly affected that the law intervenes to protect his rights. Legal regulation is much more evident when the intervention is focussed on the individual family or child. Even then the range of possible actions is enormous, varying with the nature of the situation requiring attention, the personalities of those concerned, the function and policy of the worker's agency, and the availability of resources. For legal purposes all the various things a social work agency can do have to be reduced to broad categories even at the risk of doing considerable violence to the realities of practice. Apart from the provision of material assistance, the main categories of action are those of "supervision" and "care".

"Supervision" has an authoritarian ring but it is used here for any relationship in which the social worker's duty is, in the traditional probation phrase, "to advise, assist and befriend" the client. In "care", again despite the overtones of the label, the intervention is more intensive, with at least the possibility of physical control over where the client lives and what he does, including perhaps some sort of institutional residence.

The motives behind the legal regulation of supervision and care are twofold. First is the awareness of the scarcity of resources and the need to define eligibility, so that resources go to the deserving and not just to the demanding. Second, and more central to the lawyers' concerns, is the question of self-determination, or as the lawyer would call it, of freedom or liberty. Institutional care obviously involves a restriction on liberty, but the same may also be true of forms of supervision, and the law must ensure that restrictions are not imposed without good reason. It follows that there is a crucial distinction between intervention which is voluntary, in that the client seeks or agrees to the social worker's action, and those cases in which the individual's objections have to be overridden. This distinction between voluntary and compulsory intervention is a central one in children's legislation.

PARENTS' RIGHTS

It is difficult, in making general statements about cases involving children, to use consistently the usual terminology of social worker and client. A sixteen-year-old offender under supervision is clearly the client, though his family cannot be ignored; but where a baby or young child is involved it is the parents who need the advice, and it is with the parents that there may be conflict. Child law is one of the few remaining areas in which it is possible to speak of one person having rights over another human being. Parents have the right, and the duty, to bring up their children as they think fit, and this includes the right to bring up children in a way which might strike more conformist neighbours as unusual or even eccentric. There is an important policy question: assuming for the moment unlimited professional child care resources, at what point is outside intervention justified? Should there be a right to be a bad parent, to make mistakes, to experiment with a child's future?

It was thought at one time that parents, and especially fathers, had a natural authority over their children. One judge of the Court of Appeal, speaking in 1883, said, "When, by birth, a child is subject to a father, it is for the general interest of families, and for the general interest of children, and really for the interest of the particular infant, that the Court should not, except to very extreme cases, interfere with the discretion of the father, but leave to him the responsibility of exercising that power which nature has given him by the birth of the child." [1] Now, not only are father and mother on an equal footing, but their rights as parents may have to give way to a higher value,

---

[1] *Re Agar-Ellis, Agar-Ellis* v. *Lascelles* (1883), 24 Ch. D. 317, at p. 334 *per* Cotton, L.J.

that of the welfare of the child himself. In a case under the Guardianship of Minors legislation, Lord MacDermott summarised the position
by saying, "The rights and wishes of parents, whether unimpeachable
or otherwise, must be assessed and weighed in their bearing on the
welfare of the child in conjunction with all other factors relevant to
that issue."[1]

But the law offers no single answer to the policy question. In some
contexts the welfare of the child is the paramount consideration, but
elsewhere, and notably in certain disputes between parent and social
services department, parental rights may still prevail, even if the child's
best interests (as judged by the professional experts) are not served as
a result.[2]

TERMINOLOGY

Child law is full of technicalities likely to trap the unwary. One
particularly nasty set of booby-traps is concealed in the innocent word
'child' itself. For many purposes including some, but by no means all,
of the provisions of the Children Act 1948, a child means a person
under 18. But the traditional usage of the criminal law is incorporated
in the other major piece of legislation, the Children and Young
Persons Act 1969: a "child" is under fourteen, and those aged fourteen,
fifteen or sixteen are "young persons". The Guardianship of Minors
Act 1971 applies to all those below the age of majority, now eighteen;
in the older cases and statutes a minor was called an "infant" and
the upper age-limit was twenty-one. Many proceedings concerning
children are in the Juvenile Court; "juvenile" usually means one
under seventeen.

There really is no easy rule to help sort out that jungle. The only
possible advice is to check the relevant statute, especially the interpretation section in which key words are defined and which is usually
printed at the end of the statute, whenever a teenager is involved in a
case.[3] A warning might be added that there is an unusually large
amount of unreliable "folk-law" in circulation in agencies, often giving
much exaggerated significance to the sixteenth birthday which is of
much greater interest to young lovers than to social workers.

Another series of terms which may cause confusion is that of
"guardianship", "custody", "care", "control"; all describe a relationship between some person and a child, but legal usage is perplexing
and surprisingly inexact. Parents have both rights and duties in
respect of their children; for example, a duty to maintain, and rights
to make decisions as to education or medical treatment. The whole
relationship, both rights and duties, is one of "guardianship". The
parents are the natural guardians of the child, but in some cases, as

---

[1] *J. v. C.,* [1970] A.C. 668, at p. 715, H.L.
[2] See further pp. 84–7.
[3] See Appendix, p. 161 *et seq.*

where the parents are both dead, it may be necessary to appoint other guardians, and the courts can do this under the Guardianship of Minors Act 1971. If the parents separate or are divorced, something must be done to avoid possible conflicts, and "custody"—the right to possession and control of the child—will normally be given to one or other party either in the domestic or matrimonial proceedings or (confusingly) in guardianship proceedings. It sometimes happens that a court will give custody to one party but actual "care and control" to the other, in which case custody has little immediate significance; but in some disputes with social services departments it is only a parent with custody who enjoys any rights,[1] and custody is sometimes given to *both* parents. Unfortunately the draftsmen of statutes pay little respect to tradition: in some Acts, "guardian" means anyone with actual charge of or control over a child and is distinguished from "legal guardian" with a much more limited definition;[2] all one can advise, once again, is great circumspection in cases involving persons claiming to be, or described as, a child's guardian.

WARDSHIP

In a number of different types of case involving children one or other party might be well advised to consider wardship proceedings. This possibility will be mentioned several times in the discussion which follows, and it will be helpful to give an indication of the nature of wardship at this point.

We have seen that a child's guardian has comprehensive powers over the child, and he can determine where the child will live, how he will be educated, and even with whom he should make friends. When a child is made a ward of court, these same functions are exercised by the court, in practice by a judge of the Family Division of the High Court. Taking wardship proceedings is one way of taking a dispute to court and the court has the widest possible powers in the orders it can make.

Wardship is still sometimes thought of as something peculiar to the propertied classes. Historically this was certainly true:[3] wardship originated in the feudal system of property, and in later centuries had real, and not just comic-opera, associations with heiresses;[4] until recent years the whole proceedings had to be based upon an issue arising out of a settlement of property, if need be one especially executed

---

[1] Children Act 1948, s. 6 (2); see p. 47, below.
[2] Children and Young Persons Act 1933, s. 107.
[3] A lucid and entertaining account of the development of wardship by a judge with much experience of its administration is in Cross, "Wards of Court" (1967), 83 L.Q.R. 201; this section relies heavily on that article.
[4] See *Iolanthe* for another judge's view.

for the purposes of the wardship. Now, the wardship jurisdiction applies to any child and the property aspects have quite vanished.

A child becomes a ward of court when someone (it can be anyone, but is most likely to be a parent or perhaps a social services department) takes out an originating summons in a local office of the High Court. This initial wardship continues for up to twenty-one days, but if satisfied that the proceedings are started for some good reason (and not, as has been known to happen, for publicity for a night-club artiste) the judge will continue the wardship until a full hearing can be arranged.[1]

The courts have very wide powers to make orders relating to children, either in the matrimonial jurisdiction or under the Guardianship of Minors Act 1971. It may be asked, why is there a need for a separate wardship jurisdiction? Wardship has a number of advantages over all over forms of procedure.

1. Wardship proceedings can be initiated by anyone, not just by the parents or guardian of the child. A relative or concerned outsider, including the social work agency, may only be able to take a matter to court via wardship.

2. The High Court in its wardship procedure has a number of advantages denied to other courts. It has the time, personnel and machinery to make detailed orders and to keep these under review. The court will of course receive reports from welfare officers, but a very special function is discharged by the Official Solicitor. He can take part in proceedings, representing the interests of the child and in the case of older children, presenting their own views. If the child remains a ward he can keep an eye upon the case, rather as an avuncular family solicitor might do; and he can secure the re-examination of the case by the judge if need arises.

3. A very practical advantage of taking wardship proceedings is that the situation is frozen, and whoever has possession of the child gains time. The court will not allow its procedure to be abused: the unmeritorious applicant will gain little as the judge will promptly end the proceedings and "deward" the child. In some cases this freezing effect may spare the child unnecessary changes of environment.

    A special application of the freezing effect is that the court may prohibit the removal of the child from the country. If a child is removed from the jurisdiction of the English courts there are formidable obstacles in the way of the English parent seeking to recover custody, especially for an English mother in a case where the father has taken the child to a country in which he is still regarded as having a prior natural right to possession. The immigration

---

[1] The procedure is governed by Law Reform (Miscellaneous Provisions) Act 1949, s. 9; R.S.C. Ord. 90, rr. 3–12.

authorities will cooperate in enforcing the court order by keeping a lookout at the ports, so the court order is not an altogether empty gesture.[1]

4. Most important of all, especially from the point of view of the local authority social services department, is that the court in wardship regards the welfare of the child as the first and paramount consideration. We have already noted that in some situations of conflict between the parents and the department the law may regard the parents' right to possession as decisive whatever the interests of the child. By using wardship the department can in effect appeal against that situation, and may persuade the court to override the parents in the interests of the child. An example, considered in more detail below, is where a parent without suitable accommodation for the child demands the child's return from the care of the local authority.[2] In some situations, wardship may be the only way in which the authority can keep the child in care and prevent it suffering unnecessary hardship.

On the other hand there are serious restraints on the use of wardship which explain why it is not used in more cases. It is a High Court procedure and expensive (though legal aid is available in appropriate cases). Even more important are the limitations which the judges have imposed on their own powers. Where the court takes the view that the power to make decisions about the child is vested in someone by the operation of some statute, for example where a care order made under the Children and Young Persons Act 1969 has committed the child to the care of the local authority, the court will not use its wardship powers to intervene. This limitation is very important in the sort of case with which local authority social workers are likely to be concerned and seriously restricts the use of wardship proceedings. Unfortunately the case-law is difficult and confused and the precise limits of the courts' powers are uncertain; this aspect will be examined below in relation to the various situations which present themselves.

VOLUNTARY AND COMPULSORY INTERVENTION

The point has already been made that the lawyer sees the distinction between voluntary and compulsory intervention as of the first importance. This distinction is central to the legislation relating to children.

---

[1] For the procedure see *Supreme Court Practice*, notes to Ord. 90, r. 3; *Practice Note*, [1963] 3 All E.R. 66; *Practice Direction*, [1973] 3 All E.R. 194, [1973] 1 W.L.R. 1014. Similar orders prohibiting the removal of a child can be made in matrimonial proceedings once the petition has been presented: Matrimonial Causes Rules 1973, r. 94 (1).

[2] I.e. under Children Act 1948, s. 1 (3); see pp. 84–7, below.

VOLUNTARY CASES

Under section 1 of the Children and Young Persons Act 1963,[1] it is the duty of every local authority to "make available such advice, guidance and assistance as may promote the welfare of children by diminishing the need to receive children into or keep them in care . . . or to bring children before a juvenile court". This will authorise the social services department to offer advice and guidance where its workers see that it is needed, and to respond to requests for help from parents or children. This covers voluntary forms of what we term "supervision".

If it becomes necessary for a child to be received into care because the parents cannot look after it, this can be effected under section 1 of the Children Act 1948[2] provided that certain criteria are satisfied and the parents consent.

In all these cases the agency is acting at the request or with the consent of the parents. The parent has lost no rights over the child, can break off the relationship with the agency at any time and recover possession of a child who has been received into care.

COMPULSORY SUPERVISION OR CARE

In other cases the local authority will provide supervision or take a child into care without the consent of the parents. Sometimes this happens because the parents have deliberately decided to part with the child who is being looked after by someone else. So the local authority has the right and duty to supervise "protected children", either foster-children under the Children Act 1958[3] or children placed for adoption and protected under Part IV of the Adoption Act 1958.[4]

Where the child is being looked after by its own parents and in most situations in which the child is in the care of strangers, the local authority can only intervene compulsorily if it first secures the approval of the courts. This usually involves an application to the juvenile court by way of care proceedings under the Children and Young Persons Act 1969[5] (which also provides for the emergency removal of children to a "place of safety"[6]), or, in the case of young offenders, to the juvenile court in its criminal jurisdiction.[7] In all these cases the court hearing provides safeguards against misuse of local authority powers.

The magistrates' domestic court and the divorce courts also have power to order that a child receive supervision or be received into care.[8]

---

[1] See further pp. 46–7, below.
[2] See pp. 44–8, below.   [3] See pp. 99–103, below.
[4] See pp. 113–14.   [5] See pp. 60–70.   [6] See pp. 92–4.   [7] See pp. 58–9.
[8] Matrimonial Causes Act 1973, ss. 43, 44; Matrimonial Proceedings (Magistrates' Courts) Act 1960, ss. 2–3. Similar powers exist in certain wardship and custody cases: Family Law Reform Act 1969, s. 7; Guardianship Act 1973, ss. 2–4. See pp. 70–4, below.

Here again there is the safeguard of the court but the procedure is a touch anomalous in that the order affecting the child is brought in on a sidewind; proceedings were not taken with that object.

"SECTION 2" CASES

More anomalous still are the powers of the local authority under section 2 of the Children Act 1948.[1] Where a child is in care with the consent of the parents, the local authority may, on prescribed grounds, pass a resolution assuming parental rights. This leaves parental duties (including that of financial provision for maintenance) untouched, but decisions about the child will now rest ultimately with the social services department. Although the parent has rights of objection and of appeal to the courts, a section 2 resolution can be made by the local authority, in the lawyers' sense an "interested party", without any prior judicial review; and what began as a voluntary case is converted unilaterally into a compulsory one. On the face of it, this is a surprising and awkward exception to the usual principles applying in child law.

---

[1] See pp. 48–57, below. The Children Act 1948, ss. 1 and 2, also apply where the child's parents are dead: in such a case the voluntary/compulsory distinction is obviously inapplicable.

Chapter 4

THE CHILDREN ACT 1948

The voluntary admission of children to the care of local authorities is governed by the Children Act 1948. That Act also empowers the local authority, once it has so received a child into its care, to assume the rights of one or both parents in certain circumstances. Both aspects are examined in this chapter.

VOLUNTARY ADMISSION TO CARE

When parents cannot look after their children themselves then the social services committee of the local authority must make provision for them. Section 1 (1) of the Act authorises their reception into care. It provides:

"Where it appears to a local authority with respect to a child in their area appearing to them to be under the age of seventeen—
(a) that he has neither parent nor guardian or has been and remains abandoned by his parents or guardian or is lost; or
(b) that his parents or guardian are, for the time being or permanently, prevented by reason of mental or bodily disease or infirmity or other incapacity or any other circumstances from providing for his proper accommodation, maintenance and upbringing; and
(c) in either case, that the intervention of the local authority under this section is necessary in the interests of the welfare of the child,
it shall be the duty of the local authority to receive the child into their care under this section."

This imposes a duty on the local authority: it must receive a child into care if one or other of the grounds set out in paragraphs (a) and (b) exist and if, also, the intervention is necessary in the interests of the welfare of the child.

THE STATUTORY GROUNDS

(i) "*That he has neither parent nor guardian*"

This ground may exist, surprisingly enough, even if one or both natural parents are still alive. This is because in the case of an illegitimate child, only his mother is regarded as a parent; the death or survival of the father is ignored. Similarly "parent" in relation to a child who has been adopted means the person or person by whom he was adopted, to the exclusion of the natural parents.[1]

An orphaned child will only have a legal guardian if one has been appointed by deed or will or by a court order.[2] The relative or friend who is in fact caring for the child has no legal status of guardian (unless he has been thus appointed). A step-parent is neither a parent nor a guardian.

(ii) *"That he has been and remains abandoned by his parents or guardian or is lost"*

In practice social services departments rarely rely on this ground. It makes provision for the child who has become separated from his parents either involuntarily when he is lost, or deliberately when he is abandoned. The meaning of abandonment has never been judicially defined for the purposes of this section. In the context of a criminal prosecution, when a parent was charged with having abandoned his child,[3] it was held that the abandonment must be likely to cause the child unnecessary suffering or injury to health.[4] Probably the only realistic interpretation in the present context is that if the parent has deserted the child, in the sense of walking out on him, the child will be abandoned. So, if a parent leaves his child with relatives, friends or foster-parents and then loses contact with him, he will be regarded as having abandoned his child. The same is true of the parent who leaves his child in a safe place, for example in the office of the local social services department. To construe abandonment in the stricter, criminal sense would mean that such a child could not lawfully be received into care.

There is no doubt that a child can be received into care in those circumstances. In fact it is not unknown in cases where it is desirable to receive a child into care but difficult to find proper legal grounds for the parents to make a notional, collusive abandonment of the child at the social services department's offices.

(iii) *"That his parents or guardian are, for the time being or permanently, prevented by reason of mental or bodily disease or infirmity or other incapacity or any other circumstance from providing for his proper accommodation, maintenance and upbringing"*

A commonplace example of the type of situation embraced by this ground is when the mother has to go into hospital, father, out at work

---

[1] Children Act 1948, s. 59.
[2] See p. 39, above.
[3] Children and Young Persons Act 1933, s. 1.
[4] *R.* v. *Whibley*, [1938] 3 All E.R. 777 (father left five children in juvenile court room; held not to be criminal abandonment).

all day, just cannot cope on his own, and the child must go into care. But illness is not the only circumstance which prevents a parent from looking after his child, and the section is deliberately framed loosely so that contingencies, which might not have been foreseen at the time of drafting, will fall within its scope. This ground cannot be used by the parent as a convenient means of taking a holiday without the children. Nor, generally speaking, can it be used to give the parent a break when the pressures of life threaten to become too much. The parent must be *prevented* from caring rather than simply not want to care. The social worker is sometimes confronted by the rather aggressive parent who "knows his rights" and demands that the child be taken into care in circumstances like these. Legally he is acting absolutely correctly when he resists this pressure.

THE WELFARE OF THE CHILD

Not only must one of the statutory grounds for intervention exist, but the welfare of the child must require this particular form of intervention. It is general social policy that wherever possible a child should be kept out of care, and local authorities through their social workers have for many years given support and assistance to families in danger of breaking up. The law encourages local authorities to secure the help and cooperation of voluntary organisations for this purpose.[1] If adverse circumstances make it seem likely that a parent will have to ask for his child to be received into care, but it becomes apparent that assistance in kind, or exceptionally in cash, might postpone or avert that possibility, the local authority is under a duty to see that such help is forthcoming.[2] There is, however, little bite to this provision, because of the limited nature of the assistance which it authorises. The local authority can make use of the professional skills of its social workers, and may be able to pay out a small cash sum; but if, for example, the real problem is homelessness, there is no duty to house the family in order to prevent the child coming into care.

The duty is to receive, not to take, children into care. This is not merely a matter of semantics; it serves to emphasise the voluntary nature of the arrangement, and it also connotes a passive rather than an active role by the local authority. The Act does not place local authorities under a duty to seek out children who are so circumstanced that they are eligible for reception into care. This means that some such children will never come to their attention. Also, even when grounds are made out, the local authority can choose whether or not to intervene. The sole criterion for the exercise of this choice is the welfare of the child. When a child is orphaned or abandoned, relatives or friends will often take over his physical care and at this stage there may be no need for

---

[1] Children and Young Persons Act 1963, s. 1 (2).
[2] *Ibid.*, s. 1 (1).

intervention by the local authority. If he stays in the care of non-relatives then he becomes a foster-child and subject to supervision as a protected child; the visits provided for under the fostering legislation afford an opportunity for consideration of any need for further intervention.[1]

Circumstances may not be quite so straightforward. The person looking after the child may be willing to continue doing so, but only if financial assistance is available. It is unlikely that the local authority would use its powers under the 1963 Act to make cash payments unless some short-term temporary assistance was all that was required. The usual procedure in these circumstances is to receive the child into care and then to board him back with the same person who thereby becomes eligible for a boarding-out allowance. This procedure is carried out on paper, that is to say there is no need physically to take the child into care and then return him home again.[2]

The local authority is empowered by the Children Act 1948 to receive, but not to take, a child from strangers who may be caring for him. If they are not willing to part with the child the local authority must go to court; either taking Care Proceedings, or applying for a court order for the removal of a foster-child.

CHILDREN SUBJECT TO CUSTODY ORDERS

The legal position is more complicated when the child has been the subject of court proceedings which resulted in a custody order. Only the parent who has been awarded custody is included in the phrase "parent or guardian" for the purposes of the relevant legislation.[3] This can give rise to some real difficulties which can be illustrated by the following hypothetical facts:

Alfred left his wife Betty to go to live with another woman. Betty went to the magistrates' court and obtained a maintenance order and custody of Colin, the child of the marriage. Betty has now become ill, and is about to go into hospital for a considerable period. She refuses to ask Alfred to look after the child, but Alfred is ready and willing to do so.

The position is that Colin has in fact a parent who is able to look after him; but in law the custody order means that Betty is the only person recognised as a parent. As she is prevented from caring for him, the local authority has grounds for receiving the child into care should it decide to do so. Having done so, the local authority could accommodate Colin wherever it wished, even in theory boarding him out with Alfred. On the other hand the authority might feel that, although

---

[1] Children Act 1958, s. 2; see pp. 99–103.
[2] Boarding Out of Children Regulations 1955 (S.I. 1955 No. 1377), reg. 1 (4).
[3] Children Act 1948, s. 6 (2).

the legal grounds for reception into care existed, intervention was not necessary in the interests of the welfare of Colin; in practice Betty might, as a result of this policy of non-involvement, find herself forced to let Alfred look after the child. Any of these decisions by the local authority is legally proper; yet another possibility would be to persuade Alfred to seek a variation of the custody order to avert any possibility of an apparent conflict between the court order and the effect of the authority's decisions. It must be stressed that any such conflict would be apparent and not real; the magistrates were resolving the issue between husband and wife, and the authority has a wholly distinct duty to the child.

If the facts in the example are altered slightly to include what is known as a "split order", with custody given to one parent (Alfred) but care and control to the mother,[1] the practicalities of the problem are more complex. If Betty finds herself unable to care for the child she cannot expect the local authority to take the child into care under section 1, for any reference to a parent will only include Alfred. If she tries to get Alfred to look after the child and *he* is prevented by circumstances from taking the child, there may be grounds for reception into care. If his refusal is through an obstinate refusal to cooperate with Betty, this ground does not apply, though it might be possible to treat the child as having been abandoned. The Act was not drafted with split orders in mind, and some inspired improvisation (or some turning of blind eyes to legal niceties) may be needed to sort out actual problem cases.

PROCEDURE

There is no formal procedure necessary for the reception of a child into care. It simply happens. In practice it is almost always the case that the parents, if alive and available, will be asked to sign some sort of consent form. This serves a useful bureaucratic function as page one of a file, but is of no legal significance in itself. It may, however, contain particular terms, such as a general consent to medical treatment being administered, which are important, and may also contain general information about the position of children in care which needs to be brought in some formal way to the attention of the parents.

ASSUMPTION OF PARENTAL RIGHTS

Section 2 of the Children Act 1948 enables a local authority to assume parental rights over any child in its care by a passing a resolution to that effect. These "section 2 resolutions" can be passed by the full

---

[1] Such an order can be made in the magistrates' court after proceedings under the Guardianship of Minors Act 1971, or in the higher courts in matrimonial cases.

Council of the local authority, but in practice authority to do so is delegated to the social services committee or further to a special sub-committee.[1]

The legal consequences of an assumption of parental rights are that, with a few exceptions,[2] the local authority can make decisions relating to the child without prior consultation with or authorisation from the parents. It means that the social services department can decide where and with whom the child should live; whether he should go home to his parents; who should have access to him; where he should go to school; whether he should have medical treatment. The most important effect is seen in a case in which the department considers that the child would be at risk, either physically or emotionally, if he were to go out of care. If parental rights have been taken, the parent no longer has the right to take the child home against the wishes of the social services department.[3]

Before parental rights can be assumed the child must be in the care of the local authority under section 1 of the Act. That means that the child must have come into care in the first instance with the consent of the parents, assuming them to be alive and then caring for the child. Once the child is in care, the decision to assume parental rights can be made at any time; in practice it will tend to arise when there is some development in the case or as a result of the review which local authorities are required to make every six months of the case of every child in their care.[4] Wherever possible the assumption of parental rights will be with the consent of the parents, but in the nature of things this is not always obtained. Even if the parents are entirely happy for the resolution to be passed, there must exist one or more of the grounds set out in the statutory provisions; if grounds do not exist any resolution will be improper and can be set aside by the courts.

THE STATUTORY GROUNDS[5]

(i) *The child's parents are dead and he has no guardian*

As was noted in connection with reception into care under section 1, the words "parent" and "guardian" are both given restrictive definitions in the Act.[7] This means that whether a child is orphaned for our present purposes depends upon his status. When he is illegitimate he

---

[1] Authority must be delegated in clear terms; for a case in which this was not done, leading to doubts as to the validity of a section 2 resolution, see *Re L. (A.C.) (an infant)*, [1971] 3 All E.R. 743.

[2] The local authority cannot alter the child's religious upbringing (Children Act 1948, s. 3 (7)) or consent to the child's adoption (Adoption Act 1958, s. 4 (3) (c)).

[3] Children Act 1948, s. 3 (2).

[4] Children and Young Persons Act 1969, s. 27 (4).

[5] Children Act 1948, s. 2; Children and Young Persons Act 1963, s. 48. The Children Bill (see Appendix, p. 161 *et seq.*) restates these grounds, giving effect to the proposals of the Houghton Committee and making other minor changes.

[6] Children Act 1948, s. 59; see pp. 44-5.

has no parents when his mother dies; consequently a local authority can assume parental rights over him on this basis, even though his natural father is alive, in contact with his child, and paying money towards his maintenance. When both parents of a legitimate child are dead he has no parent even though he has a living step-parent. When the child has been adopted the death or survival of his natural parents is irrelevant.

(ii) *A parent or guardian has abandoned the child*

Abandoned will have the same meaning as for section 1, that is to say it is used in the sense that the parent has deserted his child. Once the parent has deserted the child the local authority is entitled to assume parental rights at once. In practice the authority will normally wait to see whether the parent returns to claim his child; but in an urgent necessity immediate action can be taken. If, for example, a surgeon was refusing to perform an operation on the child without first obtaining the consent of a person with parental rights,[1] it might need to do so.

The child must still be abandoned when the resolution is made, so if the parent has resumed some form of contact with the child, such as visiting him or sending him letters, he will no longer be abandoned and it will be too late to make a section 2 resolution on this ground.

(iii) *A parent or guardian is deemed to have abandoned the child, the whereabouts of the parent or guardian having remained unknown for not less than twelve months.*

This ground was added by the Children and Young Persons Act 1963, because social workers found the existing abandonment ground, ground (ii), difficult to operate. The type of case which gave trouble was one in which a child had been received into care and the parent gradually lost contact and eventually failed to notify the authority of a change of address. The authority would have no means of knowing what had happened to the parent. For some time at least it would be difficult to say with certainty that the parent had deserted the child; the parent's disappearance might be due to illness or force of circumstances. The authority needed some statutory guideline on how soon it was right to treat the child as having been abandoned. This is provided in ground (iii). It is suggested that in applying this ground, a parent's whereabouts should only be treated as unknown when reasonable attempts have been made to trace him.

When the additional ground was added in 1963, Parliament could have deleted the existing ground (ii) but did not do so. If the authority

---

[1] If the consent was needed for a life-saving operation or blood transfusion this would seem an unnecessary precaution on his part; see Ministry of Health Circular F/P9/1B, April 14th, 1967. However the operation might not be so serious, in which case the surgeon's position is not so straightforward.

is satisfied that a parent has abandoned his child, and he may for example have made this clear in letters or by actions such as emigrating, there is no need to wait until twelve months have expired. It is only when there is a lack of real information about the parent's attitude that ground (iii) must be relied upon. Some local authorities appear to treat ground (ii) as a dead letter and impose a twelve-month waiting period in all cases; this is unnecessarily cautious.

(iv) *The parent or guardian suffers from a permanent disability rendering him incapable of caring for the child*

This disability can be due to either physical or mental illness and so overlaps with the next ground.

(v) *The parent or guardian suffers from a mental disorder (within the meaning of the Mental Health Act 1959[1]) which renders him unfit to have the care of the child*

This ground was also added in 1963 because of practical difficulties in the operation of ground (iv). That ground requires a permanent disability, and can only be relied upon when there is no likelihood of the patient recovering his full capacities. Often the social worker's main difficulty was in obtaining the appropriate medical or psychiatric evidence. It is difficult in many cases to give a firm prognosis, particularly where a mental condition is involved. In any event, the doctor's primary concern is with the interests of his patient; it may be thought undesirable that the patient should know of his future prospects as he would do when notified of the grounds on which the resolution was made.

The addition of the new ground using the established categories of the Mental Health Act was designed to ease this problem, but the medical practitioner may still hesitate to venture an opinion on the question of fitness to have the care of the child.

In these medical matters, common sense and caution suggest that the social services committee should have expert medical evidence before them. As a matter of strict law it seems that this is not essential. In one High Court case an argument that medical evidence was essential was rejected, the judge saying, "As long as the committee act bona fide, apply their minds to the right question and take only relevant considerations into account, it is for them to decide how to set about collecting and receiving information."[2] The case concerned ground (iv) but the statement would seem to apply to ground (v) as well, but it should be taken as a statement of the legal position and not as any encouragement to social services committees to dispense with expert advice in favour of hunches and assumptions.

---

[1] See pp. 136–40.
[2] *Re L. (A.C.) (an infant)*, [1971] 3 All E.R. 743, at p. 754 *per* Cumming-Bruce, J.

(vi) *The parent or guardian is of such habits or mode of life as to be unfit to have the care of the child*

Some local authorities make a lot of use of this ground, others rely on it less often. It is a phrase which covers a wide spectrum of behaviour and must turn in part upon current standards of conduct and morality. The words "habits and mode of life" imply that there must be a pattern of behaviour; but in one case in 1973, not fully reported, a court held a father convicted of murdering the mother to be unfit to have the care of his child on his release from prison. The decision is entirely understandable but does perhaps involve some straining of the strict words of the Act. Persistent drunkenness, drug addition, vagrancy, prostitution where the child is exposed to moral danger, and some forms of criminal conduct involving children, for example incest or cruelty, would all fall within this ground. This is a difficult phrase to interpret and little guidance can be given on what other types of behaviour the court would hold to fall within its range if the resolution was challenged by the parent.

Consider the case of Billy, aged thirteen. His father has been in and out of prison for burglary and petty theft. Unlike the actual case mentioned above, these crimes were in no sense directed against any members of the family. During one of his spells inside Billy came into care. Father is now out of prison and wanting Billy home again. There seems a real likelihood that father will "apprentice" Billy to his criminal pursuits as he has already done this with an older son. If the local authority decided to make a section 2 resolution it would be entitled to take the father's past life into account when deciding whether he was a fit person to care for Billy. What is not certain is whether there are sufficient grounds. Is the father of Billy of such habits or mode of life as to be unfit to care for Billy?

(vii) *The parent or guardian has so persistently failed without reasonable cause to discharge the obligations of a parent or guardian as to be unfit to have the care of the child*

A parent has both legal and moral obligations. Legally he is obliged to maintain his child, morally he should show affection, care and interest towards his child.[1] If the parent does not contribute towards the child's support, does not visit him or write to him and shows no interest in his progress then he is failing as a parent. This failure could stem from illness or lack of money; if this was the case then the parent would have reasonable cause for falling down on his obligations. The margin between the indifferent and the inadequate parent is indefinable, but if the resolution was challenged the court would need to be satisfied that the parent fell within the former category.

---

[1] See judgment of Pennycuick, J., in *Re P.*, [1962] 3 All E.R. 789; [1962] 1 W.L.R. 1296.

Because the indifferent parent poses no immediate threat to his child's well-being, in the sense that he does not seem likely to take his child out of care, some local authorites do not bother to assume parental rights on this ground. This could prove disastrous for the child. Social workers are unfortunately all too familiar with the situation in which a parent, who has ignored his child for years, suddenly resumes an interest in him when the child approaches school-leaving age, presumably because he now has potential earning capacity. The child may have been settled and happy for years in a community home or foster-home and a change could be very damaging to his mental and emotional development. Yet unless parental rights have been taken by the local authority the child is always at risk of a sudden removal from care. In some respects his position is more critical than for example that of the child who must be protected from his mentally ill parent. In that case even if the local authority did not assume parental rights and the child went home, and subsequently the child was at risk because of the mental illness, then he could be the subject of care proceedings. But the child who is gravely disturbed by a change of care may well not fall within the scope of the 1969 Act. The local authority can anticipate this problem by making a section 2 resolution once it is satisfied that the parent has no intention of fulfilling his obligations.

PROPOSED EXTENSIONS

Amongst its other proposals, the Departmental Committee on the Adoption of Children, the Houghton Committee, proposed an additional ground for the assumption of parental rights, that the child had remained in the care of the local authority for a continuous period of three years. The committee's view was that "this would provide machinery for local authority intervention at a time when the parents, for whatever reason, have not been undertaking parental care for a considerable period, and at a stage in the history of the child in care where decisions as to his long-term future may be required".[1] This would represent a considerable extension of local authority powers and it remains to be seen whether it is accepted by Parliament.

ASSUMPTION OF THE RIGHTS OF ONE PARENT

A section 2 resolution is made with respect to each parent as an individual. Sometimes grounds only exist in the case of one parent, and parental rights will be assumed in relation to that parent but not the other. This can lead to practical difficulties, one example of which troubled the Houghton Committee:

"We have in mind the situation where a mentally ill mother [in respect of whom parental rights had been assumed by the local authority] may not, on discharge from hospital, be sufficiently recovered to have the care of her

---

[1] *Report*, Cmnd. 5107, para. 156. See Appendix, p. 161 *et seq.*

child; she may even need further periods in hospital. Yet the father against whom parental rights cannot be taken may exercise his right to withdraw his child from care, thus returning him to the care of his wife despite her continuing incapacity."[1]

The committee recommended that in such cases, the local authority should be given power to retain the child in care despite the father's request. This would, of course, be limited to cases in which the two parents were living together so that discharge of the child to either parent was in effect discharge into the care of them both.

There is a related difficulty which can arise when one parent has been given custody by a court order. A section 2 resolution can only be made in such a case in relation to the parent with custody. It cannot be made against the parent without custody. While both parents are alive this makes practical sense. But on the death of the parent with custody, the other parent acquires the right to his child's custody by survivorship.[2] This means that the child will merely be in care under section 1 in relation to the surviving parent, who can demand the return of the child at any time. If the local authority wishes to forestall this it should take prompt steps, if grounds exist, to pass a section 2 resolution assuming the rights of the surviving parent; but there is no way of anticipating the problem by taking action before the death of the first parent. If the authority fails to take prompt action the child may have to be returned at least temporarily to the surviving parent, and the resulting chopping and changing may be harmful to the child.[3]

PROCEDURE

When the resolution is considered by the appropriate committee, the committee members will necessarily rely on the information provided by the professional staff of the department. It is obviously important that the information provided should be full and accurate. Similarly, the committee must give precise information to the parents, making it clear which particular ground or grounds are being relied upon.

These points were both relevant in the case of *Re L. (A.C.)*,[4] which reached the High Court after a series of alarming muddles in Plymouth. These involved difficulties over the delegation of authority to a sub-committee, complex and technical procedural tangles, but also two failures over information. A section 2 resolution was passed and notice was given to the parent. The notice gave no details of the grounds for the resolution, merely referring to the text of the resolution itself. That referred compendiously to all available statutory grounds

---

[1] *Report*, Cmnd. 5107, para. 157. See Appendix, p. 161 *et seq.*
[2] Guardianship of Minors Act 1971, s. 3 (unless the surviving parent has been formally declared unfit to have custody).
[3] The general problem arising in cases in which an unsuitable parent seeks the return of his child from care is discussed in more detail at pp. 84–7, below.
[4] [1971] 3 All E.R. 743.

so was entirely unhelpful. The High Court judge said that he was disturbed by all this: there was no inkling given as to the grounds on which the committee had acted. In fact it had based its resolution on the ground that the parent was suffering from a permanent disability rendering her incapable of caring for one of her children. This it did under the mistaken impression based on false information supplied to it that another child of the family was also in care, whereas in fact the mother was looking after him. This obviously threw quite a different light on her ability to care for the child in question. Yet unless she was told of the ground which was being relied upon she would not know how important was the committee's mistake of fact.

SAFEGUARDS

Once a section 2 resolution has been made, the parent or guardian may sometimes be able to object to it. If he has consented in writing to the passing of the resolution, this right is not available; there are no procedural safeguards against the social worker who persuades the parent to sign away his rights as a parent without proper consideration of the consequences.[1]

If the parent has not consented and his whereabouts are known, he must be served with a notice in writing of the resolution and of his right to object.[2] The parent has one month in which to object; he must do so in writing. If the parent does object, there are two courses open to the local authority. It can take no action, in which case the resolution lapses fourteen days after the parent's objection was received. Alternatively it may complain to the juvenile court for an order upholding the resolution; if the court so decides, its order declares that the resolution should not lapse despite the parent's objection. If the local authority goes to court, the resolution remains in force until the court reaches a decision.[3]

GROUNDS FOR ORDERING THAT THE RESOLUTION SHALL NOT LAPSE

The burden of proof lies on the local authority to show that there were grounds for making a resolution. It must establish that the child had been and remained abandoned at the time the resolution was passed; or that the parent or guardian is unfit to have the care of the child by reason of mental disorder, his habits or mode of life, or because of his persistent failure without reasonable cause to discharge the

---

[1] The procedure of applying for a court order terminating the resolution will be available, but that is less favourable to the parent than the right to challenge now being considered: see below.

[2] Children Act 1948, s. 2 (2). The Children Bill (see Appendix, p. 161 *et seq.*) re-enacts s. 2 of the 1948 Act in much clearer language and with some changes noted in the Appendix.

[3] *Ibid.*, s. 2 (3).

obligations of a parent.[1] Strangely, because of the drafting of the Act, the court has no power to uphold a resolution made on the ground that the parent or guardian suffers from some permanent disability rendering him incapable of caring for the child. It is therefore not advisable to make a resolution on this ground unless no alternative ground exists.

The consequence of making a section 2 resolution is legally curious. It becomes effective immediately. If the parent objects the local authority still retains parental rights for fourteen days. If the local authority lays a complaint in the juvenile court it retains parental rights for longer—until the court has made a decision. Theoretically at least this means that during those fourteen or more days the local authority could make all sorts of decisions affecting the child, some irreversible such as consenting to an operation or even marriage; some immediately practical such as refusing to allow the parent to take his child home, or refusing him access to his child. There would be no legal redress against the local authority even if eventually a court found that there were no grounds for making the resolution in the first place.

DURATION AND TERMINATION OF RESOLUTION

The resolution continues in force until the child is eighteen unless it is earlier rescinded by the local authority. It may also be brought to an end by the juvenile court as a result of a complaint by the parent or guardian.[2] This procedure is quite distinct from that considered above, and even a parent who had consented to the making of a resolution can invoke this procedure.

During the first six months after the resolution was made the parent can challenge the resolution on the basis that there was no ground for making it.[3] He can rely at any time on the alternative ground that it is now in the interests of the child that the resolution should be determinted.[4]

A parent using this procedure is in a weaker position than one objecting as soon as the resolution is made. In particular he has the burden of proof, that is he must convince the court that the local authority is wrong to have made or to wish to continue the resolution. Contrast this with the parent's position under the objection procedure; in that case it is for the local authority to convince the court that it has acted correctly.[5] Also, under the objection procedure, if the local

---

[1] Children Act 1948, s. 2(3); Children and Young Persons Act 1963, s. 48 (2). If the court upholds the resolution there is no right of appeal to a higher court. The Houghton Committee recommended that such an appeal should be made available: *Report*, para. 159. See Appendix, p. 161 *et seq.*

[2] Children Act 1948, s. 4.

[3] See Magistrates Courts Act 1952, s. 104.

[4] Children Act 1948, s. 4 (3).

[5] The importance of the distinction was emphasised in *Re L. (A.C.) (an infant)*, [1971] 3 All E.R. 743.

authority cannot prove one of the grounds, then the court must allow the resolution to lapse. Under the alternative procedure of seeking the termination of the resolution, even if the parent does establish that no grounds existed or that it is in the interests of the child that the resolution be determined, the court is not bound to rescind the resolution, but has a discretion.[1]

If the child has no surviving parent or guardian, the only way in which the section 2 resolution can be challenged is by an application under the Guardianship of Minors Act 1971. Anyone may apply to be appointed a guardian for a child in these circumstances, and if the application is successful, the section 2 resolution ceases to have effect. In this way a grandparent or other surviving relation of the child can exercise a right of challenge which the parent would have been able to exercise had he been alive.[2]

THE POSITION OF A PUTATIVE FATHER

We have already seen that the father of an illegitimate child is not a "parent" for the purposes of the Children Act 1948.[3] This means that there is no possibility of the assumption of parental rights as against him. In the ordinary case, where an illegitimate child is living with its mother, the father has the right to seek a custody order by an application under the Guardianship of Minors Act 1971.[4] It was decided in *R. v. Oxford City Justices, ex parte H.*[5] that he continues to have this right, even if the child is in care and the mother's parental rights have been assumed by a local authority under a section 2 resolution. In the custody proceedings the court will consider the welfare of the child, having regard to the history of the case including the fact of the resolution. In that case the mother became mentally ill, a resolution was passed, and the father sought custody. If he obtained it, the resolution would continue in force; it was concerned only with the rights of the other parent, the mother.

---

[1] Compare Children Act 1948, s. 2 (3) and s. 4 (3); s. 2 (3) needs to be read with especial care because of its tortuous drafting. See p. 55, n. 2.

[2] Guardianship of Minors Act 1971, s. 5. The Children Bill (see Appendix, p. 161 *et seq.*) would enable a resolution to be challenged by an application for a custodianship order; and also give a right of appeal against a decision of magistrates to uphold or terminate a resolution.

[3] S. 59.

[4] S. 14 (1).

[5] [1974] 2 All E.R. 356; [1974] 3 W.L.R. 1.

Chapter 5

CHILDREN: COMPULSORY
MEASURES

As a general rule there can be no care or supervision of a child against its parents' wishes without the authority of a court order. The social agency concerned must justify its wish to intervene by proving in a neutral and independent forum that it has grounds for its action. The Ingleby Committee on Children and Young Persons reporting in 1960 declared itself "in favour of retaining the present basic principle that specific and definable matters must be alleged and that there should be no power to intervene until those allegations have been adequately proved . . . The maintenance of this basis is essential if State intervention is to be fitted into our general system of government and be acceptable to the community."[1]

Acceptance of that basic principle leaves open questions as to the nature of the court or tribunal before which the agency must justify itself and as to the grounds on which it may rely. During the 1960s there was strong pressure for the abolition of the juvenile court which is the court principally involved, and for the substitution of some less formal body which could give the parents a real part in decision-making; others argued that many parents would be insufficiently articulate and at ease to play a real part, and that parental participation in some decisions, for example that the child should receive institutional treatment, was positively undesirable.[2] In the event, the juvenile courts survived the debate, but with their powers curtailed; the debate continues on the related question whether a new court, a family court with wide jurisdiction, should be created.

The same debate focussed attention on the existing grounds for intervention, which were reflected in the dual nature of the juvenile courts' jurisdiction. The courts had a civil jurisdiction concerned with the

---

[1] *Report*, Cmnd. 1191, para. 66.
[2] See the White Paper, *The Child, the Family and the Young Offender* (1965), Cmnd. 2742. In Scotland, where juvenile courts in the English sense never became established, a more informal system of "children's hearings" has been adopted: Social Work (Scotland) Act 1968.

question whether the child was "in need of care, protection or control", and also a criminal jurisdiction based on proof of a criminal offence by the child. The existence of this criminal jurisdiction came under sharp attack. It seemed to depend upon the distinction between "deprived" and "depraved" children which was increasingly unacceptable; the stigma of criminality was thought to be harmful to the child and a part of the deviance amplification process; and the courts themselves found themselves in difficulty in putting into practice the conflicting principles on which the jurisdiction was based. The court was required to have regard to the welfare of the child,[1] with results which did not accord with what would be expected as an appropriate penalty. Writing of this conflict, the Ingleby Committee observed,

> "It results, for example, in a child being charged with a petty theft or other wrongful act for which most people would say that no great penalty should be imposed, and the case apparently ending in a disproportionate sentence. For when the court orders enquiries to be made, if those enquiries show seriously disturbed home conditions, or one or more of many other circumstances, the court may determine that the welfare of the child requires some very substantial interference which may amount to taking the child away from his home for a prolonged period."[2]

The outcome of this debate was the Children and Young Persons Act 1969. Although the juvenile court remains, the policy behind the Act is that so far as possible children's cases should be resolved by informal agreement with the parents, leading for example to informal supervision rather than a court hearing. The Act has not been fully brought into force. If it is ever fully implemented it will severely restrict the criminal jurisdiction of the juvenile court, limiting it to a portion of the cases involving those over fourteen years of age. Despite the failure to implement the crucial sections 4 and 5 which have that effect, the civil jurisdiction has already been expanded in anticipation of the corresponding restriction of the criminal side. In the new "care proceedings" the commission of a criminal offence can be taken into account but is never itself a sufficient justification for intervention. At the treatment stage, the Act deliberately blurred the distinction between custodial and non-custodial treatment, and reduced the powers of the courts so that they can in effect merely determine the range of options open to the staff of the treatment agencies with whom the final decisions rest.

The partial implementation of the Act means that criminal proceedings based solely on the allegation of an offence continue to be available as an alternative to care proceedings. This has thrown the whole design of the Act out of balance,[3] and incidentally made it harder for the student to understand the new structure.

---

[1] Children and Young Persons Act 1933, s. 44 (1).   [2] *Report*, Cmnd. 1191, para. 66.
[3] See the collection of articles under the general title "Children's Act in Trouble", [1972] Crim. L.R. 670.

CARE PROCEEDINGS

The legal framework of care proceedings is laid down in section 1 (2) of the Children and Young Persons Act 1969:

> "If the court before which a child or young person is brought under this section is of opinion that any of the following conditions is satisfied with respect to him, that is to say—
> (a) his proper development is being avoidably prevented or neglected or his health is being avoidably impaired or neglected or he is being ill-treated; or
> (b) it is probable that the condition set out in the preceding paragraph will be satisfied in his case, having regard to the fact that the court or another court has found that that condition is or was satisfied in the case of another child or young person who is or was a member of the household to which he belongs; or
> (c) he is is exposed to moral danger; or
> (d) he is beyond the control of his parent or guardian; or
> (e) he is of compulsory school age within the meaning of the Education Act 1944 and is not receiving efficient full-time education suitable to his age, ability and aptitude; or
> (f) he is guilty of an offence, excluding homicide,
> and also that he is in need of care or control which he is unlikely to receive unless the court makes an order under this section in respect of him, then, . . . the court may if it thinks fit make such an order."

It will be seen that care proceedings can only succeed if two matters are proved, the existence of one of the listed conditions (a) to (f) and the care or control requirement; it is not sufficient to establish one without the other.

THE CARE OR CONTROL REQUIREMENT

In all care proceedings the applicant must satisfy the court that the child is "in need of care or control which he is unlikely to receive unless the court makes an order". These words give practical expression to much of the basic philosophy behind care proceedings.

One principle is that a specific incident, or piece of behaviour, or one aspect of the child's total situation, should not be relied upon to justify compulsory intervention. The court is required to consider the overall needs of the child and to consider not merely past events but the likely future circumstances as well. It is to satisfy this principle that the Act requires proof of need of care or control.

The term "care or control" has a fairly broad meaning; the Act makes it clear that care includes protection and guidance and that control includes discipline.[1] In many cases the requirement will not be a major hurdle, once the relevant condition has been proved.

---

[1] Children and Young Persons Act 1969, s. 70 (1).

For example, if condition (*d*), that the child is beyond the control of his parents, is established, the need for care or control will be evident. But truancy or the commission of a criminal offence may be proved without there being any evidence of a need for care or control.

A second principle is also involved, that cases should be disposed of, so far as possible, without resort to court proceedings. The social agency is expected to pursue all available alternatives. The parents may be able to take the necessary action themselves, perhaps making use of advice or recreational facilities in the community; they may accept informal supervision from the social services department or the NSPCC. It may be that the case can be disposed of by a police caution, or some form of court proceedings not directly involving the child. It is only if these alternatives are not available that care proceedings are proper.

This is the significance of the words "care or control *which he is unlikely to receive unless the court makes an order*". The court must be satisfied not only that care or control is needed but also that it is only by means of a court order that it can be given. The court should be provided with evidence that alternatives were considered, and with the reasons for their rejection.

It was perhaps inevitable that the Act should contain no direct provisions about the alternative methods of dealing with the case; but the notion of voluntary agreement between parents and agency presents a number of practical problems.

The first is indicated by the question "how voluntary is voluntary?" Is there a danger that a relatively inarticulate parent will be swept into the semblance of agreement by the more forceful social worker? This is a recurrent danger in social work, but there is a special difficulty in the present situation. The lawyer would expect the social worker to explain to the parents the full implications of the decision they are being asked to take. This would include the point that continued disagreement between the parents and the agency can only be resolved by the courts. The problem is how to prevent this sounding like a *threat* to take court proceedings in the absence of agreement.

This point was fully aired during the debates both inside and outside Parliament when the Act was being considered. To meet it, assurances were given that there would be no attempt to secure an informal agreement to residential treatment. If a period in a community home seemed advisable, care proceedings would be taken. Subsequently the Home Office, which was then responsible for children's legislation,[1] issued advice which included the suggestion that amongst the alternatives to court proceedings was reception into care with parental consent under section 1 of the Children Act 1948.[2] In some cases this would seem

---

[1] Responsibility now lies with the Department of Health and Social Security.
[2] *Part 1 of the Children and Young Persons Act 1969, a Guide for Courts and Practitioners*, H.M.S.O. (1970), para. 34.

wholly unobjectionable: for example an offence by a child might
reveal a situation in which a single parent was seriously ill and unable
properly to look after the child, and temporary reception into care
would be a welcome solution. But a resort to the Children Act provisions to avoid the difficulties of evidence which might arise in care
proceedings would be open to serious objections; the grounds for intervention under the two Acts are distinct and a blurring of the distinctions for the convenience of the agency is to be deplored.

Another matter to be borne in mind when voluntary agreements are
contemplated is the position which arises if an agreement is made and
not honoured, as when an offer of informal supervision is accepted but
no contact is made with the supervisor. The official answer is that
there is no direct sanction,[1] but there may be situations, and areas, in
which inaction would be dangerous, as a bad example to others.
Arguably parental non-cooperation might itself be used to support
allegations in care proceedings; it would certainly go a long way
towards making out the "care or control" requirement.

CONDITION (*a*)

"*his proper development is being avoidably prevented or neglected or his
health is being avoidably impaired or neglected or he is being ill-treated*"

Under this condition will come cases of cruelty to children and of child
neglect, but the concept of the child's "proper development" is a broad
one and a number of less obvious fact-situations will also be covered. If
we assume that mental and emotional development is included, the
condition would cover the case of a single parent whose mental condition is abnormal to the point that the child suffers as a result by coming
to share the parent's distorted perceptions. There is clearly no need to
prove *physical* hardship.

The example of the mentally abnormal parent raises a difficult
question on the interpretation of this condition which has never been
considered in any reported case. The paragraph uses the word
"avoidably". On one view this implies an element of blameworthiness.
The parent could have done better and has failed. On this view there
is a contrast between the 1969 Act and the Children Act 1948 provisions for reception into care: the 1948 provisions are concerned with
the incapacity of the parent, who is prevented by circumstances from
giving proper care, with no hint of blame. The parent who suffers
from an abnormal mental condition is incapacitated but (in the absence
of factors such as the abuse of drugs which led to mental deterioration)
in no way open to criticism; the consequences are not *avoidable* in the
sense we have been considering. But it is equally possible that "avoidably" simply means that the harmful consequences could be averted by

---

[1] See *Children in Trouble*, Cmnd. 3601, Appendix A, para. 3 (5); but this is, of course,
not a legal provision.

appropriate steps such as social work intervention and are not the inevitable result of some other condition. Take the case of a child who is kept indoors and seldom allowed to enjoy play and adventure with other children. In an extreme case his development would be hindered. If the child is sickly or has some condition like haemophilia (a dangerous tendency to excessive bleeding at the slightest cut) it may be inevitable that his life should be confined and sheltered. If the child is a normal healthy child such confinement is "avoidable", i.e. *not* inevitable; the state of his parents' mental health is, on this view, quite irrelevant, and the decision to confine the child can be the result of malice, folly or mental breakdown without the issue being affected.

CONDITION (*b*)

"it is probable that the condition set out in the preceding paragraph will be satisfied in his case, having regard to the fact that the court or another court has found that that condition is or was satisfied in the case of another child or young person who is or was a member of the household to which he belongs"

Although the wording of this paragraph is difficult, the intention is clear enough. It has been proved that one child has been ill-treated. Depending on the circumstances, it may be all too likely that other children in the same household will receive similar treatment. Those children can be taken into care, or at least placed under supervision, as a preventive measure and in advance of any evidence of actual harm to them. Intervention is justified because the child is very clearly at risk, just as is a child "exposed to moral danger" under the next condition.

The obvious application of this paragraph is to the case in which a definite finding has been made in respect of one child under condition (*a*); the other child or children are brought to court at a later date under condition (*b*).

The decision of the Court of Appeal in *Surrey County Council* v. *S.*[1] shows that this condition can sometimes be used in cases where there has been no such earlier court hearing in respect of the first child. In January 1972 care proceedings were begun in respect of a three-month-old girl, and an interim care order was made. The case came before the juvenile court in July 1972. There was no evidence that the baby girl had ever been ill-treated, but the local authority wanted to rely on condition (*b*) and to bring evidence relating to her elder sister who had died in December 1971. (The girls' father had subsequently been charged with her murder but was acquitted.) Counsel for the parents argued that the Act required a finding as to the other child by a competent court on a previous occasion, but the Court of Appeal decided that the same court could at one and the same sitting decide both that condition (*a*) had been satisfied in the past in relation to the dead girl

---

[1] [1974] Q.B. at p. 130; [1973] 3 All E.R. 1074.

and also that condition (*b*) was satisfied in relation to the surviving sister.

A possible variant of the facts would be if the other child survived ill-treatment and care proceedings were taken in its case, but for some reason condition (*a*) was not used; instead it might have been shown, for example, that he was "exposed to moral danger" under condition (*c*). Presumably, applying the reasoning in *Surrey County Council* v. *S.*, it would be open to a later court to apply condition (*b*) on the footing that condition (*a*), though never relied on in the earlier proceedings, could have been relied on.

CONDITION (*c*)

"he is exposed to moral danger"

The idea of "moral danger" must be limited in some way, but it is not at all clear what the limitations should be. It is not limited to sexual cases,[1] but those must be the most frequent in practice. Some courts would accept without hesitation that a child living in the same house as a person who uses drugs like cannabis was exposed to moral danger, but other courts might well be surprised by such a suggestion. The leading case, *Alhaji Mohamed* v. *Knott*,[2] supports a number of propositions: that participation in a crime does not necessarily expose a person to moral danger; that marital intercourse does not; and that, at least in sexual cases involving immigrants, regard must be had to the customs and ways of life of the country in which the parties grew up. The courts seem to have given no further guidance as to the meaning of this condition.

The natural alarm which such a wide and ill-defined provision excites amongst lawyers is increased by a reading of *Alhaji Mohamed* v. *Knott*. This concerned a couple married under Nigerian law, and the marriage was valid in England. The facts can be gathered from the following extract from the judgment of the magistrates:[3]

> "Here is a girl, aged 13 or possibly less, unable to speak English, living in London with a man twice her age to whom she has been married by Muslim law. He admits having had sexual intercourse with her at a time when according to the medical evidence the development of puberty had almost certainly not begun. He intends to resume intercourse as soon as he is satisfied that she is adequately protected by contraceptives from the fear of pregnancy. He admits that before the marriage he had intercourse with a woman by whom he has three illegitimate children. He further admits that since the marriage, which took place as recently as January of this year [the judgment was delivered in June], he has had sexual relations with a prostitute in Nigeria from whom he contracted venereal disease. In our opinion a

---

[1] See the Home Office guidance in their Guide to Part I of the 1969 Act, cited above, p. 61, n. 2, at para. 18.
[2] [1969] 1 Q.B. 1; [1968] 2 All E.R. 563, decided under the corresponding provision in the Children and Young Persons Act 1963 (repealed).
[3] Set out in full at [1969] 1 Q.B. 5.

continuance of such an association notwithstanding the marriage, would be repugnant to any decent-minded English man or woman."

The magistrates' decision to commit the wife to the care of the local authority[1] was reversed by the Divisional Court. The court had some sympathy with the magistrates, describing the husband as "a bad lot", but the magistrates' decision was clearly wrong in law, involving as it did the conclusion that a validly married woman is exposed to moral danger because of the likelihood that her husband will have sexual intercourse with her.

Alhaji Mohamed v. *Knott* presented an unusual set of facts which raise some far-reaching questions of legal as well as social policy about the recognition in England of marriages entered into under legal systems very different from our own; though, as Lord Parker points out,[2] it was only in 1929 that English law imposed any minimum age for marriage. But there is a more general point which can be important in cases whose facts are much more mundane: that the use in a statute of a phrase as vague as "moral danger" gives too much scope for the subjective preferences of those whom the statute empowers to act, and encourages unpredictable local variations in its interpretation.

CONDITION (*d*)

"he is beyond the control of his parent or guardian"

It was the practice at one time for the parents themselves to initiate proceedings against children beyond their control,[3] but this formal public opposition of parent and child was scarcely calculated to improve their relationship. Care proceedings on this as on the other grounds can now only be taken by the local authority or the police[4] but the parents are given special powers. They may send a written request to the local authority asking that proceedings be taken, and if the authority refuses to act may seek an order from the juvenile court directing the authority to take proceedings.[5] The court has a discretion and will consider all the circumstances, including a social enquiry report[6] and in appropriate cases the views of any parent of the child who is living apart from the complainant.[7]

If this condition is proved, there will be no difficulty about the "need for care and control" in the general requirement, but it must be stressed once again that what must be shown is a need which is unlikely to be met unless the court makes an order. It is possible for the

[1] By a fit person order, a precursor of the care order, under Children and Young Persons Act 1933, s. 62 (repealed).
[2] [1969] 1 Q.B. 1, at p. 15.
[3] Children and Young Persons Act 1933, s. 64 (repealed).
[4] Children and Young Persons Act 1969, s. 1 (1).
[5] Children and Young Persons Act 1963, s. 3 (1).
[6] *Ibid.*, s. 3 (2). The child is not present.
[7] Magistrates' Courts (Children and Young Persons) Rules 1970 (S.I. 1970 No. 1792), r. 22 (1).

court to decide that satisfactory arrangements could be made without a court order, though in practice these should have been thoroughly explored before court proceedings were taken.

CONDITION (*e*)

"*he is of compulsory school age within the meaning of the Education Act 1944 and is not receiving efficient full-time education suitable to his age, ability and aptitude*"

The Education Act 1944 imposes a duty on the parent of every child of compulsory school age to cause the child "to receive efficient full-time education suitable to his age, ability and aptitude, either by regular attendance at school or otherwise".[1] The enforcement of this duty either by taking steps against the parents or by means of care proceedings is a matter for the local education authority, and care proceedings based on this condition may only be brought by that authority.[2]

Compulsory school age covers any age between five and sixteen.[3] If the local education authority believe that any parent of a child of compulsory school age is failing in his duty, they must serve a notice requiring the parent to satisfy the authority that he is in fact meeting his obligations. The parent may argue that he is providing education at home; this may be accepted if there is evidence of a properly directed programme of work, but not if the children are given no guidance but merely encouraged to pursue their own interests.[4] If the authority is not satisfied, it must serve a school attendance order requiring the parent to register the child as a pupil at a named school.[5] Failure to obey the order is an offence, unless the parent satisfies the court that he is, contrary to the authority's view, discharging his duty to provide suitable full-time education.[6]

The parent of a registered pupil commits an offence if the pupil fails to attend regularly.[7] Obviously absence through illness is to be disregarded, as are absences on days "exclusively set apart for religious observance" by the parents' religious group,[8] and absence when the pupil's home is not within "walking distance", three miles for most age-

---

[1] Education Act 1944, s. 36.
[2] Children and Young Persons Act 1969, s. 2 (8) (*a*).
[3] Education Act 1944, s. 35; Raising of the School Leaving Age Order 1972 (S.I. 1972 No. 444). School-leaving dates are fixed by the Education Act 1962, s. 9.
[4] Compare *Baker* v. *Earl* (1960), *Times*, February 6, with *R.* v. *Surrey Quarter Sessions Appeals Committee, ex parte Tweedie* (1963), 107 Sol. Jo. 555 (where the parent also produced reports on work done but denied the authority access to inspect, to which it was held entitled).
[5] Education Act 1944, s. 37 (1), (2). The parent may apply for the name of a different school to be inserted.
[6] Education Act 1944, s. 37 (5).
[7] *Ibid.*, s. 39.
[8] Children who are "C of E" might like to know that this includes Ascension Day and perhaps other days commonly falling within school terms, and that actual religious observance is not required. *Marshall* v. *Graham*, [1907] 2 K.B. 112.

groups,[1] of the school and neither transport nor boarding arrangements have been made.[2]

The courts have considered a number of marginal cases. In one case, *Jenkins* v. *Howells*,[3] a girl stayed at home to do housework for her invalid mother. The Act does allow absence for some "unavoidable cause", but it was held that the cause must relate to the child himself and not to some other person.[4] More common are what might be termed the "long hair" cases, where the pupil is sent daily to school wearing the wrong clothes or hairstyle or otherwise failing to conform to a school rule and is repeatedly sent home. In these circumstances the parent is guilty of an offence under section 39; the fact that the child presents himself is irrelevant when everyone knows he will not be admitted.[5] These cases are notoriously difficult to deal with, as headmaster and parent both adopt entrenched attitudes; it is perhaps unfortunate that the wording of this offence is such that a parent convicted in these circumstances will be left with a distinct sense of injustice.

A third offence in connection with school attendance is committed by nomadic parents who "habitually wander from place to place" and take with them a child of compulsory school age who is prevented from having suitable full-time education.[6]

The relevant statutes provide, in relation to all three types of offence, that before instituting criminal proceedings against the parents the local education authority should consider whether it would be appropriate, instead of or as well as instituting these proceedings, to take care proceedings relying on condition (*e*).[7] Here as in other contexts, criminal proceedings are seen as likely to create further ill-feeling and obstruction; care proceedings may be a more direct means of ensuring that the child receives the education he needs.

Now that Education Act cases have been brought within the framework of the 1969 Act care proceedings, the "care and control" requirement must be made out in every case. It will not necessarily be easy to prove that a child who is not attending school, perhaps as a result of a "long-hair" dispute, is in need of care and control which he is unlikely

---

1 Education Act 1944, s. 39 (5); two miles for those under eight.
2 *Ibid.*, ss. 39 (2), 54 (7).
3 [1949] 2 K.B. 218; [1949] 1 All E.R. 942.
4 Education Act 1944, s. 39 (2) (*a*). The same facts might have constituted a "reasonable excuse" allowed under the pre-1944 law: cf. *London School Board* v. *Duggan* (1884), 13 Q.B.D. 176 (child working to support poor, industrious and respectable parents).
5 *Spiers* v. *Warrington Corporation*, [1954] 1 Q.B. 61; [1953] 2 All E.R. 1052 (girl subject to attacks of rheumatic fever refused admittance for wearing trousers).
6 Children and Young Persons Act 1933, s. 10. For parents whose employment requires them to travel from place to place, see Education Act 1944, s. 39 (3).
7 Children and Young Persons Act 1933, s. 10 (1A); Education Act 1944, s. 40 (2). Both these provisions were inserted in 1969.

to receive unless the court makes an order. The result may be that, although the legislation is designed to encourage the use of care proceedings rather than criminal prosecution of the parents, the presence of the "care and control" requirement may force the local education authority to fall back on to criminal charges in certain types of case.

CONDITION (f)

"he is guilty of an offence, excluding homicide"

Special rules for homicide cases are a recurring feature of the law, perhaps because of the high emotions they create or perhaps because of the former association with capital punishment. A young child accused of murder or manslaughter must be taken through the full Crown Court procedure.

In all other cases there is, as we have seen, a choice between criminal proceedings and care proceedings based on condition (f), "the offence condition". This choice will continue to exist until sections 4 and 5 of the Children and Young Persons Act 1969 are implemented, prohibiting criminal proceedings against children in the 10–14 age-group and restricting their use against young persons aged between 14 and 17. Criminal proceedings are less desirable in theory but have a number of practical advantages for the prosecution: there is no need to bother with the "care and control" requirement (which makes it much easier for a police officer to handle the whole proceedings) and a greater range of penalties is available to the courts. So, a fine, a discharge, an attendance centre or detention centre order, or committal to the Crown Court with a view to borstal training are all only available after criminal proceedings. So it is not surprising that in almost all areas of the country, criminal proceedings continue to be used rather than care proceedings based on the offence condition.

Care proceedings are essentially civil rather than criminal in nature.[1] The rules of evidence and procedure in civil cases are less favourable to the defendant than those which apply in criminal cases, where so much may be at stake that the defendant is given special protection. So the case against him must be proved not merely on "the balance of probabilities" but at the higher standard of "beyond reasonable doubt"; certain types of evidence, especially hearsay evidence, are forbidden to the prosecution in criminal cases. From the defendant's point of view, and from that of his parents, just as much is at stake when he is alleged to have committed an offence in care proceedings as when he is charged in criminal proceedings. To meet this point the 1969 Act provides in effect that when the court is considering whether the offence condition is satisfied, the rules of criminal evidence and procedure apply;[2] if the

---

[1] Though it is *criminal* legal aid which is available: Legal Aid Act 1974, s. 28 (3).

[2] Children and Young Persons Act 1969, s. 3, especially s. 3 (3) (proof) and s. 3 (8) (right of appeal); Magistrates' Courts (Children and Young Persons) Rules 1970 (S.I. 1970 No. 1792), r. 16 (2).

offence condition is proved, the court then turns to the "care and control" requirement acting under the rules of evidence and procedure appropriate to civil cases. Procedurally care proceedings based on the offence condition involve a criminal trial set in a civil framework. In practice it is only in contested cases that these procedural complexities become obvious. The Home Office advised local authorities that when they, rather than the police, were presenting an offence condition case, they should consider whether it would be desirable for them to be legally represented, presumably because of the procedural pitfalls.[1]

ORDERS IN CARE PROCEEDINGS

When the court is satisfied both as to one of conditions (*a*) to (*f*) and of the "care and control" requirement, it "may if it thinks fit"[2] (and it almost invariably will think fit) make one of a number of orders. Of these the two most important are the supervision order, which places the child under supervision and may also authorise "intermediate treatment" in his case,[3] and the care order. A care order commits a child to the care of the local authority in whose area he resides[4] until he reaches eighteen, or, where the child was already sixteen when the order was made, until he reaches nineteen.[5] Both supervision and care orders are discussed further below.[6] The court may choose instead to order the parents to enter into a recognisance[7] to take proper care of the child and to exercise proper control over him; or, in appropriate cases, make a hospital or guardianship order under the Mental Health Act;[8] and in offence condition cases a young person may himself be required to enter into a recognisance[9] and (in addition to any other order) pay compensation for damage caused.[10]

Compulsory care or supervision after a court order generally means a care order or supervision order made by a juvenile court in care proceedings or criminal proceedings. Although much less frequently

---

[1] In the *Guide to Part 1 of the Act*, para. 50.
[2] Children and Young Persons Act 1969, s. 1 (2).
[3] See pp. 96–8, below.
[4] Children and Young Persons Act 1969, s. 20 (2); if there is no such local authority, the authority for the area in which the offence was committed or the other circumstances on which the proceedings were based arose.
[5] *Ibid.*, s. 20 (3). A court may in some cases order the extension of a care order due to expire at age 18 to age 19: the mental condition or behaviour of the child must necessitate his further detention in his own or the public interest: *ibid.*, s. 21 (1).
[6] For supervision orders, see pp. 75–83; for the treatment of children in care, see pp. 95–8; for the discharge of care orders, see p. 83.
[7] This is an undertaking involving a financial penalty in case of breach within the period of operation of the undertaking. See Children and Young Persons Act 1969, s. 1 (3) (*a*).
[8] *Ibid.*, s. 1 (3) (*c*), (*d*). A hospital order may be combined with a care order. For the Mental Health Act, see generally chapter 9.
[9] Children and Young Persons Act 1969, s. 3 (7).
[10] *Ibid.*, s. 3 (6).

encountered in practice, orders with similar effects can be made by courts which have been dealing with certain matrimonial, wardship or custody cases.

MATRIMONIAL CASES

There are two distinct sets of courts dealing with matrimonial cases. Magistrates' domestic courts can make matrimonial orders under the Matrimonial Proceedings (Magistrates' Courts) Act 1960, including separation and maintenance orders. Only the higher courts can grant decrees of divorce or of nullity of marriage; their powers in connection with maintenance and matrimonial property are much more comprehensive than those of the magistrates' courts, and litigants seeking an exercise of these powers may go to the higher courts even when they do not seek a divorce, by means of an application for judicial separation or proceedings for wilful neglect to maintain. This jurisdiction, under the Matrimonial Causes Act 1973, is exercised by the High Court and certain county courts, the latter handling undefended cases.

Orders affecting children can be made in either jurisdiction, and the powers we are particularly concerned with are expressed in similar language in the two sets of legal provisions. Unfortunately there are differences and the two jurisdictions must be treated separately.

MAGISTRATES' COURTS

When a magistrates' court hears a complaint under the Matrimonial Proceedings (Magistrates' Courts) Act 1960, it has power to include in the matrimonial order provisions affecting any child of the family who is under sixteen years of age.[1] The court may call for a report from a probation officer or from the local authority social services department before making its order.[2] The usual provisions deal with the legal custody of the child, which may be given to either of the parties or to a third person, and with access to the child. The court cannot make an order as to access if the child is already in the care of the local authority;[3] the decisions about access are within the competence of the authority under its statutory powers, and confusion would result if the court were to intervene.

In addition the court is given powers "in exceptional circumstances" to commit the child[4] to the care of the local authority or to place him

---

[1] Matrimonial Proceedings (Magistrates' Courts) Act 1960, s. 2 (1) (*d*)–(*g*); payments in respect of maintenance may be ordered under *ibid.*, s. 2 (1) (*h*) even when the child is over 21. "Child of the family" includes the child of one party who has been accepted as one of the family by the other party: *ibid.*, s. 16 (1).

[2] *Ibid.*, s. 4 (2). See further pp. 28–31.

[3] *Ibid.*, s. 2 (4) (*b*).

[4] I.e. a child of the family aged under 16.

under supervision. There is little judicial guidance on the nature of the "exceptional circumstances"; the intention is that the court should only make an order after very careful consideration of all the alternatives. In one case the magistrates' court found that it was unsuitable for the mother to have the care of a diabetic child and refused to give custody of the child to his father because the father was living in adultery. The magistrates held that "exceptional circumstances" were established, but their order was quashed on appeal; the Divisional Court, taking into account the nursing experience of the woman with whom the father was living, awarded custody to him.[1] In a High Court case under corresponding legislation, "exceptional circumstances" were found where the mother had no suitable accommodation for the child and the father was (for reasons which are not reported) not a fit and proper person to care for him.[2] Neither case, as reported, contains a full discussion of the possible fact-situations.

Committal to care

Before the court commits a child to the care of the local authority it must be satisfied that there are exceptional circumstances making it impracticable or undesirable for the child to be entrusted to either of the parties, or to any other individual.[3] In practice the court has to consider this matter twice, for once it has in mind the possibility of making an order it must give notice to the local authority, inviting the authority to make representations, including representations as to an order for payments towards the cost of maintaining the child in care.[4] An order cannot be made if the child is already in care, or if some court has already given custody of him to some person.[5]

If the order is made it continues in force until the child is eighteen unless it is earlier revoked. The local authority cannot discharge a child from care of its own volition, but it can initiate court proceedings for revocation of the order.[6] While the child remains in care, the rights and duties of the authority are the same as if the child had been received into care under the Children Act 1948 with a few technical differences[7] and one important one, that the parents have no right to the return of their child on demand; they must go to court and seek revocation of the order.[8]

---

[1] *G.* v. *G.* (1962), 106 Sol. Jo. 858.
[2] *F.* v. *F.*, [1959] 3 All E.R. 180, n.
[3] Matrimonial Proceedings (Magistrates' Courts) Act 1960. s. 2 (1) (*e*).
[4] *Ibid.*, s. 3 (1).
[5] *Ibid.*, s. 2 (4) (*a*), (*b*).
[6] *Ibid.*, ss. 3 (4), 10 (1) (*e*).
[7] For the general provisions see pp. 74–82. Contributions towards maintenance expenses are a matter for the magistrates' court to deal with in its order and the normal contribution procedures do not apply; nor does s. 17 of the Children Act 1948 (emigration of the child).
[8] Matrimonial Proceedings (Magistrates' Courts) Act 1960, s. 3 (3).

Supervision

When the court makes a custody order but finds that there are exceptional circumstances making it desirable that the child should be under the supervision of an independent person, it may make an order placing the child under the supervision of either a probation officer or of the local authority.[1]   An order cannot be made if the child is already in care or is being committed to the care of the local authority;[2] plainly there would be no point in requiring a probation officer to supervise a child in care, and it would do little to improve professional relationships between the services.

This form of supervision continues until the child is sixteen years of age, unless the order is earlier revoked. The supervisor may himself commence proceedings for its revocation.[3]

THE HIGH COURT AND COUNTY COURTS

The jurisdiction of the higher courts in respect of the custody and education of children affected by matrimonial cases is wider than that of the magistrates. There is greater flexibility as to the type of order that can be made so that, for example, the child may be made a ward of court and so subject to the court's continuing oversight. In addition the court's powers apply in general to children who are below eighteen years of age, and to a wider class of children: if a child other than one boarded-out with the parties by a local authority or voluntary organisation has been treated by both parties as a child of their family, he falls within the scope of the court's powers whether or not either party is a parent of his.[4]

Committal to care

When a child of the family is under seventeen, the court may commit him to the care of the local authority on the same grounds as apply in the magistrates' courts, that is that there are exceptional circumstances making it impracticable or undesirable for the child to be entrusted to either of the parties to the marriage or to any other individual.[5] Before doing so the court will often have ordered a report from the Court Welfare Officer[6] and must give the local authority an opportunity to submit representations.[7]

The higher courts can make such an order even if the child is already in the care of the local authority, the effect being to exclude the parents' right to demand the return of their child; and can secure the

---

[1] Matrimonial Proceedings Act 1960, s. 2 (1) (*f*).
[2] *Ibid.*, s. 2 (4) (*b*), (*c*).
[3] *Ibid.*, ss. 3 (*a*), 10 (1) (*f*).
[4] Matrimonial Causes Act 1973, ss. 42, 52 (1).
[5] *Ibid.*, s. 43 (1).
[6] Under Matrimonial Causes Rules 1973, r. 95.
[7] Matrimonial Causes Act 1973, s. 43 (2).

same result by directing the local authority, under the court's general power to make such order relating to custody as it thinks fit, to have the care and control of the child and not to relinquish it to a parent unless to do so would be consistent with the welfare of the child.[1]

When an order is made the local authority's powers under the Children Act 1948[2] apply subject not only to the qualification that the parents cannot recall their child but also to the overriding provision that the authority must exercise its powers subject to any directions given by the court.[3]

An order committing the child to care continues in force until the child is eighteen unless it is earlier discharged. The local authority may itself apply for the order to be discharged, or for other directions of the court as to the exercise of the authority's functions.[4]

Supervision

The powers of the higher courts to place a child under supervision in a matrimonial case are almost identical to those of the magistrates' court.[5] Apart from minor procedural matters, the only significant distinction is that the higher courts' power extends to any child under eighteen who is subject to a custody order;[6] the period of supervision similarly extends to the eighteenth birthday.

WARDSHIP CASES

Under s. 7 of the Family Law Reform Act 1969, the High Court has power in wardship cases to commit a ward of court to the care of a local authority or to place him under supervision. The grounds for such orders and their consequences are the same as the corresponding powers of the higher courts in matrimonial cases.

GUARDIANSHIP OF MINORS ACT CASES

Applications for the custody of a child under sixteen years of age can be made to the High Court, a county court or a magistrates' court under the Guardianship of Minors Act 1971. This Act was amended by the Guardianship Act 1973 which gave the courts power to commit

---

[1] *Practice Direction* (1955), 23 May.
[2] See pp. 75–81.
[3] Matrimonial Causes Act 1973, s. 43 (5); Children Act 1948, s. 17 (emigration of children) is also excluded.
[4] Matrimonial Causes Rules 1971, r. 93 (4). In a case of urgency, or where no opposition is expected, the procedure is simple: a letter is written addressed to the court.
[5] See p. 72, above.
[6] Matrimonial Causes Act 1973, s. 44.

the child to the care of the local authority in exceptional cases.[1]   The
detailed rules[2] are similar to those applying to the corresponding
order in the matrimonial jurisdiction of the magistrates' court; in the
case of a High Court order the powers of the local authority are
subject, in some respects, to the directions of that court.[3]

The 1973 Act also gave the courts power to place the child under the
supervision of a probation officer or of the local authority.   The
supervision can continue until the child is sixteen, but may be termin-
ated by the court on the application of the supervisor or a parent or
guardian of the child.   The court ordering supervision may include
in its order a provision that the order should be suspended for any
period during which the parents are living together, and may also
provide that supervision shall lapse altogether if the parents live
together for a period of three months.[4]

---

[1] Guardianship Act 1973, s. 2 (2) (*b*).
[2] See *ibid.*, ss. 2 (3) (8), 4.
[3] *Ibid.*, s. 4 (4) (*a*).
[4] *Ibid.*, ss. 2 (2) (*a*), 3.

Chapter 6

CHILDREN IN CARE

A. RIGHTS AND DUTIES

Even the normal relationship of parent and child is subject to legal regulation. As we have seen, the parent's position as the child's natural guardian gives him legal rights, and the law imposes obligations upon him. Once a child is received into care, it is even more important that the relationships of the various parties in terms of legal rights and duties should be clear. The local authority undertakes responsibility for the child, and the law must indicate in general terms how that responsibility is to be discharged; and also how far it extends, for the parents are not absolved from continuing obligations. There are immediate practical questions of accommodation and the cost of the child's maintenance, but also questions of policy as to the purpose and duration of the authority's intervention.[1]

A code of general provisions regulating these questions is to be found in the Children Act 1948.[2] This applies, subject to technical modifications in particular classes of case to all children in care, whether by voluntary agreement or court order.[3] The general principle is stated in these words:

> "Where a child is in the care of a local authority, it shall be the duty of that authority to exercise their powers with respect to him so as to further his best interests, and to afford him opportunity for the proper development of his character and abilities."[4]

---

[1] An example of the latter is the duty imposed on the local authority by s. 1 (3) of the Children Act 1948 to secure that the care of the child is taken over by a parent, relative or friend wherever considerations of the child's welfare permit. See p. 88, below.

[2] As amended, especially by the Children and Young Persons Act 1969. References below to particular provisions of the 1948 Act are to those provisions as amended, sometimes radically, by the later legislation.

[3] Children Act 1948, s. 11 specifies children in care under *ibid.*, s. 1, under a care order, or remanded in the care of the local authority; but the provisions are applied by other legislation to children in care after matrimonial or wardship proceedings, or after custody proceedings under the Guardianship of Minors Act 1971.

[4] *Ibid.*, s. 12 (1). In the case of children in care after High Court or county court matrimonial or wardship proceedings, ss. 12–14 apply subject to any directions of the court: Family Law Reform Act 1969, s. 7 (3); Matrimonial Causes Act 1973, s. 43 (5). Similar provisions apply in the case of High Court orders under the Guardianship Act 1973: see s. 4 (4) (a).

The authority is directed to make appropriate use of the normal facilities available for children who live with their own parents.[1] This expresses the policy that children in care should not be treated as a class apart, but should have as normal a life as possible.

In the 1969 Act this unexceptional general duty to further the child's best interests was qualified by a new provision.[2] The local authority was expressly given the power to act in a manner which might be inconsistent with that duty if they felt it necessary for the purpose of protecting members of the public. In effect, the protection of the public takes priority. This provision was introduced as a result of the enlarged responsibility of local authorities for community homes; some homes have special "secure provision", and most will from time to time impose restrictions for disciplinary reasons. It is perfectly possible to argue that the use of these methods was within the authority's powers under the existing legislation as being in accordance with the child's best interests, at least in the long term; the 1969 provision puts the legality of the authority's actions beyond dispute.

ACCOMMODATION

A child in care may be accommodated in an institution, a community home[3] or a voluntary home; or he may be boarded out with foster-parents; or allowed to live either as a temporary or as a long-term measure with his own parents or with a relative or friend; or under other arrangements, such as in a boarding-school, considered appropriate by the authority.[4] It is entirely up to the social services department to decide what should be done with the child. There are of course external restraints such as the problem of finding a vacant place in the right sort of home, but no outside body can interfere and order that the child should be accommodated in one way rather than another. Similarly no outside body has to approve changes of accommodation; a child originally received into care by a voluntary arrangement under section 1 of the 1948 Act could in theory end up in secure accommodation in a community home without any person other than the staff of the social services department and of the relevant institutions having considered the case. Reliance is placed on the professional skills of the social workers rather than on any machinery for lay review.[5]

When the Children Act 1948 permits the local authority to allow a child to be under the charge or control of its parents, guardian, relative

[1] Children Act 1948, s. 12 (2).
[2] Children and Young Persons Act 1969, s. 27 (2). Note also the reserve powers of the Secretary of State to intervene: s. 27 (3).
[3] Or in one of the special "s. 64 homes" provided by the central government under *ibid.*, s. 64.
[4] Children Act 1948, s. 13.
[5] There can be review in the sense that a court can be asked to have the child sent out of care, e.g. by discharging a care order (see p. 83); but unless circumstances were wholly exceptional the accommodation used would not be relevant.

or friend, it speaks of this as being "either for a fixed period or until the local authority otherwise determines".[1] It appears that when the fixed period alternative is used, the local authority has no power to recall the child before the end of the period.[2] If things go badly wrong, it may be possible to achieve the same result by taking fresh proceedings in court, but the authority cannot simply rely on its general powers over the child. This makes it quite important to be clear just what are the terms on which the child is allowed home: expressions like "a month's trial; and we will see how it goes" leave room for doubt whether there is or is not a fixed period.

When a child is boarded out with foster-parents he is, by definition, not under the immediate control either of his own parents or of the professional staff of the authority. Special care is called for in selecting foster-parents and in providing adequate supervision, and legal provisions are contained in the Boarding-Out of Children Regulations 1955.[3]

SELECTION OF FOSTER-PARENTS

A child can only be boarded-out with a married couple, a single woman, or a man who is grandfather, uncle or elder brother of the child.[4] In the case of longer-term fostering,[5] the foster-parents should so far as possible be of the same religious persuasion as the child or at least undertake to bring him up in that persuasion.[6] The foster-parents and the accommodation must have been visited before the boarding-out begins. In longer-term cases, the visit must be by a visitor who is personally acquainted with the child and his needs, or if that is impracticable is fully informed about them, and the visitor must be satisfied that all the conditions of the dwelling and the household generally would suit the child's particular needs. The visitor must report on the reputation, religious persuasion, age, character, temperament and health of the foster-parents, and as to any illness or criminality in the household which might adversely affect the child.[7] The child himself must be the subject of a report as to physical and mental health based on an examination made within the last three months; regular examinations must be held during the fostering period.[8]

---

1 Children Act 1948, s. 13 (2).
2 See Children and Young Persons Act 1963, s. 49 (1), which is primarily concerned with the offence of harbouring a child whose return has been requested; no offence is committed until the end of any fixed period.
3 S.I. 1955 No. 1377, made under Children Act 1948, s. 14. The Home Office published a helpful *Memorandum* on these Regulations, which also apply with modifications to children boarded-out by voluntary organisations.
4 Reg. 2, which contains provision for special situations; e.g. the child may remain even if the foster-mother dies.
5 I.e. for a period exceeding 8 weeks; regs. 16 to 23 only apply to such cases.
6 Reg. 19.
7 Reg. 17. For shorter-term fostering, see the much simpler reg. 25.
8 Regs. 6, 7, 8; for emergency placement without a medical report, see reg. 6.

If all seems well and the child is boarded-out, the foster-parent must sign a statutory undertaking, the important terms of which include a promise to bring up the child as the foster-parent would bring up a child of his own, to allow authorised visits by local authority staff, and to permit the child to be removed by an authorised person.[1]

SUPERVISION

There are elaborate provisions for the visiting of the foster-parents. A visitor must see the child and his accommodation within the first month of the boarding-out period, once every two months during the first two years (once every six weeks if the child is under five), and once every three months thereafter. The visits are more frequent in the case of short-term fostering,[2] and in all cases the visits must be as frequent as the child's welfare requires, with an immediate visit on the receipt of any complaint by the child or about him (unless action is deemed unnecessary, as where a similar complaint from another source has just been investigated).[3] Every visit must be the subject of a written report which forms part of the case records which the authority must maintain.[4]

REVIEW AND TERMINATION

A review must be held of each longer-term fostering case within the first three months, and once every six months thereafter, or more often if necessary. This amounts to a review of the case record with its visitors' reports, and should be conducted by members of the social services department staff who are not currently acting as visitors themselves.[5] If the authority concludes, as a result of such a review or at any other time, that it would not be in the child's best interests to continue the boarding-out, they must bring it to an end.[6] In addition any visitor who considers that the conditions in which the child is boarded-out endanger his health, safety or morals is empowered to remove the child from the foster-parents forthwith, and the foster-parent has no right of appeal or review.[7]

It occasionally happens that a foster-parent (or indeed a natural parent with whom a child in care is living on trial) refuses to hand over the child as requested. The persuasive blandishments of the social workers, with reference in appropriate cases to the undertaking which the foster-parent has signed, may be ineffective; the door is barred and an impasse is reached. If the child is subject to a care order and is

---

[1] Reg. 20 and Schedule; in short-term cases the conditions can be notified in a letter rather than incorporated in a formal undertaking: reg. 27.
[2] Within 2 weeks, then every 4 weeks; but if the child is over 16 only one visit, within the first month, is essential: reg. 28.
[3] Reg. 21.
[4] Regs. 9, 10, 11.
[5] Reg. 22.
[6] Reg. 4.
[7] Reg. 5.

"absent from premises at which he is required by the local authority to live" (which seems to cover this type of case), he may be arrested without warrant by a constable and removed to those premises.[1] But if the child is in care under the 1948 Act the position is more difficult; there is no power of arrest in such cases. In some cases a place of safety order may be obtained;[2] if a section 2 resolution is in force, it is an offence to harbour or conceal a child recalled by the local authority at or after the expiry of any fixed period for which charge of the child was handed over;[3] but ultimately the authority may have to use the remedy of *habeas corpus* to obtain possession of the child.[4]

REVIEW OF LOCAL AUTHORITY DECISIONS

The powers possessed by the local authority over the children in its care are very great, and those in respect of the child's accommodation are particularly important: it is not only where the child is to be housed that is involved but also, and much more sensitive, who controls his upbringing.

These matters are exclusively within the control of the authority, and the courts will not intervene. The position was made clear in the Court of Appeal decision in *Re M.*[5] The case concerned a boy of eight who had been looked after by a foster-mother for almost six years. He was in the care of the local authority, which had also assumed parental rights by a section 2 resolution, and had been boarded-out with the foster-mother. The authority decided that it was no longer in the child's best interests for him to remain with the foster-mother; she was asked to hand the child over, refused, and made him a ward of court.

The Court of Appeal held that Parliament had created a clear and comprehensive scheme which formulated precisely the powers of the local authorities, and that the matter of judging the best interests of the child was, in the circumstances of the case, in the exclusive jurisdiction of the authority. In other words the courts will not review the wisdom of the local authority's decision, and, while a child may be made a ward of court, wardship proceedings cannot be used as an appeal from the authority.[6]

The decision in *Re M. (an infant)* was followed in the later case of

---

1 Children and Young Persons Act 1969, s. 32 (1); the foster-parents may also be guilty of criminal offences in such cases: see *ibid.*, s. 32 (2), (3).
2 See pp. 92–3.
3 Children and Young Persons Act 1963, s. 49 (1), as amended in 1969.
4 This remedy was used in *Re A.B.*, [1954] 2 Q.B. 385, [1954] 2 All E.R. 287 and in *Re M. (an infant)* [1961] Ch. 328. The latter case (discussed below) led to unsuccessful attempts during the passage of the 1963 Act to create a power of arrest.
5 [1961] Ch. 328; [1961] 1 All E.R. 788, affirming [1961] Ch. 81; [1961] 1 All E.R. 201.
6 [1961] Ch. 328, at pp. 341–3. In *Re M.* the court ordered that the child should cease to be a ward, but this will not always happen.

Re K (an infant)[1] in the Divisional Court of the Family Division. The natural father of two illegitimate children applied to the Hertfordshire County Council for access to them. There was some disagreement about the conditions of access, apparently related to the fact that the father was a convicted offender, and he eventually sought a court order for access under the Guardianship of Minors Act 1971. The magistrates granted the order but this was set aside on appeal. The Divisional Court accepted the argument for the Council that decisions as to access were for the Council alone to take, and that the courts would not intervene either to take decisions or to substitute their own view for that of the local authority.[2]

The technical legal position in these cases is that the courts do have jurisdiction, but will not in fact use their powers to intervene in matters such as access "which must necessarily be under the day to day and continuing control and discretion of the local authority'.[3] The courts will intervene in other types of case: if someone has independent statutory rights to apply for custody under the Guardianship of Minors Act 1971, those rights will not be destroyed by the circumstance that the child is in care;[4] and the courts will also intervene if "bad faith" is alleged. If councillors, or the social workers concerned, bear some malice towards the parties, and the authority reaches its decisions under the influence of those feelings and not on the real merits of the case, the courts may intervene. Then the question would not be the wisdom of a decision taken under the authority's powers but whether the authority was in breach of its statutory duties.[5]

THE PARENTS

The legal position of the parents depends very much on how the child came to be in care and on whether or not a section 2 resolution has been passed, but the Children Act contains some general provisions designed to advance the policy of keeping alive the relationship between the child and his parents. The parents must keep the authority informed of their address, and failure is a criminal offence.[6] More positively, the authority may give financial assistance to parents wishing to visit their child (or, sadly, to attend his funeral) and for whom the expenses of the visit would entail undue hardship.[7] The main legal

---

[1] [1972] 3 All E.R. 769. See also *Re B. (a minor)*, [1974] 3 All E.R. 915; *S. v. Huddersfield B.C.*, [1974] 3 All E.R. 296.
[2] See also *Re T. (A.J.J.)*, [1970] Ch. 688; [1970] 2 All E.R. 865 (child in care under a court order; dispute between foster-parents and local authority).
[3] *R. v. Oxford City Justices, ex parte H.*, [1974] 2 All E.R. 356, at p. 360.
[4] E.g. the rights of a putative father under that Act: see p. 57, above, and *R. v. Oxford City Justices, ex parte H.*, [1974] 2 All E.R. 356; [1974] 3 W.L.R. 1.
[5] See *Re M. (an infant)*, [1961] Ch. 328, especially at pp. 341–2, 345.
[6] Children Act 1948, s. 10; Matrimonial Proceedings (Magistrates' Courts) Act 1960, s. 3 (5); Children and Young Persons Act 1969, s. 24 (8); Matrimonial Causes Act 1973, s. 43(6).
[7] Children Act 1948, s. 22.

obligation of the parents is to make financial contributions towards the cost of maintaining their child.

FINANCIAL CONTRIBUTIONS

When a child under sixteen is in care either under section 1 of the 1948 Act[1] or under a care order (but not an interim care order) the father and mother of the child are liable to pay contributions towards his maintenance.[2] If the child is over sixteen and earning money from whole-time work, he is liable to pay contributions on his own account.[3] These liabilities can be enforced by obtaining a contribution order from a magistrates' court which fixes a weekly sum after taking the means of the contributor into account.[4] Where the child is illegitimate, the court may order that payments under an affiliation order be made over to the local authority, and an affiliation order may be applied for by the local authority itself.[5]

When anyone is liable to pay contributions, the local authority must seek his voluntary agreement, proposing a sum as the amount he should contribute. The maximum sum is that which the authority would pay in respect of the child as a boarding-out allowance to foster-parents. It is only after the failure of negotiations that a court order can be made and the court cannot order payment of a sum larger than that proposed by the local authority during the negotiations.[6]

LOCAL AUTHORITY FINANCIAL OBLIGATIONS

The sums recovered as parental contributions are in fact derisory in relation to the cost of maintaining the child, and the bulk of the expenditure is a charge on the funds of the local authority. This leads to a certain amount of not altogether edifying wrangling as to which local authority is responsible. The basic principle is that the financial responsibility rests with the local authority within whose area the child is ordinarily resident, ignoring for this purpose residence in a school or institution, under the conditions as to residence of a supervision order or recognisance, or while boarded-out.[7]

Suppose for example that Michael's parents now live in Sheffield;

---

[1] Including protected children removed from unsuitable places under the Children Act 1958 or the Adoption Act 1958.

[2] Children and Young Persons Act 1933, s. 86; Children Act 1948, ss. 23, 24. When a minor is committed to the care of the local authority after Guardianship of Minors Act proceedings, either parent may be required to make contributions: Guardianship Act 1973, s. 2 (3).

[3] Children Act 1948, s. 24 (3); this last provision also applies to children in care after matrimonial proceedings in magistrates' courts (1960 Act, s. 3 (2) (*b*)) but any question of payments by the parents is to be dealt with by way of a maintenance order in the matrimonial proceedings: see p. 71.

[4] Children and Young Persons Act 1933, s. 87.

[5] *Ibid.*, s. 88; Children Act 1948, s. 26.

[6] Children and Young Persons Act 1969, s. 62.

[7] Children Act 1948, s. 1 (4), (5).

they have lived there for five years having earlier been in Leeds. Michael, now aged thirteen, was received into care in Sheffield soon after his parents moved there and was boarded-out with foster-parents who lived just over the Derbyshire border. He was recently discharged from care and returned home. He soon ran away from home and has been received into the care of the local authority for a Lancashire holiday resort. For most of the last five years he has been living in Derbyshire; but that was while he was boarded-out and is to be disregarded. There is little doubt that his ordinary residence is in Sheffield where his parents live.

It is easy to construct more difficult problems, especially where the parents live apart, or change addresses frequently, and the legal interpretation of "ordinarily resident" is notoriously difficult. Disputes as to the application of the phrase to particular cases are resolved by the Department of Health and Social Security.[1]

Not only does the local authority in which the child is ordinarily resident bear financial responsibility, but in many cases it should also take over the care of the child. This is not a matter of legal obligation but merely of good practice: if a child runs away to a holiday resort and gets himself into trouble, the legal responsibility for providing care is on the resort's authority; but it obviously makes good sense in most cases to bring him back to his own home area even if he has to remain in care. The Act authorises his home authority to take over his care.[2] A long-delayed transfer might be disruptive if the child has settled to his new environment; after the first three months the home authority may only take over the child with the agreement of the authority which received him into care.[3]

CARE ORDER CHILDREN

The position of children in care under a care order is generally the same as that of other children in care. The local authority is given an express power to restrict the liberty of a care order child to such an extent as they consider appropriate,[4] but it is doubtful whether that adds anything to the powers generally applicable.

The main special provision concerns the appointment of visitors to certain care order children. It is important that a child who is living in an institution should have some contact with an outsider, someone quite independent of the institution; this is socially desirable, but has the additional value of giving the child an independent source of advice as to the exercise of certain legal rights, especially that of

---

[1] Children Act, 1948, s. 1 (4).
[2] *Ibid.*, s. 1 (4) (*a*).
[3] *Ibid.* The 3 months begins to run from the time it is decided which is in fact the local authority within whose area the child is ordinarily resident; this determination may take some time.
[4] Children and Young Persons Act 1969, s. 24 (2).

applying for the discharge of the care order. Most children will be in contact with some outside person, their parents, the staff of the school they attend or people with whom they work; if for some reason this is not the case a visitor must be appointed.

The legal rules provide that if the child has not been allowed to leave his institution to go to school or work for three months, and has not seen his parents for a year or has had minimal contact with them in other ways, the local authority is under a duty to appoint a visitor, to visit, advise and befriend the child and advise the child especially as to his right to apply for a discharge of care order.[1] The visitor must have no connection with the authority, the institution or any voluntary body running the institution.[2]

B. GOING OUT OF CARE

This section summarises the rules governing the discharge of a child from the care of a local authority, and examines the somewhat uncertain and complex legal position which can arise in disputed cases.

CHILDREN IN CARE UNDER A COURT ORDER

If the authority itself feels that the time has come for the child to be discharged from care it can apply to the court for the order to be discharged.[3] The child may in fact have been living at home for some considerable period, this having been allowed on a trial basis;[4] what is in issue is not the physical location of the child but the legal rights and duties attached to his being "in care". In the case of a child subject to a care order, the court which discharges that order can substitute a supervision order;[5] in this way the authority maintains contact and continues to enjoy considerable powers with which to influence the child's upbringing.

If the child or his parents are seeking a discharge, they must also proceed by making an application to the court. In the case of a care order, application may be made to the juvenile court as often as once every three months, or even more often if the court consents (which it is unlikely to do), and an appeal against a refusal lies to the Crown Court.[6] In matrimonial cases the parents can apply,[7] but the rights of the child to do so are wholly unclear.

---

[1] *Ibid.*, s. 24 (5), (6).
[2] For details see Children and Young Persons (Definition of Independent Persons) Regulations 1971 (S.I. 1971 No. 486).
[3] Matrimonial Proceedings (Magistrates' Courts) Act 1960, s. 10 (1); Children and Young Persons Act 1969, ss. 21 (2), 70 (2); Matrimonial Causes Act 1973, s. 43 (7).
[4] I.e. under Children Act 1948, s. 13 (2); see pp. 76-7.
[5] Children and Young Persons Act 1969, s. 21 (2).
[6] *Ibid.*, s. 21 (2), (3).
[7] Matrimonial Proceedings (Magistrates' Courts) Act 1960, s. 10 (1); Matrimonial Causes Act 1973, s. 43 (7).

CHILDREN SUBJECT TO A SECTION 2 RESOLUTION

The various procedures for challenging a resolution assuming parental rights have already been examined.[1] If a section 2 resolution is successfully challenged it does not necessarily mean that the child will be discharged from care; if the resolution ceases to have effect the child is still in care under section 1 of the Children Act. The matter will normally be taken to court by parents anxious to have their child at home, but in some cases a parent who is quite unable to take over the care of the child may wish to challenge an attempt to deprive him of parental rights, so as to retain the right to recover his child when his own circumstances permit.

CHILDREN RECEIVED INTO CARE UNDER CHILDREN ACT
1948, s. 1

The position of children received into care under section 1 of the 1948 Act is governed by the important subsection 1 (3). The first part of that subsection reads:

> "Nothing in this section shall authorise a local authority to keep a child in their care under this section if any parent or guardian of his desires to take over the care of the child. . . ."

So if a parent or guardian (in the restricted sense which those terms have in the Children Act)[2] asks for the return of the child, the local authority cannot insist on keeping the child against the parent's wishes, unless of course they have assumed parental rights by a section 2 resolution. The Act speaks of a parent who "desires to take over the care of the child": this does not necessarily mean that the parent will actually look after the child himself. If the mother of the child seeks to recover her illegitimate child from the local authority, her intention being that the child's putative father and his wife should look after the child, she is seeking to "take over the care of the child", for she rather than the authority will be seeing to it that proper provision is made for him. This was established by the Queen's Bench Divisional Court in *Re A.B.*,[3] but over the dissent on this point of one of the judges.

In almost all cases the local authority will be only too happy for the child to return home. Whatever emergency led to the reception into care will have passed; scarce resources will be available for other cases. But there may be cases where the local authority's social workers are convinced that it would be most harmful to the child for him to return home, that to allow his parent to recover him would be directly contrary to his best interests. Is there anything that can be done where this is the case? There are four possibilities to be considered:

---

[1] See pp. 55–7.
[2] See pp. 44–5.
[3] [1954] 2 Q.B. 385; [1954] 2 All E.R. 287.

1. *Pass a belated section 2 resolution*

The situation would never have arisen if the authority had antici-
pated it and (assuming that grounds existed) had passed a section 2
resolution. Might it be possible to rush through the necessary procedures and so prevent the removal of the child? In many cases this
can be done. The authority has some advance warning that the parent
is about to demand the child's return; the parent may enquire about
the possibilities of its being returned, or make the beginnings of an
approach. What is uncertain is whether the authority can still pass a
section 2 resolution once the child's return has actually been demanded
in unambiguous terms. The point has never presented itself directly
for decision, but has been the subject of comment from judges. One
view is that of Pearson, L.J. speaking in the Court of Appeal in 1965.[1]
A section 2 resolution can only be made while a child is in care; if the
parent's demand ends the right of the authority to keep a child in care,
then it is at least arguable that there is no longer any basis upon which
to make a section 2 resolution.

The alternative view is that a child remains "in care", and the
authority retains the right to pass a resolution, so long as he is physically
in the authority's care, that is until his care is actually taken over by the
parent. This view was apparently favoured by Goff J. in *Krishnan* v.
Sutton London Borough Council;[2] his decision in the case was affirmed by
the Court of Appeal but this particular point was not referred to in the
higher court.

The result is that we have conflicting dicta, that is judicial statements
which are influential but not binding on any future court, and the legal
position remains unresolved.

2. *Ignore the parent's request*

At first sight this is an outrageous suggestion. The Act makes it clear
that the authority has no right to keep the child; any idea that the
parent's demand for the return of his child should be ignored is likely to
have lawyers reaching for their pens with words like "bureaucratic
oppression" ready for use. But the decision of the Court of Appeal in
Krishnan v. *Sutton London Borough Council*[3] gives some semblance of re-
spectability to what has been proposed. The Court of Appeal, resolving earlier doubts, accepted that the words of section 1 (3) quoted
above impose no mandatory obligation on the authority to return the
child to his parents. That is, the authority has no right to keep the
child, but is under no duty to do anything to return the child. In the
Krishnan case itself the child was a girl of seventeen living with foster-
parents, and persuasion having failed there was little that the authority

---

[1] *Re S.*, [1965] 1 All E.R. 865, at p. 871.
[2] [1970] Ch. 181, at pp. 185–6.
[3] *Ibid.*, at p. 192.

could do to ensure that the girl was returned to her father.[1] If we consider a more usual case, of a young child in a local authority home, the legal position still seems to be that the authority are under no positive duty to facilitate the transfer of the child; non-cooperation might in effect overcome the parent's resolve.

It must be added, with all respect to the judicial view, that for an authority to resort to this sort of behaviour, when on the plain words of the Act it has no right to keep the child in care, would be contrary to the spirit of the legislation. It would be not illegal; but it would be improper.

3. *Take wardship proceedings*

A much more respectable alternative would be to make the child a ward of court. Although the courts will not allow wardship proceedings to be used as a form of appeal from the exercise of local authority powers,[2] there are situations in which wardship can be used successfully. For example, the authority may invoke the wardship jurisdiction to supplement its own powers, for example to prevent the removal of a child from the country.[3]

In the present context the parent's request for the return of his child brings to an end the rights of the authority to keep the child. The courts have taken the view that once that has happened (and perhaps even when it is about to happen[4]) the wardship jurisdiction comes into full play; there is no need to restrict the scope of wardship in deference to the local authority's own expiring statutory powers.[5] Accordingly the local authority on receipt of a demand for the return of the child can make him a ward of court and secure an examination of the case in which the welfare of the child will be the paramount consideration. The court has full powers to order with whom the child should stay, both in the immediate future while the case awaits a hearing and in the longer term.

4. *Care proceedings*

A final possibility, available in some cases, is for the child to be returned to the parents but promptly retaken under a place of safety order pending care proceedings.[6] Whether or not this possibility is available will of course depend on the existence of the statutory

---

[1] The authority might institute *habeas corpus* proceedings to recover the child from the foster-parents: see p. 79; but that would not necessarily help, especially in the case of an independent-minded teenager.

[2] See p. 41.

[3] As in *Re G. (infants)*, [1963] 3 All E.R. 370; [1963] 1 W.L.R. 1169. See also *Re Hetherington* (Court of Appeal, 1964; unreported, but see [1965] 1 All E.R. 41).

[4] See *Re S. (an infant)*, [1965] 1 All E.R. 865, at p. 868 *per* Lord Denning, M.R.

[5] *Re K.R. (an infant)*, [1964] Ch. 455; [1963] 3 All E.R. 337.

[6] See pp. 92–3.

grounds. It can lead to distressing scenes and disturb the child considerably, so that the other alternatives are perhaps to be preferred.

LEGAL ACTION BY THE PARENT

It sometimes happens that a parent will himself begin legal proceedings, perhaps when his request for the return of his child fails to produce a satisfactory response. There are many different types of proceedings which might be used: wardship, the Guardianship of Minors legislation, possibly a residual inherent jurisdiction in the Family Division to safeguard children, *habeas corpus*, or an injunction applied for in an action against the authority for breach of statutory duty.[1] Whichever form of procedure is used, it is now clear that the court will regard the welfare of the child as the first and paramount consideration, as it will in, for example, wardship proceedings begun by the authority.[2] The parent secures no added advantage by being the first at the courthouse.

LEGAL ACTION BY A FOSTER-PARENT

The saddest cases in which the future of a child is disputed are those involving foster-parents. If a child has been received into care and boarded-out, perhaps for many years, it is not surprising that the foster-parents should resent the natural parents' attempts to recover possession of the child. If the local authority support the natural parents, there is little likelihood of the foster-parents retaining the child. The authority can recover the child, using *habeas corpus* if necessary;[3] although the child's welfare is paramount even in *habeas corpus*,[4] the court would hesitate to challenge the local authority's view on that question.[5] But if the local authority is sympathetic to the foster-parents' case, wardship proceedings may be taken (by the foster-parents, the authority or both together) so that the court will determine the matter on the basis of the child's welfare.[6]

One final complication was revealed in *Re S. (an infant)*[7] in 1965. There the local authority was in effect neutral. Its mistaken view was that section 1 (3) left it with no alternative but to agree to return the child to its natural parents. The Court of Appeal allowed the child's foster-parents to continue wardship proceedings so that their claim to

---

1 *Krishnan* v. *Sutton London Borough Council, supra,* is an example of the last named.
2 *J.* v. *C.,* [1970] A.C. 668; [1969] 1 All E.R. 788; Guardianship of Minors Act 1971, s. 1. The historical development of the various forms of action and of earlier statutes such as the Custody of Children Act 1891, still unrepealed, is of great complexity; it is reviewed, and the proposition in the text established, in the House of Lords decision in *J.* v. *C.*
3 *Re A.B. (infant),* [1954] 2 Q.B. 385; [1954] 2 All E.R. 287.
4 See *Re S.,* [1965] 1 All E.R. 865, at p. 868, *per* Lord Denning, M.R.
5 See *Re S.,* [1965] 1 All E.R. 865, at p. 870, *per* Pearson, L.J., who seems to be applying, perhaps out of context, the principle that the court will not normally investigate the wisdom of an authority's exercise of its powers.
6 *Re K.R. (an infant),* [1964] Ch. 455; [1963] 3 All E.R. 337.
7 [1965] 1 All E.R. 865; [1965] 1 W.L.R.

the child, based on their assertion that it was in the child's interests that he remain with them, could be fully investigated.

THE DUTY TO TRANSFER CARE

Section 1 (3) of the Children Act 1948, in addition to the words previously set out and which are the basis of the technical matters just discussed, contains a wholly separate provision. Their proximity has led to confusion in some of the cases but the two parts of the subsection are quite distinct.

> ". . . and the local authority shall, in all cases where it appears to them consistent with the welfare of the child so to do, endeavour to secure that the care of the child is taken over either
> (a) by a parent or guardian[1] of his, or
> (b) by a relative or friend of his, being, where possible, a person of the same religious persuasion as the child or who gives an undertaking that the child will be brought up in that religious persuasion."

In effect this is a policy directive to local authorities. They are to ensure that someone close to the child takes over the care of him as and when that accords with their view of his welfare. If they take the view that his welfare is best served by his remaining in care, then this part of section 1 (3) never applies.

This is illustrated by the facts of *Re C. (A) (infant)*.[2] A seven-year-old illegitimate boy had been in care and had lived with foster-parents for almost the whole of his life. The putative father whose home was in South Africa was anxious to take the child there to be brought up by himself and his wife. The putative father of an illegitimate child is not a "parent", and so could not demand the return of the child under the *first* limb of section 1 (3). Instead he tried to make use of wardship proceedings to compel the local authority to hand over the care of the child under the *second* limb. This attempt failed. If the court had continued the wardship it would have been reviewing the wisdom of a decision of the authority made under the authority's statutory powers. As we have seen the court will only do this in exceptional circumstances, none of which applied here. The authority's decision as to the child's needs was final, and there could therefore be no duty to hand over the care of the child.

AFTER-CARE

A local authority's responsibility does not necessarily end once a child is discharged from care. In some circumstances there may continue to be a formal supervision requirement; but even when this is not the case

---

[1] These words have the usual restricted meanings: see pp. 44–5. But in this context the limitations are of little practical importance: the putative father of an illegitimate child is a "relative" (*Re A.B. (infant)*, [1954] 2 Q.B. 385, at p. 393), and an unofficial "guardian" would doubtless qualify as a "friend".

[2] [1966] 1 All E.R. 560; [1966] 1 W.L.R. 415.

continued contact may have preventive value and be a source of support, and even pleasure, for the child.

The most obvious need is for the continuing care of those who spent many years of childhood in care and may have no parents or relatives who accept any responsibility for them. The law imposes a more general duty, to be found in a number of rather scattered legal provisions. In particular, a local authority is under a duty to advise and befriend anyone under the age of eighteen who was, at or after his sixteenth birthday, in the care of a local authority or voluntary organisation, unless that organisation provides after-care or the child's welfare does not require it, as for example when he is happily married.[1]

The authority is also under a general duty to provide after-care at the request of a person under twenty-one who was in care at, or at any time after, his seventeenth birthday but has now ceased to be in care. The duty is to visit, advise and befriend him, and "in exceptional circumstances" to give financial assistance.[2]

Presumably the expectation is that most financial needs will be met from social security sources, but the children's legislation contains some rather complicated provisions authorising the local authority to give financial help for special purposes, in addition to the exceptional power already mentioned. If a child has been in care at any time after reaching the age of sixteen, he becomes eligible for financial assistance from the local authority if certain further conditions are met. These are that he is *either* seventeen or more and is no longer in the care of the authority *or* that he is eighteen (whether or not he is still in care). In these cases assistance can be given at any time up to his reaching the age of twenty-one towards the cost of accommodation and maintenance near his place of employment, education or training.[3]

In addition, if a child was in care at any time after he reached the age of seventeen, grants may be given to him while he is aged between seventeen and twenty-one towards the cost of education or training. These grants may be continued even when the recipient has reached twenty-one if his course of study or training is still continuing, or is later resumed after some interruption.[4]

A local authority also has power, not limited to children who are or have been in care, to provide accommodation in a community home to persons aged between sixteen and twenty-one who are working, seeking employment, or studying nearby.[5]

---

[1] Children Act 1948, s. 34, which also contains notification provisions to ensure that the relevant authority is aware, so far as possible, of children in this category.
[2] Children and Young Persons Act 1963, s. 58.
[3] Children Act 1948, s. 20 (1).
[4] *Ibid.*, s. 20 (2), (3).
[5] *Ibid.*, s. 19.

C. THE INITIAL DETENTION OF A CHILD

Under this rather forbidding title, there fall to be examined some of the legal rules which apply when a child is physically detained, or removed from a particular place, by someone in authority. The most obvious example of this procedure is an arrest. If the reader will imagine himself being arrested by the police one day, he will soon sympathise with the concerns which excite a lawyer reacting to any type of detention. The person detained will want to know exactly why this is happening to him; if no good reason exists he is legally entitled to resist, to use reasonable force to maintain his freedom. The legal principle that an arrested person must be told why he is arrested was stated in the lawyers' books as early as 1755, and emphatically reaffirmed by the House of Lords in 1947.[1] Similarly the detained person will want to know how long he can be kept in custody, and how soon he must be brought to court.

In this context we naturally tend to think of action by the police. Both at common law and under more recent statutory provisions constables have greater powers of arrest than other citizens. But other citizens do have powers of arrest, and in some situations special classes of citizens, and especially social workers, have (or may be given) the very similar power of removing a child to a place of safety. Emergency intervention to rehouse a child found to be living in a brothel, or wandering with a vagrant, is socially highly desirable, but the questions of the legality of what is done, and the time within which judicial safeguards operate, are still important. They are important not only to the child and his parents, but also to the social worker who could face actions for trespass or false imprisonment if he put a foot wrong in this highly technical as well as highly emotive area.

OFFENDERS

If the child has committed an offence there are extensive powers of arrest granted to the police and to private citizens; a social worker may have occasion to use these latter powers himself. If an "arrestable offence", defined as one punishable in the case of an adult with five years' imprisonment, which includes common crimes like theft and criminal damage to property, has been committed, a private person may arrest anyone he suspects on reasonable grounds of being guilty of the offence; similar provisions apply to a person caught in the act of committing the offence.[2]

A child arrested in this way will be taken to a police station. There

---

[1] *Christie* v. *Leachinsky*, [1947] A.C. 573; [1947] 1 All E.R. 567.
[2] Criminal Law Act 1967, s. 2 (2), (3). The law of arrest is complex and its details are outside the scope of this book. Short summaries appear in such books as *Stone's Justices' Manual* (Butterworths, annually).

the matter will be looked into and a decision taken, by an Inspector or more senior officer, to release the child or detain him further. The child[1] must be released unless detention is in the child's own interests; or he is thought to have committed homicide or another grave crime; or that his release would defeat the ends of justice; or that he would fail to appear to answer a charge.[2] These phrases are fairly imprecise: no indication is given of what is meant by a "grave" crime, nor are "the ends of justice" specified. The latter phrase is meant to cover cases in which, for example, evidence might be destroyed if the child were prematurely released.

If the child is detained, the police make arrangements for him to be taken into the care of the local authority, but he has to be brought before a court (unless prevented by illness or accident) within seventy-two hours.[3]

ABSCONDERS

If the child is an absconder, absent without leave from some place where he is lawfully detained,[4] there will be power for a constable to arrest him without warrant, but a private citizen has no such power.[5] In this situation, where the child is already subject to lawful detention, there is no fresh court hearing; he is taken back to the institution or place from which he absconded.

OTHER CASES—POLICE POWERS

A wide power is given to the police by the Children and Young Persons Act 1969. A constable may detain, without any form of warrant, a child whom he reasonably believes to fall within one of conditions (*a*), (*b*), (*c*) or (*d*) of section 1 (2) of the Act.[6] He need not concern himself with the "care and control" requirement. This power does not cover the school attendance cases under condition (*e*), but there is a special power of detention in the case of the children of vagrants who are not receiving proper education.[7]

---

[1] In the relevant provisions of the Children and Young Persons Act 1969, a distinction is drawn between children and young persons; in bringing the Act into force, the Government modified its terms, so that the provisions set out for young persons do in fact apply to all cases.

[2] The position is slightly different if a child is arrested under a warrant. See *ibid.*, s. 29 (1), (2).

[3] *Ibid.*, s. 29 (3), (5).

[4] For the related situation in which persons with whom a child has been boarded-out refuse to return him, see pp. 78–9.

[5] See Prison Act 1952, s. 49 (1) (borstals and detention centres); Children and Young Persons Act 1969, s. 32 (children subject to a care order, remanded to the care of a local authority, detained in a community home as a place of safety, or in the custody of a local authority after an arrest). Prison officers acting as such have the powers of constables: Prison Act 1952, s. 8.

[6] Children and Young Persons Act 1969, s. 28 (2): for the conditions under *ibid.*, s. 1 (2), see pp. 60–9.

[7] *Ibid.*, s. 28 (2); i.e. where an offence is committed under Children and Young Persons Act 1933, s. 10 (1): see p. 67.

When a child is detained under this power he and his parents must be told of the reasons as soon as possible. He must be released as soon as the police have investigated the matter unless an Inspector or more senior officer decides that he should be further detained in his own interests. If he is detained it must be in a place of safety (defined as including a community home, hospital, police station, or other suitable place the occupier of which is willing temporarily to receive the child; a local authority home or foster-home would be the usual place of safety). In any event, the detention cannot exceed eight days unless reserved by a court or justice; and before then the child and his parents can apply to a justice for earlier release, so that they have in effect an appeal from the police decision.[1]

These powers of detention do not include a power to search premises. If it is thought on reasonable grounds that a child has been or is being assaulted, ill-treated or neglected, or that one of a number of specified offences involving cruelty or sexual assaults has been committed against the child, wider powers may be obtained, but only after prior application to a justice. He can issue a warrant, on the application of any person acting in the interests of the child (plainly including a social worker), authorising a constable to search for and remove such a child, who can afterwards be kept in a place of safety for up to twenty-eight days before there need be a court hearing.[2]

ACTION BY THE SOCIAL WORKER

Social workers as such do not enjoy anything corresponding to the police power of arrest without warrant. Intervention involving removal or detention requires prior authority from a justice of the peace. Specific procedures exist for obtaining removal orders in the case of foster-children protected under the Children Act 1958[3] and of protected children under the Adoption Act 1958.[4] In those cases detention for up to twenty-eight days in a place of safety is lawful before a court hearing which will either lead to an interim order committing the child temporarily to the care of the local authority or to the child's release. In practice the child will almost always have been received into the care of the local authority before the period elapses, and no hearing is then needed.[5]

In all other cases in which the social worker wishes to act himself, and it may be very desirable that the police should not be involved, he should seek a place of safety order under the Children and Young

---

[1] Children and Young Persons Act 1969, s. 28 (3)–(6).
[2] Children and Young Persons Act 1933, s. 40; Children and Young Persons Act 1963, s. 23. See also Children Act 1958, s. 8 (refusal to allow visiting of foster-child a ground for issuing a warrant to search under this power).
[3] Children Act 1958, s. 7; see p. 102.
[4] Adoption Act 1958, s. 43; see p. 114.
[5] Children and Young Persons Act 1963, s. 23.

Persons Act 1969. A justice of the peace can give this order on an application from any person who reasonably believes that any of conditions (*a*) to (*e*)[1] is satisfied in respect of the child,[2] or in the special case of a child about to be taken abroad as a juvenile entertainer.[3] There is no need to consider the "care and control" requirement. It will be seen that school attendance cases within condition (*e*) are included here, but not in the powers given by the Act to the police. The place of safety order authorises detention for a maximum of twenty-eight days; the justice may fix a shorter period. As usual, there is a statutory duty to take steps to tell the child why he is being detained and his parents of the fact of his detention and those reasons.[4]

Place of safety orders are used for a variety of purposes. The twenty-eight-day period gives time for steps to be taken, for example, to arrange for the voluntary reception of the child into care. But it must be stressed that the order can only be obtained on the prescribed grounds linked closely with the conditions in the 1969 Act; it is not necessary that care proceedings should actually be contemplated, but the primary conditions for those proceedings none the less govern.

It will be appreciated that there is some element of overlap between these various powers. The power to go to court for a removal order in respect of a foster-child under the Children Act 1958[5] is widely drawn, but the emergency procedure under that Act, under which an order can be made by a single justice, requires proof of "imminent danger to the health or well-being of the child". Where there is acute suspicion falling short of proof, it could be easier to seek a place of safety order under the 1969 Act, which is also a matter for a single justice.

---

[1] See pp. 60–9.
[2] Children and Young Persons Act 1969, s. 28.
[3] See *ibid.*, s. 25.
[4] *Ibid.*, s. 28 (1), (3).
[5] See p. 102.

Chapter 7

CHILDREN UNDER
SUPERVISION

It must be stressed once again that supervision, however beneficial and well-intentioned, can be seen as an intrusion and as an interference with liberty. Of course the intrusive element is very much less than in a "care" situation where accommodation and upbringing may be taken over comprehensively, but a supervisor may exert a very great influence. He needs to bear that in mind, partly because it is crucial to his own professional work, but also because it makes relevant the lawyer's concern with legality and the dangers of the abuse of power.

The common element in the various forms of supervision is the relationship in which the supervisor "advises, assists and befriends". Legal rules deal with the start and finish of that relationship, but hardly at all with its content; that is essentially within the domain of the professional social worker. But this common element seldom exists on its own. In many contexts supervision contains an element of inspection which can in turn lead to sanctions being applied. For example, in fostering a supervisor is there to give advice and encouragement but also to see that the child is properly looked after; if the foster-parents prove unsatisfactory, the child may have to be removed, an act of intervention affecting rights and duties.

A similar point can be made about supervision orders under the Children and Young Persons Act 1969. In some circumstances the supervisor can require the attendance of the child at an institution for some months. This is far removed from simple supervision; as the label "intermediate treatment" suggests, it has elements of the "care" situation. This is just one aspect of the gradual playing-down of distinctions between residential and community care.

OCCASIONS FOR SUPERVISION

There are five principal types of situation in which supervision can arise. The first is where a court has ordered that there shall be supervision. We have seen that this can be done under the Children and

Young Persons Act 1969 and in certain wardship, matrimonial, and Guardianship of Minors Act cases. These have already been discussed,[1] but detailed treatment of supervision orders under the 1969 Act has been reserved for this chapter.

In the last chapter it was noted that children in care could be boarded-out with foster-parents, a situation which gives rise to powers and duties of supervision under the Boarding-Out of Children Regulations.[2] Children fostered privately are not within those provisions, but are protected (not, as we shall see, entirely satisfactorily) under the Children Act 1958. Children placed for adoption may become "protected children" under the Adoption Act 1958,[3] and are then in a very similar position as regards supervision to the privately fostered children. Finally, children minded on a daily basis are subject to the Nurseries and Child-Minders Regulation Act 1948.

So in this chapter, three groups must be dealt with: those subject to supervision under the 1969 Act, privately fostered children, and children left with child-minders.

A. SUPERVISION ORDERS UNDER THE 1969 ACT[4]

A supervision order may be made by a juvenile court in either care proceedings or in its criminal jurisdiction. For the most part, the same rules apply whatever the nature of the proceedings.

The basic pattern is quite straightforward. The court fixes a period up to a maximum of three years during which the supervision order can remain in force; an order made in care proceedings must end on the eighteenth birthday, one made in a criminal case need not.[5] The court will also appoint a supervisor, naming either the local authority (normally the one in whose area the child will be living) or a probation officer. In the case of a child aged below thirteen,[6] the local authority must be appointed unless it requests otherwise and a probation officer has been working with some other member of the household to which the child belongs, such as his older brother.[7]

The court may include a number of special terms in the supervision order. It may, and normally will, include requirements that any change of address or employment must be notified, and that the child should keep in touch with his supervisor, making and receiving visits as

---

[1] See chap. 5, above.
[2] See pp. 76–9, above.
[3] See further, p. 114.
[4] For the grounds for proceedings under this Act, see pp. 60–9, above.
[5] Children and Young Persons Act 1969, s. 17.
[6] The age was fixed at 13 by S.I. 1974 No. 1083; it may be raised to 14 in the future.
[7] Children and Young Persons Act 1969, s. 13.

required.[1] A supervision order may also contain a requirement of mental treatment either as an in-patient or as an out-patient, on terms very similar to those which apply to adults on probation.[2]

A more intensive requirement still may be included: that the supervised person should live with a named person for the duration of the order.[3] The intention is that this should be used where it is desirable that the child should live with, say, an uncle, or a married sister, or a particular friend of the family. There is no requirement that he should live at a particular place, and a requirement that he live, for example, with the Head Teacher of a named residential school would be quite outside the spirit of the Act; a care order is appropriate when any sort of institutional treatment is contemplated.

INTERMEDIATE TREATMENT

The most important of the special terms which can be included in a supervision order are those relating to "intermediate treatment". The object of this form of treatment has been officially described as "to bring the child into contact with a different environment and to give him the opportunity of forming new personal relationships and developing new interests. To do this he may spend one or more relatively brief periods away from home, or take part in constructive activities of a social, educational or therapeutic nature."[4]

There are two sorts of intermediate treatment. One involves a period of residence at a particular place for a single period which cannot exceed ninety days; this period must normally begin within the first year of the order.[5] In truth this is institutional treatment, the novelty being that there is maximum flexibility as to when it takes place, how long it lasts, and even if it takes place at all.

The second type of intermediate treatment may also include short periods away from home, but is essentially participation under the charge of the supervisor or other responsible person, and as far as possible in the company of children who are taking part voluntarily, in "activities of a recreational, educational or cultural nature or of social value . . . including (but not limited to) the following:

> physical education, competitive sports or games, adventure training, camping, cycling, walking, climbing, sailing, boating, canoeing, riding, swimming, amateur dramatics, arts, crafts, music, dancing, remedial education, further education, evening classes, vocational education, group counselling, group discussion, debating, attendance at lectures or talks, first aid, training in survival or rescue techniques,

---

[1] Children and Young Persons Act 1969, s. 18 (2) (b); Magistrates' Courts (Children and Young Persons) Rules 1970 (S.I. 1970 No. 1792), Sched. 2, para. 45.
[2] Children and Young Persons Act 1969, s. 12 (4), (5); see further, pp. 149–50.
[3] *Ibid.*, s. 12 (1).
[4] *Intermediate Treatment* (D.H.S.S. 1972), para. 14.
[5] If the power to give directions as to this type of treatment is inserted in the order by variation, the year begins at the date of variation: 1969 Act, s. 12 (3) (b).

community or social service projects, charity fund-raising projects pursuit of hobbies, work experience."[1]

Compulsory participation cannot exceed thirty days a year; as a part of a day is treated as a day this usually means thirty attendances. The aggregate number of days to be spent in both types of intermediate treatment must not exceed ninety days, and the court may specify periods shorter than the ninety- and thirty-day maxima given in the Act.[2]

The legal framework is unusually complicated in that decisions by both the court and the supervisor are involved. The court has to decide in the light of the reports before it what sort of supervision order to make—one for simple supervision; one authorising a certain type of intermediate treatment such as the second, "activities", type; or one authorising the full range of intermediate treatment. The supervisor, if he is given the power to use intermediate treatment, must then decide if and when to use his power, and what form of treatment to direct. Once he takes the decision, he directs the child accordingly; in the extreme case, he, the social worker, decides to activate the ninety-day residence in an institution. This is a novel power, with which some social workers are understandably unhappy.

In the "activities" type of treatment the supervisor will instruct the child, perhaps in writing but that is not essential, to report to a particular place or person or join in particular activities. The range of facilities available to him are those, falling within the general types set out above, included in the Scheme prepared in his area by a Children's Regional Planning Committee set up under the Act. So to take examples from a fictional "dummy" scheme published by the Department of Health and Social Security, the supervisor may direct the child to join a Scout troop, and attend for at least thirty Friday evenings; or report to Superintendent Jones and join a group of police cadets who are reclaiming a derelict canal at weekends; or (rather oddly at first sight) spend every Saturday night for the next few months at the Harbour Café, a base for a detached worker.

If these directions are not obeyed, what are the sanctions available to the supervisor? If the child is under seventeen, the supervisor's only remedy is to apply to the court for a variation of the order (perhaps to include the ninety-day type of intermediate treatment, though that can only be inserted within the first twelve months of the order's life) or for its discharge and replacement by a care order.[3] Both steps are fairly drastic: the thinking behind the Act seems to have been that if the

---

[1] See *Intermediate Treatment*, Appendix B, reproducing the list of approved types of facility for s. 19 (5) of the Act.

[2] S. 12 (3).

[3] S. 15 (1); application is to the supervising court, which may not be the court which made the order: s. 16 (11).

supervisor was being at all effective he would be able so to judge the timing and nature of intermediate treatment that refusals would seldom occur. If the child is over seventeen and the order was made in criminal proceedings there are special powers, akin to those applying to adults in breach of probation, including the power to fine for disobeying a supervisor's directions as to intermediate treatment.

DISCHARGE AND VARIATION

An application for the discharge or variation of the order may be made at any time by the supervisor, the child or his parent or guardian.[1] This procedure can be used for a number of different purposes. One, just mentioned, is the supervisor's application for a strengthening of the order; and this can include the insertion of a mental treatment requirement if the application is made within the first three months of the order's existence. The supervisor may also apply for the supervision to be ended or lightened: the period may be reduced, or intermediate treatment powers removed. In this last case, and where the variation is formal, e.g. a new supervisor takes over, there is no need for the child to be present in court, as he must be if the variation is to strengthen the order.[2]

When the application is by or on behalf of the child, the proceedings serve a different purpose. They are then a review of the order. If the child is seeking a discharge, as he usually will be in these cases, he may do so once every three months, and if he fails he can appeal to the Crown Court.[3]

In considering major variations in or the discharge of an order the court must bear in mind the "care or control" requirement which is central to the Act. So, it must not add to the requirements of a supervision order, or replace it by a care order unless it is satisfied that the child is unlikely to receive the care or control he needs unless the court so orders. This carries with it implications as to seeking parental cooperation and informal settlement.[4] Correspondingly, the order must not be weakened or discharged unless the court is satisfied that the child will continue to receive the care or control that he needs despite the change which is proposed.[5] This should mean that no application for variation can ever be treated as a formality. If a supervisor wishes to end the supervision after two years, he must explain his reasons to the court, saying why the child's circumstances, or the attitude of his parents, now permit the ending of the order. The procedural rules governing the court's handling of an application for a discharge are in fact the same as those applying when care proceedings are first taken.

---

[1] See last note, and s. 70 (2).
[2] *Ibid.*, s. 16 (1), (5).
[3] *Ibid.*, s. 16 (8) (*a*).
[4] See pp. 60–2, above.
[5] Children and Young Persons Act 1969, s. 16 (6).

B. CHILDREN PRIVATELY FOSTERED

The law relating to children who are privately fostered has something of the quality of a fantasy. It lays down procedures which are seldom followed, and gives to local authority social service departments powers and duties which they do not, and indeed cannot, discharge. As research has clearly demonstrated, this is an area in which legal provisions are impotent.[1]

FOSTER-CHILDREN

The Children Act 1958 contains an elaborate scheme designed to protect the interests of children who are given into the charge of foster-parents. Such children are seen as being at risk and in need of the protection which supervision by a social worker can provide.

A foster-child for these purposes is a child below sixteen years of age "whose care and maintenance are undertaken by a person who is not a relative or guardian of his".[2] This statutory definition needs some interpretation. "Undertaken" has a certain ambiguity; it is sometimes used in the sense of "agreed to", but it is now clear that in this context it means "actually provided".[3] "Relative" means a grandparent, brother or sister, uncle or aunt, and relationships by marriage or by adoption are included. In the case of an illegitimate child, his father and relatives traced through him are included.[4]

The class of children included in this definition is potentially very large indeed and the Act contains a large number of exclusions. So a child who is in care, or in a voluntary home, residential school in which he is receiving full-time education,[5] hospital or institution maintained by a public or local authority is not within the scope of the Act. Nor are children receiving supervision for other reasons, by virtue of a supervision order under the 1969 Act, guardianship under the Mental Health Act 1959,[6] or because they have been placed for adoption.[7] If the child is living in the same premises as any parent or guardian or adult relative then he is not a foster-child even if he is in the charge of someone else.[8]

It will be noted that the question of payment is irrelevant. A child who is invited to spend six weeks with the parents of a school-friend while his own parents take an extended holiday abroad will be a foster-child whether or not any money is paid towards his upkeep. But

---

[1] R. Holman, *Trading in Children: a study of private fostering* (Routledge 1973).
[2] Children Act 1958, s. 2 (1); a child still fostered at age 16 may continue to be a foster-child until he is 18: s. 13.
[3] *Surrey County Council* v. *Battersby*, [1965] 2 Q.B. 194; [1965] 1 All E.R. 273.
[4] Children Act 1958, s. 17, referring to Adoption Act 1958, s. 57.
[5] Unless (Children Act 1958, s. 12) he stays in the school for more than 2 weeks of the holidays.
[6] See p. 147.   [7] Children Act 1958, s. 2 (2), (3), (4), (4A).   [8] *Ibid.*, s. 2 (3) (*a*).

shorter stays are excluded. If the person taking care of the child does not intend at the outset to and does not in fact keep the child for a continuous period of more than twenty-eight days[1] the Act does not apply, unless the person is "a regular foster-parent"[2] in which case the limit is six days.[3]

These rules are horribly technical. It is not surprising that in one of the few reported cases, *Surrey County Council* v. *Battersby*,[4] the local authority social workers had given incorrect legal advice to a foster-mother. She had arranged to look after twins for an indefinite period, which in fact lasted for several months. On the advice of the social worker, she arranged for the children to go home for weekends so that at no time did a continuous period of twenty-eight days elapse; this was so that she need not register as a foster-parent. Unfortunately some higher authority on the Council's staff took a different view of the law. Despite the advice given, and the fact that the foster-mother was entirely acceptable as a suitable person to have the care of the children, she was prosecuted for failing to notify the authority of the fostering arrangement, which is all the more extraordinary in view of the widespread disregard of the notification provisions. The Queen's Bench Divisional Court held that she should have been convicted: there was a continuous period of care and maintenance of more than twenty-eight days despite the weekend interruptions. But the Court did suggest an absolute discharge.

BEFORE FOSTERING COMMENCES

The main problem in this area of social work is to find the client. In a supervision case, or where a child in care is boarded-out, the case is known to the authorities; there is a file. But who is to know that a fostering arrangement has been made? The law's, rather ineffective, answer is to impose a duty on persons proposing to act as foster-parents to notify the local authority not less than two weeks nor more than four weeks before they receive the child; failure to notify is an offence. The Act itself seems to recognise the unreality of the provision: in "an emergency" it is enough to notify within forty-eight hours of receiving the child.[5]

Holman's study of private fostering in one particular area gives a very clear view of what this amounts to in practice. Of his sample of 143 foster-parents, all of whom were known to the local authority, only three (2·1%) had notified within the statutory time-limit. A half of the

---

[1] Short interruptions of a day or a weekend may be ignored: *Surrey County Council* v. *Battersby*, [1965] 2 Q.B. 194; [1965] 1 All E.R. 273; see below.

[2] One who has had a foster child for 3 months, or for 3 periods each of more than 6 days, in the last 12 months.

[3] Children Act 1958, s. 2 (3A).

[4] [1965] 2 Q.B. 194; [1965] 1 All E.R. 273.

[5] Children Act 1958, s. 3 (1). Where a foster-parent already has foster-children there is generally no need for fresh notification for additional children.

group had notified by the end of the first month of fostering, well out of time. Twelve (8·4%) gave notice after the first year, or not at all.[1] This, it must be stressed, is a sample of parents known to the authority; we can only guess at the number remaining unknown.

The point of notification is to enable the local authority to check the suitability of the prospective foster-parents and their accommodation before fostering begins. Some groups of people are disqualified from acting as foster-parents unless the authority gives express consent: these are persons who have previously had children removed from their care,[2] or have lost their parental rights, been convicted of an offence against a child, or been refused registration as a child-minder.[3] This disqualification also applies to persons living in the same premises as the disqualified person or in premises at which he is employed: a resident caretaker at an office-block might fall foul of this provision if one of the employees should happen to be a disqualified person.

Even if the prospective foster-parent is not disqualified, the fostering arrangement might still be highly unsuitable. If the local authority considers this to be the case, it can impose a prohibition. This can prohibit the prospective foster-parent from acting as such anywhere in the local authority's area; or it can relate to particular premises only, on the grounds that the accommodation is unsuitable; or it can be quite specific, relating to a particular foster-child whom it was proposed to foster in particular premises. The prospective foster-parent can appeal to the local juvenile court and again to the Crown Court.[4] In practice this power of prohibition is seldom used; a prohibition can only be imposed in advance, before the child has actually been received, and the unsuitable foster-parent is unlikely, in the nature of things, to be found in the very small group of persons who give notice to the local authority in time for proper enquiries to be made.[5]

A distinct power is also given to the local authority to impose "requirements" on the foster-parents. These requirements can be imposed after the reception of the child as well as in advance, and the foster-parent can be made the subject of a prohibition if he fails to comply within a specified time. There are rights of appeal against requirements as in the case of prohibitions. Requirements can cover such matters as the number, age and sex of foster-children who may be received; the accommodation and equipment (including fire precautions) to be provided; medical arrangements; the number, qualifications and experience of any staff employed; and the keeping of

---

[1] Holman, *op. cit.*, Table 10.1, p. 221.
[2] Under the Children and Young Persons Act 1969, or the provisions as to foster-children or children placed for adoption, including the corresponding Scottish provisions.
[3] Children Act 1958, s. 6.
[4] *Ibid.*, ss. 4 (3), (3A), 5, 11.
[5] In Holman's study (*op. cit.*, p. 223) none of the local authorities concerned could find any instance of the power having been used.

records and furnishing of particulars relating to staff and children.[1] This is a comprehensive list which should give the local authority adequate powers of control, especially in those cases in which regular fostering of a number of children is carried on.

The research study already referred to indicates the ineffectiveness of these powers. Child care staff of the local authority were invited to assess, on the basis of material on the authority's files, the suitability of 100 private foster-parents, and to consider whether they would approve them as local authority foster-parents. 37 per cent of parents would not have been approved; another 18 per cent were scored as doubtful. Three parents were in fact disqualified; another six had serious convictions.

POWERS AND DUTIES OF LOCAL AUTHORITIES DURING
FOSTERING

The Children Act 1958 contains one of those general, and optimistic, statements about the function of local authorities:

> "It shall be the duty of every local authority to satisfy themselves as to the well-being of children within their area who are foster-children, . . ., and, for that purpose, to secure that, so far as appears to the authority to be appropriate, the children are visited from time to time by officers of the authority and that such advice is given as to the care and maintenance of the children as appears to be needed."[2]

To give some teeth to this provision, a right of entry to premises in which a foster-child is, or is to be, kept is given to duly authorised officers. If such an officer is refused entry to premises in which there is reasonable cause to believe that a foster-child is being kept, he can obtain a warrant from a Justice of the Peace, on a sworn application in writing, which authorises him to enter the premises at any reasonable time within the next forty-eight hours, using force if need be.[3]

The ultimate sanction is the removal of the foster-child. The juvenile court may make a removal order authorising a local authority officer or a police constable to remove a foster-child to a place of safety. The grounds for the application are that the child is being kept or is about to be received by a person who is unfit to have the care of him, or who is disqualified or prohibited from acting as his foster-parent, or "in any premises or any environment detrimental or likely to be detrimental to him". In an emergency, on proof of imminent danger to the health or well-being of the child, a justice may make the order alone, without a court hearing.[4]

---

[1] Children Act 1958, s. 4 (2).
[2] Children Act 1958, s. 1.
[3] *Ibid.*, s. 4 (1), (1A). Refusal to allow visits is also a ground for seeking a warrant to search for and remove a child under Children and Young Persons Act 1933, s. 40: see Children Act 1958, s. 8, and p. 92.
[4] *Ibid.*, s. 7. The parents or guardian of the child must be notified at once.

It must be recorded that Holman found very little use of removal orders; difficulties of proof, and the unlikelihood of the child being found a better alternative home, were the main reasons given. It is certainly the case that the removal of a privately fostered child is a more complicated procedure—the juvenile court is involved, with a possible appeal to the Crown Court—than applies to children fostered by the local authority, who can be peremptorily removed by the visiting social worker acting under the Boarding-Out of Children Regulations.[1] It is right that the protections for the private foster-parent should be maintained; unlike the local authority foster-parent he has not entered into any undertaking to the authority; but it is to be regretted that court procedures seem to present themselves as such discouragingly large hurdles that steps to protect children who are at risk are neglected.

C. NURSERIES AND CHILD-MINDERS

The same problems of enforcement apply, perhaps with even greater force, in the area of child-minding. The fostering legislation is designed to protect children left in the care of others for periods of more than six days; the child-minding legislation is designed to safeguard children left for shorter periods. The principal enforcement problem is again that of discovering what is actually happening. The fact that Mrs A's little boy is often playing in and around Mrs B's house does not immediately suggest a need for investigation; in fact the legislation may well apply, and in some cases intervention may be urgently needed.

The Nurseries and Child-Minders Regulation Act 1948 is a complex statute. It requires local authorities to maintain public registers, one relating to premises, the other to persons.

Premises must be registered if children are received there to be looked after for the day, or for more than two hours a day, or for a longer period not exceeding six days. Premises "wholly or mainly used as private dwellings" are excluded, as are hospitals, homes and institutions excluded from the fostering rules previously considered.[2] Registration may be refused if any person employed to look after children is thought not to be a fit person to do so,[3] or if the premises or equipment available are unfit.[4] If the premises are registered, the local authority may impose requirements as to numbers of children, staff, repairs to the premises, safety and maintenance, feeding and medical arrangements, and records. Failure to comply with the requirement is an offence and

---

[1] Reg. 5 (1).
[2] See p. 99, above.
[3] The application for registration must contain details of all such persons, in particular of any facts which would make the person a disqualified person under the fostering legislation: Health Services and Public Health Act 1968, s. 60 (7).
[4] Nurseries and Child-Minders Regulation Act 1948, s. 1 (1)–(3).

a ground for cancelling the registration. There is a right of entry to inspect premises, which may be backed by a warrant.[1]

These rules give extensive powers to the local authority, and as one would expect there are rights of appeal to the courts against the exercise of many of them. So, there is an appeal to the magistrates' court (not the juvenile court) and thence to the Crown Court, against a refusal of registration, the cancellation of registration, or the imposition of a requirement.[2]

Even if the premises do not need to be registered, and Mrs B's house would not because it falls within the "dwelling-house" exemption, the child-minder may have to apply for inclusion on the second register, a register of persons. Persons who can be included in the register are those who receive children under the age of five into their homes for the periods set out above in connection with the premises register, for reward. If the child received is a relative of the child-minder, registration is unnecessary in the sense that it is not an offence to receive such a child without registration.[3] Registration may be refused on grounds relating either to the applicant or the premises proposed to be used,[4] and the provisions relating to inclusion in the premises register (including rights or appeal) apply equally to this second register.

The sanction behind this legislation is that it is an offence to receive a child on to premises which need to be but are not registered, the offence being committed by the occupier of the premises; or for a person who should be but is not registered as a child-minder to receive children (other than relatives).[5] It is well known that prosecutions under these provisions are very seldom undertaken.

---

[1] Nurseries and Child-Minders Regulation Act 1968, ss. 2, 4, 5, 7.
[2] *Ibid.*, s. 6.
[3] *Ibid.*, ss. 1 (1), (2), 4 (2).
[4] *Ibid.*, s. 1 (4).
[5] *Ibid.*, s. 4 (1), (2).

Chapter 8

ADOPTION

Although social work is almost always carried out in a legal context, it is only in a few special areas that the powers and duties of the social worker are prominent in the actual legislation. Probation is an obvious example; adoption is another. Although adoption could be seen as primarily a legal operation, a fairly recent product of statute law[1] designed to regulate the legal status of a child, it is obviously a field in which human needs and relationships are crucial; the law recognises this by giving much attention to the role of the agencies and social workers concerned.

From their point of view this means that their activities are governed, more closely than usual, by technical legal rules which have to be observed before a court can or will make an adoption order. These legal rules impinge on the social worker's activities at various stages in the adoptive process.

The law relating to adoption was thoroughly reviewed by a Departmental Committee on the Adoption of Children, generally known as the Houghton Committee, after its first chairman, which reported in 1972.[2] It seems likely that many of its recommendations will be implemented and they are noted at appropriate points in this chapter.

MAKING ARRANGEMENTS FOR ADOPTION

The most significant step in the adoptive process is the selection of adopters and the placing with them of a child. It is true that the final decision is taken by the court, but the success rate of adoption applications is so high, over 95 per cent of cases resulting in adoption orders on the initial application, that the court can often fairly be described as merely placing a seal of approval on decisions already taken by others. This makes it important to see who takes those earlier decisions, and how closely they are controlled by the law.

---

[1] Legal adoption in England dates from 1926.
[2] *Report*, Cmnd. 5107. A Government Bill to give effect to the Report was introduced into Parliament in December 1974: see Appendix, p. 161 *et seq.*

In almost a third of all adoptions there is no selection problem, for the child is being adopted by its own parent who has had the care of the child throughout; the typical case is one in which the mother of an illegitimate child later marries and she and the step-father join in seeking an adoption order. In all other types of case, somebody had selected the prospective adopters and effected a "placement".

Under the existing law, anybody may place a child for adoption. The only qualifications to this are that it is an offence either to give or receive payment for making adoption arrangements,[1] or to send a child for adoption abroad without first obtaining a provisional adoption order.[2] In practice the great majority of placements are arranged by adoption agencies, either registered adoption societies (56% of placements) or local authorities (28%), but in quite a number of cases the child will be placed directly, by the mother herself, or by some third party, a doctor or clergyman, or a relative or friend of the mother.[3]

In the case of adoption societies, there are safeguards in that the societies are subject to a measure of outside control. An adoption society can only operate if it is registered by the local authority for the area within which it has its administrative centre. The local authority will only register a society, or keep it on the register, if it is satisfied that the society is a charity, controlled by a responsible committee, and that its staff is sufficient in number and consists of fit and competent persons.[4] The local authority can require a registered society to open its books, accounts and other documents for inspection so that it can obtain materials relevant to the matters affecting the continued registration of the society.[5] It can be seen that control over adoption agencies is not exercised directly by the courts. It is the duty and responsibility of the local authority to ensure that only suitable organisations take part in this service. However, as curtailment of corporate liberty is in issue if the local authority refuses or cancels registration the aggrieved society is given a right of appeal to the Crown Court.[6]

Another method of controlling placements is to prescribe a detailed procedure which must be followed before the child is placed. This is done for agency placements[7] but not for direct or third-party placements. The only requirement in non-agency cases is that a third party making adoption arrangements must give not less than two weeks' notice of the intended placement of a child below the upper limit of compulsory school age to the local authority for the area in which the

---

[1] Adoption Act 1958, s. 50.
[2] *Ibid.*, s. 52; and see *Re M. (a minor)*, [1973] Fam. 66; [1973] 1 All E.R. 852.
[3] Detailed statistics of adoptions can be found in *A Survey of Adoption in Great Britain* (H.M.S.O. 1971), based on a sample of adoptions in 1966.
[4] Adoption Act 1958, ss. 29, 30.   [5] *Ibid.*, s. 33.
[6] See *ibid.*, s. 31 for details as to procedure.
[7] I.e. local authority or adoption society placements. The procedure is laid down in Adoption Agencies Regulations 1959 (S.I. 1959 No. 639, as amended by S.I. 1961 No. 900, S.I. 1965 No. 2054 and S.I. 1973 No. 1203); see pp. 112–13, below.

child is to be placed.[1] This notice can be given before the child is born so that he can be placed with adopters soon after birth. If the notified local authority considers that it would be detrimental to the child to be placed with a particular person in the proposed premises, it may prohibit the placement. This is only done "in the relatively few cases where the placement is patently damaging";[2] there is a right of appeal to the juvenile court.[3]

If the Houghton Committee's recommendations are implemented, the provision of an adoption service would become the responsibility of local authorities. They would be expected to integrate adoption work in their general child care and family casework provision, but would cooperate with the continuing voluntary societies. The registration of adoption societies would be transferred to the Department of Health and Social Security. Once the new system was in operation direct and third-party placements would be prohibited, though private placement with a relative would still be allowed.[4]

WHO MAY ADOPT?

The selection of adopters involves a careful assessment of such factors as the personal qualities, motivation and marital stability of the applicants, and the process is complicated by the varying policies of particular agencies and (to use terms which may seem insensitive) the supply and demand situation in adoption. The social worker, whether making an assessment for the agency or acting as guardian *ad litem*, must bear in mind that while some of these factors are matters of discretion and judgment, some are statutory provisions.

An applicant for a full order must be domiciled in England or Scotland[5] and resident in England.[6] A person is domiciled in England if his home is here and he intends to remain here permanently. A foreign student or businessman planning to return to his own country at some future date is not domiciled here, and careful enquiries are necessary before a person with foreign connections is approved as an adopter. The law on this point is very difficult, and likely to change at any time if further provisions of the Adoption Act 1968 are brought into force, and expert legal advice should be sought in case of difficulty.

Only one person can adopt a child unless a joint application is made by husband and wife. If joint applicants obtain an adoption order and it is later discovered that they are not validly married, the order is

---

[1] Adoption Act 1958, s. 40. In an "emergency", which is not defined, the notice may be given up to one week after placement; it is, of course, then too late to prohibit the placement: Adoption Act 1958, s. 40 (3). Cf. the similar situation in the private fostering area: p. 101, above.
[2] *Guide to Adoption Practice* (H.M.S.O. 1970), p. 93.
[3] Adoption Act 1958, s. 42.
[4] *Report*, Recommendations 2–10, 13–16, paras. 30–61 and 81–92.
[5] *Ibid.*, s. 1 (1).
[6] *Ibid.*, s. 1 (5); Scottish courts have jurisdiction if the applicant is resident in Scotland.

wholly void.[1] In practice 99 per cent of applications are by spouses. If a married person applies to adopt alone he or she must first obtain the consent of the other spouse.[2] This rule can be difficult where the spouses are no longer living together, or where one spouse is mentally ill. However, in these and similar situations the court may dispense with the consent of the applicant's spouse "if it is satisfied that the person whose consent is to be dispensed with cannot be found or is incapable of giving his consent or that the spouses have separated and are living apart and that the separation is likely to be permanent".[3] This procedure cannot be used if the spouse is only temporarily absent for on his return he will be faced with responsibilities, financial or emotional, which he might not wish to accept; and while he will be under no legal duty to maintain the child, in practical terms the pressure will be real.[4]

Potential adopters must satisfy minimum age requirements. If the applicant or one of joint applicants is the mother or father of the child there is no minimum age. For this purpose "father" includes the natural father of an illegitimate child. Otherwise a sole applicant must be at least twenty-five years of age unless he is a relative of the child when he must be at least twenty-one. In the case of applications by husband and wife, one must be twenty-five and the other twenty-one, unless one is a relative when both need only be twenty-one. Relative means grandparent, brother, sister, uncle or aunt, whether of full blood or half blood or by affinity. It makes no difference whether the child is legitimate or illegitimate or that the relationship depends on some other adoption order.[5] The Houghton Committee recommended a simplification of the age requirements with a uniform minimum age of twenty-one in all cases.[6]

Section 2 (3) of the Adoption Act 1958 draws attention to the special situation in which a single man wishes to adopt a female child. The court must be satisfied that there are special circumstances which justify as an exceptional measure the making of such an order. The thinking is that a girl should normally be brought up by a woman, and of course in an extreme case there may be a danger of sexual corruption if a man is allowed to adopt.

The sort of case in which this problem arises is one in which a widowed step-father wishes to adopt his dead wife's daughter; or where the father of an illegitimate child wishes to care for the daughter whose mother is unable or unwilling to keep her.[7] This sort of relationship may well be treated as amounting to a "special circumstance"; it is very

---

[1] *Re R.A. (minors)*, (1974) *Times*, June 10th.
[2] Adoption Act 1958, s. 4 (1) (*b*).
[3] *Ibid.*, s. 5 (4).
[4] In the event of subsequent marriage breakdown he might be ordered to maintain the child as a child of the family.
[5] Adoption Act 1958, ss. 2, 57 (1).
[6] *Report*, Recommendation 11, paras. 75–7.
[7] Two orders were made in favour of fathers of illegitimate girls in 1970.

doubtful whether *Re R.M.*,[1] sometimes cited as authority for the proposition that paternity of an illegitimate child is not such a circumstance, really supports it, and the father is certainly entitled to apply for custody of his child.[2] The court will want to consider all the circumstances, such as the presence of a female relative in the household. A guardian *ad litem* should probably prepare a special report so that the court has all available information; an order made without the court giving careful attention to this special provision may be quashed on appeal.[3]

The Houghton Committee recommended the repeal of section 2 (3). The problem could be dealt with under the general provision that the court must in every case consider the welfare of the child.[4]

A mother sometimes seeks to adopt her own illegitimate child.[5] This in no way alters her legal obligations. If her motive is to conceal from the child the nature of his parentage the court may not be satisfied that the order will be for his welfare, for current opinion is that a child should grow up in the knowledge of his origins.[6] She may seek an order because she wishes to sever all connection with the child's natural father.[7] So long as she only has custody he can apply to the courts for custody of or access to his child, and he has equal status with the mother in any such application.[8] Any such rights terminate when the child is adopted, but the duty to maintain under an affiliation order survives, and an affiliation order can even be made after the adoption order.[9] The guardian *ad litem* is required to report to court on the applicant's reasons for wanting to adopt; this part of the report would seem especially important when the applicant is an unmarried mother.

Another recurring situation is adoption by a parent and a stepparent; this can be of an illegitimate child, or of a legitimate child where one parent has died or there has been a divorce. The Divisional Court of the Family Division has stressed that a wish to give the child the mother's new surname, or to disguise from neighbours the fact of an earlier divorce, could not be legitimate grounds for adoption.[10] The

---

[1] [1941] W.N. 244.
[2] *Re R.M.* involved an appeal by the child's adoptive mother against an adoption order made in favour of the child's natural father 9 years after the original order was made, because the adoptive mother was in breach of an (unenforceable) undertaking as to access.
[3] *R.* v. *Liverpool Justices, ex parte W.*, [1959] 1 All E.R. 337; [1959] 1 W.L.R. 149.
[4] *Report*, Recommendation 11, para. 78.
[5] In 1970, 84 such orders were made in England.
[6] See Houghton *Report*, para. 98.
[7] E.g. *Re E.(P.)*, [1969] 1 All E.R. 323; [1968] 1 W.L.R. 1913. See also *F.* v. *S.* [1973] 1 All E.R. 722, at p. 24.
[8] Guardianship of Minors Act 1971.
[9] Adoption Act 1958, s. 15. The Houghton Committee would permit adoption orders in favour of a natural parent as a sole applicant only in exceptional cases; and though that where an order was made, the father's obligation to maintain should be extinguished: *Report*, para. 102.
[10] *Re D. (Minors)*, [1973] 3 All E.R. 1001, at p. 1007.

Court referred to the Houghton Committee's Report[1] where the same view was taken: it is wrong to extinguish by law the links which a legitimate child has with one half of his family. The Committee's view is that the concept of guardianship should be extended and step-parents enabled to become guardians of their step-children.

The Adoption Act makes specific provision for adoption by parents and relatives, consequently any refusal by the court to make an order cannot be based on the fact of this tie as such,[2] but must turn upon the overriding consideration of the child's best interests. The courts are somewhat reluctant to impose an artificial adoptive relationship where there is a pre-existing genetic kinship; the success rate of applications by relatives is still very high (about 90%) but this is distinctly lower than in other types of application. In a case where grandparents sought an order in respect of their illegitimate grandchild, Vaisey, J. made the order but emphasised that it should only be made in special circumstances and not as a matter of course.[3] In a Scottish case[4] grandparents were refused an order as the court feared that the mother might not have severed her connection with them and the child, and such an order would create the artificial relationship of sister and brother between mother and son. In this type of case also the Houghton Committee proposed that the concept of guardianship should be used: a relative caring for a child should be able to apply for guardianship and should only be allowed to adopt if in the circumstances that was preferable to guardianship in the interests of the child's long-term welfare.[5]

ARBITRARY LOCAL RULES

Agencies operate their own rules when choosing adopters and apply their own selection criteria. In particular many agencies are affiliated to a certain religious persuasion. Unfortunately some judges have created further special local rules as to the qualifications of adopters. The social worker can find himself faced with what, for want of a better phrase, can be termed problems of "non-law" when dealing with adoption applications. He may come across the judge who will not make an order permitting a white couple to adopt a coloured child; the judge who sets his own age-limits which are additional to those laid down in the Act; the judge who requires that in all cases the applicants should have been married for a minimum period; the judge who requires evidence of infertility of the marriage before he will make an order.[6]

---

[1] Paras. 103–10.

[2] *Re D. (infant)*, [1959] 1 Q.B. 229; [1958] 3 All E.R. 716.

[3] *Re D.X. (infant)*, [1949] Ch. 320; [1949] 1 All E.R. 709.

[4] *C.D. Petitioners*, 1963 S.L.T. (Sh. Ct.) 7.

[5] *Report*, Recommendations 20 and 21, paras. 111–22.

[6] Some of these idiosyncrasies are mentioned in *The Report to the Home Office on Difficulties Arising from the Adoption Act 1958* made by the Standing Conference of Societies Registered for Adoption in 1968. See also the views of the Houghton Committee: *Report*, para. 73.

This is where the social worker can profit from knowing his local courts. If the personal whims and prejudices of a judge or magistrates' bench are known to him he can take advantage of the multiple jurisdiction of the courts, and suggest that application should be made in the juvenile court rather than the County Court, or vice versa, and thereby save the applicants anxiety and distress. He can explain to the applicants that there may be problems concerning their suitability to adopt and suggest to them that it would be advisable to obtain legal representation. A solicitor might be able to remind the judge or bench that to superimpose arbitrary rules over and above the provisions of the Adoption Act is a wrongful exercise of judicial discretion.

If the court refuses to make an order for some such arbitrary reason the placing agency could encourage the applicants to appeal. If the guardian *ad litem* has reported that adoption would be in the best interests of the child, the local authority could appeal. There are difficulties in appealing against the exercise of judicial discretion, the appellate court taking the view that the trial court having seen the parties and heard the evidence is best suited to make a decision, and this should not be upset. But a judge is not entitled to exercise his discretion with total freedom; he must operate within certain limits. If the applicants can establish that he was influenced by legally irrelevant facts a rehearing will be ordered before a different judge or bench, or the order will be made on appeal.

A very clear illustration is provided by *Re G.*[1] This concerned an application made by a Jewish couple. Their solicitor described the hearing to the Court of Appeal in these terms:

> "Upon my entering the judge's room at the Marylebone County Court, and before I had an opportunity of addressing him, he told me that I was in difficulties over the application because the applicants were of the Jewish faith whereas the infant was a Protestant Christian child born of a Protestant Christian mother, that he [sc. the judge] was a Protestant Christian and that England was a Protestant Christian country and that therefore he did not feel it right, nor did he propose to grant an application, for a Protestant Christian child to be adopted by persons of the Jewish faith."

The Court of Appeal held that the judge had not exercised his discretion judicially. All the evidence, including the welfare reports, favoured the making of an order, and the Court of Appeal made one itself.

WHO MAY BE ADOPTED?

A child must be under the age of eighteen, and never have been married.[2] The child must be resident in England.[3] (There are exceptions to this provision which will be examined later.[4])

---

[1] [1962] 2 Q.B. 141; [1962] 2 All E.R. 173
[2] Adoption Act 1958, ss. 1, 57.   [3] *Ibid.*, s. 1 (5).   [4] See p. 133.

SELECTION, SUPERVISION AND CONSENTS

This section examines the legal controls on the central procedures in the adoptive process. The selection of the prospective adopters leads eventually to the placement of the child; there follows a period during which the child is subject to "welfare supervision"; and before the adoption can be completed the natural mother, and sometimes others, must give consent, unless the consent is dispensed with.[1]

SELECTION

We have already noted that it is only in the case of agency placements that there exists a statutory code of procedure. This procedure applies to cases handled by adoption societies and local authorities;[2] we shall consider the usual case of the adoption by non-relatives of an illegitimate child below the upper limit of compulsory school age.

The process begins with the initial approach by the applicants to the agency seeking to be approved as prospective adopters. They must be interviewed,[3] and in practice a series of interviews will take place, and full information obtained. The Regulations prescribe in detail[4] the many particulars which must be obtained, including names of two referees, but this list is really only a starting-point. Information is statutorily required as to the duration of the applicant's marriage; the agency will want to know about its quality as well. Information will be needed at a later stage about the applicant's health, for a medical certificate must accompany the actual application to court; in practice enquiries will be made at the outset. It is also important to consider the proposed accommodation for the child; the premises must be inspected and enquiry made of the local authority for the area to see whether it raises any objection.[5]

The relationship between the agency and the natural mother is even more important. Quite apart from the embarrassment which she may feel, the adoptive process will lead to her surrendering all rights to her child; usually she will never see the child again. It is crucial that she understands what is involved, both in her own interests, and in those of the prospective adopters and the child. It is always possible that the mother will change her mind and refuse consent, or at an even later stage withdraw her consent; the Regulations seek to ensure that this is never due to a misunderstanding about the nature of adoption. The mother must be given a prescribed memorandum which explains what

---

[1] Dispensing with consent is considered at pp. 128–32, below.
[2] Adoption Agencies Regulations 1959 (as amended), r. 9.
[3] *Ibid.*, r. 5 (*c*).
[4] *Ibid.*, Sched. 4, Part II: the Houghton Committee recommended that there should no longer be statutorily prescribed information, it being left to the agencies with official guidance: *Report*, para. 79.
[5] *Ibid.*, r. 5 (*d*), (*e*).

is involved, and she signs an acknowledgment that she has received and read it.[1]

Information must also be obtained about the child and his parents. In the usual case some of this is obtained from the mother before its birth, and the interviewer will generally supplement the statutory details[2] by details as to, for example, the physique of the father, lest small adopters acquire an embarrassingly tall child. After the birth a full medical report on the child is obtained,[3] and if the timetable works smoothly this report will later be attached to the adoption application.

It is only at this stage that the local authority, or in the case of an adoption society the case committee of the society, can approve the placement of the child with the prospective adopters.[4]

SUPERVISION

When a child is being brought up or looked after by someone other than its parents, the law commonly provides for some sort of outside supervision; this is found in adoption practice in the interval between placement and the granting of the adoption order. The aim of supervision had been described as "to offer a supporting service to adopters, help them to focus on the essential task of integrating the child into their family life, and look forward confidently to the future.[5]" The adopters may well be anxious about the outcome of the adoption proceedings, or may face hostility from relatives. There is also an element of inspection, especially where the placement is not an agency placement.

The supervision can arise in a number of ways. In the case of an agency placement, the agency itself is under a duty to supervise the child until the adopters give notice to the local authority of their intention to adopt, and a specific duty to have the family visited during the first month is laid down.[6] An incidental advantage of this arrangement is that it may enable the natural mother, hesitating about giving consent, to be reassured that the child is well cared for.

The local authority is also under a duty to supervise children who become "protected children" under the Adoption Act. A child placed under an agency or a third-party placement becomes a protected child at once.[7] A child placed directly by the mother with non-relatives also becomes a protected child at once, but by virtue of being a foster-child

---

[1] *Ibid.*, r. 4 and Sched. 3.
[2] *Ibid.*, Sched. 4, Part I.
[3] *Ibid.*, r. 5 (*b*) and Sched. 5.
[4] *Ibid.*, r. 5 (*f*).
[5] *Guide to Adoption Practice*, p. 101.
[6] Adoption Agency Regulations 1959, r. 6.
[7] Adoption Act 1958, s. 37 (1) (*a*). Many agencies seem to interpret this provision as not applying to them, as if "person" did not include a member of the agency's staff; as a result many agencies do not give notice of intended placement under s. 40. Their interpretation seems to be wrong. Cf. *Guide to Adoption Practice*, p. 99.

under the Children Act 1958; the supervision duties are the same.[1] A
child placed by its mother with relatives becomes a protected child as
soon as the prospective adopters give notice of their intention to adopt,
as they must do at least three months before the date of the adoption
order.[2] This is a reflection of the State's reluctance to interfere in the
family unit. If, for example, grandparents or an aunt are able to care
for a child then the law does not require that they should be subject to
outside supervision. If, however, they want to change a *de facto*
custodial arrangement into a legal arrangement involving rights and
duties and a change of status, then the law is concerned that checks are
made on the child's proposed home environment.

The local authority has a duty "to secure that protected children
within their area are visited from time to time by officers of the
authority, who shall satisfy themselves as to the well-being of the
children and give such advice as to their care and maintenance as may
appear to be needed".[3] To carry out this duty it needs further powers,
in particular the right of entry to premises. This right is given, for the
purpose of inspecting any premises in the local authority's area in
which protected children are to be or are already being kept, to any
local authority social worker who carries, and if need be produces, a
suitable authorising document;[4] obstructing the social worker is a
criminal offence.[5]

If the local authority believes that a protected child is being kept, or
is about to be received by unsuitable people or in unsuitable surroundings, it can apply to the juvenile court for an order for the child's
removal to a place of safety. In an emergency, where there is "imminent danger to the health or well-being of the child", a single justice
of the peace may make an order on the application of any person
authorised to visit protected children.[6] The involvement of the court
is an important safeguard; no citizen may have his rights interfered
with by another, however well-intentioned, without due process of
law.

When the adoption proceedings are commenced, the local authority
are respondents. Accordingly, as we shall see, the views of the local
authority will be sought by the guardian *ad litem* and any written report
will be submitted by him to the court. In this way any doubts as to the
suitability of the applicants which the welfare supervision may have
raised can be taken into account.

---

[1] Children Act 1958, s. 2 (1).
[2] Adoption Act 1958, s. 37 (1) (*b*).
[3] *Ibid.*, s. 38. Under the Houghton Committee's proposals the local authority welfare
supervision will survive only in non-agency cases; otherwise the placing agency will
have responsibility: *Report*, paras. 237–43.
[4] Adoption Act 1958, s. 39.
[5] *Ibid.*, s. 44 (1) (*b*).
[6] *Ibid.*, s. 43.

CONSENTS

Before an adoption order can be made the consent of the child's parents must either be obtained or dispensed with.[1] The natural father of an illegitimate child is not a "parent" for consent purposes:[2] neither are those with the rights and powers of parents by virtue of the Children and Young Persons Acts or the Children Act 1948.

The present consent procedure allows the parent to give consent either before or at the adoption hearing.[3] The mother cannot give her consent until the child is at least six weeks old.[4] The parent's signature on the consent form must be witnessed by a justice of the peace, a duly authorised county court officer or a justices' clerk. Consent may be given without the parent knowing the identity of the applicant.[5] The only condition which the consenting parent may stipulate is that the child should be brought up in a particular religious persuasion.[6] Care should be taken by the social worker to ascertain whether the mother has firm views on this issue before the child is placed for adoption, as if the matter only comes to light when the consent form is signed the adopters may have cared for the child for some time. A Roman Catholic mother's religious belief has been held to be a valid reason for her withholding consent to the adoption of her child by non-Catholics.[7] The part of the consent form which gives space for the parent to stipulate the child's religion has the following footnote: "Delete 'on condition that the religious persuasion in which the infant is proposed to be brought up is . . .' if the applicant is named or if the applicant is not named but the consenting party does not desire to impose a condition as to the religious upbringing of the infant." It is submitted that this footnote is based on a misreading of section 4 (2) and that the parent may impose conditions with respect to the child's religious upbringing whether or not he knows of the identity of the applicant.

While the adoption application is pending a parent who has given consent may not remove the child from the care of the applicants except with the leave of the court.[8] But until the court hearing the parent is free to withdraw consent. This can lead to uncertainty for all

---

[1] *Ibid.*, ss. 4, 5.

[2] His position is examined at p. 123, below.

[3] In practice in 98% of the applications by non-relatives the mother's consent is attached to the application.

[4] Adoption Act 1958, s. 6 (2).

[5] *Ibid.*, s. 4 (2).

[6] *Ibid.*, s. 4 (2). The Houghton Committee recommended that it should be no longer possible to impose this condition: *Report*, Recommendation 55, paras. 228–31. Denominational adoption societies would, of course, continue to exist and retain their present selection policies.

[7] *Re E.*, [1963] 3 All E.R. 874; [1964] 1 W.L.R. 51.

[8] Adoption Act 1958, s. 34. The Houghton Committee proposed that the same prohibition on removal should apply, whether or not the parent had consented, once an application to adopt was made by foster-parents who had cared for the child for 5 years or more: *Report*, Recommendation 36, paras. 161–4.

concerned: a mother who is hesitating can continue indecisively right up to the last moment. To overcome this problem, the Houghton Committee proposed a new form of procedure, a "relinquishment" application. This would be available in any case of an agency placement. The parent and the agency would jointly apply to the court for an order transferring parental rights to the agency with a view to the child's adoption. This would in effect settle questions as to the parent's consent (and also resolve any questions raised by a putative father of an illegitimate child)[1] in advance of the adoption proceedings. A "reporting officer" would ascertain and report to the court that the consent was freely given, discharging some of the duties of the guardian *ad litem*. The rule forbidding the giving of consent before the child was six weeks old would remain. If no adoption took place the parent could in some circumstances resume the care of the child, and full parental rights.[2]

A related proposal would enable adoption agencies or local authorities who had a child in their care to apply for the parent's consent to adoption to be dispensed with in advance, on one of the statutory grounds discussed below.[3] This would amount to a sort of compulsory relinquishment procedure, and would resolve the same practical difficulties.[4]

THE MOTHER'S HUSBAND

When a married woman places her child for adoption, a particularly difficult problem may arise concerning consents. A hypothetical case will illustrate the problem:

Alice has been living apart from her husband Brian for the last ten months. Brian left her when he discovered that she was committing adultery with Charles. Alice has just given birth to a son, Donald. She is certain that the father is Charles; she says that she and Brian did not have sexual intercourse during the period when Donald could have been conceived, and that anyway they invariably used contraceptives. Alice has broken off her relationship with Charles; she is anxious to have the child Donald adopted and to conceal its birth from Brian with whom she hopes to be reconciled.

The difficulty is that the law presumes that the husband of the married woman is the father of her child, and his consent is needed, as the father of the child, to the adoption. If he is approached he may well refuse to give his consent, denying paternity: some courts in practice accept his consent expressed to be given by him as "the husband of the mother", although the statutory forms do not provide for

---

[1] See p. 123.
[2] *Report*, Recommendations 37 to 46, paras. 167–91.
[3] See p. 128–32.
[4] *Report*, Recommendation 53, paras. 221–5.

this wording and it is misleading, as his consent is required in his capacity as father, not as husband. The more difficult problem, as in the case above, is where there are strong reasons for not even approaching him.

In some cases it is possible to persuade the court to accept an affidavit from the mother that her husband is not the father. The court will generally accept this if the husband and wife lived apart for more than twelve months before the birth, or if the child is of mixed race, both the husband and wife being of the same race.[1] But in cases like the above, it is difficult to see how the existence of the adulterine child can be kept from the husband. Whenever there is a possibility that the child is the husband's, it is only right that he should learn of its existence, and wrong that the child should be bastardised, unknown to the husband and solely on the assertion of the mother. In practice the evidence problems are discussed informally with the officers of the court in advance of any hearing.

THE ADOPTION APPLICATION

As soon as the papers are ready, including in the usual case the mother's consent, the adopters can make their application to court, but the hearing will be a month or two later. There are three reasons for the delay. The first is the requirement, already noted, that the applicants notify the local authority of their intention to adopt; this must be at least three months before the date of the adoption order,[2] and the period will seldom be over when application is made. Early application is desirable so that the initial medical reports of health of the child can be relied upon; the courts are unwilling to accept reports more than one month out of date. A second reason for delay is that the court must appoint a guardian *ad litem*, whose extensive enquiries take some time to complete. His duties are discussed below.[3] The third reason is that the child must have been continuously in the care and possession of the adopters for at least three consecutive months immediately before the date of the order.[4] This three-month period is often confused with the three-month period of notice of intention to adopt, but they are distinct: once three months has passed from the date of giving notice that requirement is met; the three-month period of care and possession is counted backwards from the date of hearing, and in an extreme case may not even overlap the other three-month period.

Application may be made to the High Court, the county court or the

---

[1] The Houghton Committee strongly deplored the practice of some courts of informing the husband even in cases where he was clearly not the father: *Report*, para. 200.
[2] I.e. under Adoption Act 1958, s. 3 (2).
[3] See pp. 119-22.
[4] Adoption Act 1958, s. 3 (1); see pp. 126-7.

juvenile court.[1]   In practice adoption applications by parents or relatives of the child tend to go to the juvenile court, but agencies generally prefer the county court.   The one or two circuit judges who sit in the county court are a more predictable forum than the ever-changing benches of magistrates in the juvenile court.

Application is seldom made to the High Court.[2]   There may however be some rare occasions when an applicant should consider departing from usual practice and instituting proceedings there.   This is because the county court or juvenile court may at any stage refuse to proceed with the application if it appears to the court that owing to special circumstances it is more fit to be dealt with by the High Court.[3]   Special circumstances in this sense means that difficult points of law will be put in issue; or that the facts require that the child should be separately represented by the Official Solicitor.   When a father who had strangled the child's mother refused to give his consent to the child's adoption, the Court of Appeal, directing a rehearing, suggested it should be heard in the High Court.[4]   Although choosing to make application to the High Court initially may appear unduly expensive, if there are a number of difficult issues to be resolved by the court, or there is some likelihood of other proceedings, such as wardship, being commenced, then this choice may prove advantageous in the long run.

Although the natural father of an illegitimate child cannot prevent his child's adoption by withholding his consent,[5] he has the right to apply for custody of the child under the Guardianship of Minors Act 1971.   It is clearly desirable that both the adoption and custody proceedings should be heard together.   If both proceedings are begun in the High Court they will be heard at the same time;[6] if both are begun in a county court, the same result can be achieved, with one set of proceedings being transferred from one county court to another if necessary;[7] but in other cases difficulties can arise.   At the magistrates' court level, adoption orders are dealt with in the juvenile court, custody applications in the domestic court; there is no way in which the proceedings can be brought together, and in such a case the magistrates

---

[1] The Houghton Committee recommended that the juvenile court's jurisdiction should be transferred to the magistrate's domestic court, which has jurisdiction in custody and guardianship cases: *Report*, Recommendation 64, paras. 259–62.

[2] Applications average about forty a year.

[3] County Court Rules, r. 7; Juvenile Court Rules, r. 7.   The detailed court procedure for adoptions is set out in Rules of Court.   Separate sets of rules exist for the High Court, county courts and magistrates' courts, but the relevant content is the same unless otherwise indicated.   See Adoption (High Court) Rules 1971 (S.I. 1971 No. 1520); Adoption (County Court) Rules 1959 (S.I. 1959 No. 480; S.I. 1965 No. 2070; S.I. 1973 No. 1541); Adoption (Juvenile Court) Rules 1959 (S.I. 1959 No. 504; S.I. 1965 No. 2072; S.I. 1973 No. 1118).

[4] *Re F. (an infant)*, [1970] 1 All E.R. 344; [1970] 1 W.L.R. 192.

[5] See pp. 123–4, below.

[6] *Re Adoption Application (No. 41 of 1961)*, [1963] Ch. 315; [1962] 3 All E.R. 553.

[7] As in *Re B. (an infant)*, (1961), unreported but discussed at [1962] 2 All E.R. 835, which involved the High Court and county courts in Sheffield and Brighton.

might refuse to make an order in either set of proceedings on the ground that the matter is more conveniently dealt with in the High Court.[1] Similar conflicts could occur between the county court and the High Court, so that if determined intervention by the natural father is feared, the best course would seem to be to begin the adoption proceedings in the High Court from the outset.

Whichever court is used, it is possible for the applicants to preserve their anonymity by obtaining a serial number, the case being referred to by that number rather than by the names of the parties.

THE GUARDIAN AD LITEM

As soon as practicable after an application has been made the court must appoint a guardian *ad litem* (meaning "for the purpose of litigation") of the infant. The County Court and Juvenile Court Rules state that the person appointed must be the director of social services or one of his staff, a probation officer or some other person who appears suitably qualified.[2] If application is made in the High Court the Official Solicitor normally acts as guardian *ad litem*.[3] If the Official Solicitor does not consent, or if the applicant desires some other person to act, the court may appoint any person who appears to be suitably qualified. The Rules imply that the director of social services or one of his staff would be a suitable alternative.[4] In *Re A.B.* (*infant*)[5] applicants sought to have their family doctor appointed as guardian *ad litem* to the baby born of their daughter who was herself aged under sixteen. Roxburgh, J., refusing the application, made clear that the choice of a guardian *ad litem* was not a matter which just concerned the family, but was of public concern too, because of the nature of his duties.

For this same reason certain people may not be appointed as guardian *ad litem*, namely a person who has the rights and powers of a parent or who has taken part in the adoption agreements; or a member, officer or servant of a local authority, adoption society or other body of persons which has the rights and powers of a parent or which has taken part in the adoption arrangements.[6] This restriction is an application of a principle with which the lawyer is entirely familiar, that no man can be a judge in his own cause. During the period between the application and the hearing the guardian *ad litem* investigates all the circumstances relevant to the proposed adoption including the matters alleged in the application and those specified in the second schedule to the Rules. On completing his investigations he must make a confidential report in

---

[1] Juvenile Court Rules, r. 7; Guardianship of Minors Act 1971, s. 16 (4). For the solution proposed by the Houghton Committee see p. 118, n. 1, above.
[2] County Court and Juvenile Court Rules, r. 8.
[3] High Court Rules, r. 6.
[4] *Ibid.*, r. 7.
[5] [1948] 2 All E.R. 727.
[6] County Court and Juvenile Court Rules, r. 8 (2) (c) (i), (ii).

writing to the court.[1] If he has taken part in the placing arrangements it is recognised that he could not make a fresh and unbiased assessment of them. His duty at the hearing of the application is to safeguard the interests of the child before the court,[2] and to do this he must be independent of all other persons interested in the adoption.

The guardian's duties span a wide range. He must check the accuracy of the information given in the application form. This covers such straightforward information as the name, age, occupation and status of the applicant; and the age and health of the child and who his parents are. It also means that the guardian *ad litem* must have an understanding of what is meant by "domicile"[3] and "ordinarily resident";[4] and what constitutes "continuous care and possession" on the part of the applicants.[5] His particular duties are specified in the second schedule to the Rules. He must interview the applicant and must try to assess the applicant's personality and his suitability to adopt the particular child. He must find out about the applicant's means and his home, his own and his family's health, his religion, why he wishes to adopt and whether he understands the implications of adoption; in particular the guardian *ad litem* must make sure that the applicant realises that if an order is made this will render him responsible for the maintenance and upbringing of the infant. In the case of an application made by one of two spouses the guardian *ad litem* must discover why the other spouse did not join in the application. He must take up the references specified in the application form and ascertain whether the referee is a responsible person and whether he recommends the applicant with or without reservations. Where the applicant is not ordinarily resident in Great Britain application can be made only to the High Court or the county court; their Rules require the guardian *ad litem* to endeavour to obtain a report on the applicant's home and living conditions from a suitable agency (such as International Social Service) in the country in which he is ordinarily resident.

The guardian *ad litem* has a duty to find out and tell *the applicant* whether and when the child was baptised; whether he has been immunised against disease; whether the child has a right or interest in any property and whether he has been insured against the cost of funeral expenses. The guardian *ad litem* must ascertain whether the child is able to understand the nature of an adoption order; if the guardian *ad litem* thinks that the child is able to do so he must "forthwith" inform the court. In other words this is one of the occasions when the guardian *ad litem* should make an interim report to the court.[6] The court will

---

[1] High Court Rules, r. 15; County Court and Juvenile Court Rules, r. 9.
[2] Adoption Act 1958, s. 9 (7).
[3] P. 107, above.
[4] P. 82, above.
[5] See pp. 126-7, below.
[6] High Court Rules, r. 15 (3); County Court Rules, r. 9 (3); Juvenile Court Rules, r. 9 (3).

then inform the applicant that the personal attendance of the child at the hearing of the application is required.[1] The guardian *ad litem* must find out whether such a child wishes to be adopted by the applicant. If there is any difference in age between the applicant and the child which is less than the normal difference in age between parent and child the guardian *ad litem* must draw the court's attention to this.

The guardian *ad litem* has to obtain information from a variety of sources, categorised rather unhelpfully in the Rules as "individual respondents" and "respondents, not being individuals". These categories include anyone whose consent is needed before the adoption order can be made, persons (or local authorities) with parental rights, persons liable to maintain the child,[2] the local authority to which the applicants gave notice of their intention to adopt, and the local authority or agency which took part in the adoption arrangements. Individuals who took part in the arrangements must also be interviewed, although they are not technically respondents, and others can be brought into the picture as respondents if the court thinks that they should be given a chance to be heard. This last category may include relatives, and the guardian is under a special duty to inform the court at once if he hears of a relative of a child, one of whose parents is dead, who wishes to be heard, or of any other person or body who wishes to be, or should be, heard. Individuals must be interviewed either by the guardian in person or an agent appointed by him for the purpose. Local authorities and adoption societies will normally produce a written report which is appended to the guardian's own report to court.[3] In the case of agency placements, the agency will itself have gathered almost all the information needed by the guardian, but he must satisfy himself as to its accuracy; in cases of direct and third-party placements the guardian's duties are more onerous and perhaps more important.

The guardian *ad litem* must find out when the mother ceased to have care and possession of the child and to whom it was transferred. This information will often tie in with his duty to ascertain whether the child has been continuously in the care and possession of the applicants for the previous three months. If any interruption has occurred because the parent has removed the child he must make this clear in his report.[4]

---

[1] County Court and Juvenile Court Rules, r. 11. In High Court cases the procedure is different: the guardian merely includes his assessment of the child's wishes in his report; there is no personal attendance by the child. See High Court Rules, Sched. 2, para. 3.

[2] For the father of an illegitimate child, see p. 123, below.

[3] High Court Rules, r. 17 (where the term 'respondent' is not used); County Court Rules, r. 10; Juvenile Court Rules, r. 12; Sched. 2 (to all sets of Rules), paras. 4, 5, 8, 10.

[4] See p. 126, below.

The information which the guardian *ad litem* gathers together when complying with his specific duties (as itemised either in the application form or in the second schedule to the Rules) may not cover all matters which are relevant to the proposed adoption. He has a duty to investigate all such relevant circumstances.[1] So if, for example, a single man seeks to adopt a female child he should see whether there are any special circumstances to justify as an exceptional measure the making of an order.[2] The order if made must be for the welfare of the child,[3] and the guardian *ad litem* should provide the court with any information which seems pertinent, for example the likelihood of continued contact between the child and his natural parents after the adoption. This is not to say that an order will be refused in circumstances in which such contact will continue. Twice in recent years an appellate court has rejected appeals brought against the making of adoption orders by the local authority which regarded severance from the natural parents as being of primary importance.[4] Each time the court made it clear that there is no mandatory requirement in the Act that severance be enforced. With a view to obtaining the directions of the court on any particular matter, the guardian *ad litem* may at any time make an interim report to the court; this he should do rather than risk that the hearing be adjourned because the court is not satisfied that his report is sufficiently comprehensive, thereby causing the applicants unnecessary anxiety.

CONSENTS TO ADOPTION

The guardian *ad litem* must find out whether all consents have been given freely and with full understanding of the nature and effect of an adoption order. The guardian often finds interviewing the natural mother a painful process. Although in the large majority of cases she abides by her decision to relinquish her child, it will sometimes be evident that her decision was reached because of pressure from other people or from fear that she could not afford to keep the child. The mother's signature on the consent form is sufficient evidence of her consent,[5] and the court must rely upon the guardian to report any doubt there may be about the reality of that consent.

In these circumstances the guardian is in a difficult position. His primary duty is to report the facts to the court, and not to influence the mother's decision in any way. But there are cases in which the mother's feelings go well beyond the natural feelings of sorrow and regret, and in which the mother needs further independent advice. Legal advice is

---

[1] High Court Rules, r. 15; County Court Rules, r. 9; Juvenile Court Rules, r. 9.
[2] *Ibid.*, s. 7 (1) (*b*).
[3] *Ibid.*, s. 7 (1) (*b*).
[4] *Re G. (D.M.) (an infant)*, [1962] 2 All E.R. 546; [1962] 1 W.L.R. 730; *Re B. (M.F.) (an infant)*, [1972] 1 All E.R. 898; [1972] 1 W.L.R. 102.
[5] Adoption Act 1958, s. 6.

one possibility, and there is a suggestion in one Court of Appeal adoption case, *Re M. (an infant)*[1] that it might be a desirable solution in this type of case. In *Re M. (an infant)* Sachs, L.J. spoke[2] of the importance of legal aid in safeguarding the interests of the person concerned, and for ensuring that justice both is done and appears to be done. He suggested that there might be cases in which a rehearing of an adoption case would be ordered simply because a party was not made aware in appropriate terms of the availability of legal aid and advice.[3] The actual context of the suggestion was a contested case, in which the mother's consent, having actually been withdrawn, was dispensed with; but there might well be advantages in applying the same ideas to other cases. So if the guardian *ad litem*, in the final or in an interim report, raises the question of the nature of the mother's consent, the court might itself prompt the mother to apply for legal advice or legal aid.

THE SPECIAL POSITION OF THE FATHER OF AN ILLEGITIMATE CHILD

If the natural father of an illegitimate child is liable to maintain him by virtue of any order or agreement he is a respondent under the Rules,[4] and correspondingly the guardian *ad litem* is under a duty to interview him. If the guardian *ad litem* learns of any person claiming to be the father who wishes to be heard he must inform the court immediately; and it will then decide whether notice of the hearing of the application should be served on him.[5] But it should be noted that the guardian *ad litem* is under no obligation to seek out the putative father.[6]

The paragraph above is a statement of the law. In practice many courts require the guardian *ad litem* to interview the fathers of all children placed for adoption. Some courts insist upon obtaining signed consents from those fathers who have made some financial contribution. Hence the guardian *ad litem* may find himself working within a blurred "grey" area of mixed law and local practice, the application becoming the subject of constant adjournments while he tries to comply with the court's direction to trace the natural father.[7]

In such a case a social worker might consider advising the applicants to engage a solicitor to represent them. Some guardians *ad litem* feel that they can give such advice without compromising their neutrality,

---

[1] [1972] 3 All E.R. 321.
[2] *Ibid.*, at p. 328.
[3] Legal advice will be available to applicants of limited means under the Legal Aid Act 1974; legal aid for representation at the hearing is available under the civil legal aid scheme in the county court and in cases where there is a contested application to dispense with consent in the magistrates' court: see pp. 158-9.
[4] High Court Rules, r. 17; County Court Rules, r. 10; Juvenile Court Rules, r. 12.
[5] Second Schedule to the Rules.
[6] *Re Adoption Application (No. 41 of 1961)*, [1963] Ch. 315; [1962] 3 All E.R. 553.
[7] See *Report to the Home Office on Difficulties Arising from the Adoption Act 1958.*

which is often slightly at risk because the guardian may well also be carrying out the welfare supervision on behalf of the local authority. In particularly difficult cases it might be advisable for the guardian to arrange for another worker to take over the supervision to avoid this sort of problem.

FAILURE BY GUARDIAN AD LITEM TO MAKE AN ADEQUATE REPORT

Non-compliance with any duty laid on the guardian *ad litem* could mean that an adoption order would be quashed on the grounds that he had failed to make a full investigation, if this meant that the court had exercised its discretion on inadequate information. The case of *R.* v. *Liverpool Justices, ex parte W.*[1] is a salutary example for all guardians *ad litem*.

A husband, William Leigh, was seeking to adopt his dead wife's illegitimate daughter. The child had been brought up by her mother and grandmother from May 1952 until April 1957. The mother went to live with Leigh in April 1957, she married him in October 1957 and she died in March 1958. Two days later Leigh gave notice to the local authority that he intended to adopt the child. About the same time the child's grandmother applied for legal aid to enable her to make the child a ward of court.

Leigh made his application in the juvenile court and the local authority was appointed guardian *ad litem*. A child care officer made a report to the court; the only reference to the grandmother was couched in the following terms:

> "The maternal grandmother seems not always to be clear as to the parentage of the infant, and has on a number of occasions picked up the infant from school and removed her to another part of the country. These happenings occurred whilst the mother of the infant was still alive, and they seem to have rather upset the infant, who is now very frightened of her maternal relations and if she sees them, or thinks she sees them, she runs into the house and hides."

It appeared that this was the only information about the grandmother put before the court. In fact the guardian *ad litem* knew that the grandmother disapproved of Leigh, that she wanted custody of the little girl and that she was consulting a solicitor for this purpose.

In June 1958 Leigh's application came before the court and an adoption order was made. No notice of the proceedings were served on the grandmother, she did not appear and she was probably unaware that they were taking place. The guardian *ad litem* was clearly in breach of his duty to inform the court of the existence of any relative of a deceased parent wishing to be heard by the court.[2] The grandmother

---

[1] [1959] 1 All E.R. 337; [1959] 1 W.L.R. 149.
[2] See p. 121, above.

applied for an order of *certiorari*, which would in effect quash the adoption order, on the grounds (i) that the guardian had failed to make a full investigation; and (ii) that the justices had failed to have proper regard to the fact that this was an application by a single man to adopt a female child.[1] The Queen's Bench Divisional Court granted an order of *certiorari* on the second ground, but also said that the failure of the guardian *ad litem* to make a full report to the court might have also been a proper ground on which to act.

Another illustration is *Re C.S.C.*[2] Here the adoption order was quashed on appeal, Roxburgh, J. holding that the justices had no jurisdiction to make an order, because the child had not been continuously in the care and possession of the adopters for the previous three months.[3] It is of course one of the guardian *ad litem*'s duties to report when that period of care and possession began; clearly there was some failure, and the absence of any report in the papers supplied to the appellate court led to speculation that there may have been no report at all, or even that no guardian *ad litem* had been appointed. The consequences of the errors in this case were serious because Roxburgh, J. found that he had no power to authorise the adopters to retain the child pending a further appeal to the Court of Appeal. Presumably the child was returned to his natural parents, which may or may not have been consonant with his long-term interests.

Fortunately for the guardian *ad litem*, it is not every mistake on his part that will invalidate an adoption order.[4] The fact that most adoptions are uncontested means that no-one is concerned to upset the order; and if there is an appeal, it must be lodged within twenty-eight days, though this time-limit could be extended in very special circumstances.[5] None the less it is important that the guardian pays scrupulous attention to the rules. If the court is dissatisfied with the report, there may have to be an adjournment, with distress to all concerned; and the confidentiality of the guardian's report to court, which means that it cannot be challenged on many points, puts an additional moral duty on its author.

THE HOUGHTON COMMITTEE ON THE GUARDIAN AD LITEM

If the recommendations of the Houghton Committee are implemented the guardian *ad litem* will cease to feature in every adoption case. There are cases in which much of his work duplicates what has already been done perfectly adequately by other professionals. The

---

[1] See Adoption Act 1958, s. 2 (3); and p. 108, above.
[2] [1960] 1 All E.R. 711; [1960] 1 W.L.R. 304.
[3] See Adoption Act 1958, s. 3 (1); p. 126, below.
[4] See *Re P. (an infant)* (1954), 118 J.P. 139: misstatement that withdrawal of consent might lead to financial liability held, in all the circumstances, not to have had crucial effect on mother's decision: the order stood.
[5] *Re F. (R.) (an infant)*, [1970] 1 Q.B. 385; [1969] 3 All E.R. 1101.

Committee took the view that the appointment of a guardian *ad litem* could cease to be mandatory and be left to the discretion of the court in every case. In most cases[1] the placing agency would be under a duty to provide a full report to the court in place of that now provided by the guardian.[2]

PERIOD OF CARE AND POSSESSION

Before an order can be made the child must have been continuously in the care and possession of the applicant for at least three consecutive months immediately preceding the date of the order.[3] Time does not start to run until the child is at least six weeks old. The word "continuously" leads to difficulties of interpretation as obviously it cannot be read entirely literally: the prospective adopters are not prevented from going out for the evening leaving the child with a baby-sitter. Where a longer period of separation is involved, the leading writers provide conflicting interpretations. Clarke Hall and Morrison state "if the infant were at boarding school, and never at home continuously for three months, but being cared for by the applicants as if he were their child, spending his holidays with them, it would seem unreasonable to hold that they could not apply for an adoption order".[4] Bromley, on the other hand, writes "An extreme application would clearly defeat the purpose of the Act, if for example the child spent the whole of the time in hospital or at boarding school there would be no opportunity of seeing whether he was likely to settle down in his new home. In the absence of any other evidence the court would refuse to make an order in such a case on the ground that it was not satisfied that it would be for the child's welfare."[5] The word "possession" provides no real guidance for it is notorious among lawyers for the elusiveness of its meaning, in all sorts of legal contexts.

An applicant may seek advice from a social worker on how to complete that part of the adoption application form in which he must declare that the child has been continuously in his care and possession from a specified date. The guardian *ad litem* has a duty to investigate all matters alleged in the originating application;[6] if the child has been parted from the adopters during the relevant three months he may be uncertain whether he should mention this in his report to the court. A little guidance can be derived from case-law. When a child was taken from the applicants for three nights and a day this was held to interrupt the period of care and possession.[7] However, it is generally agreed that

---

[1] I.e. adoption applications made after "relinquishment": see p. 116, above.
[2] *Report*, Recommendations 60–3, paras. 236, 244–56.
[3] *Ibid.*, s. 3 (1).
[4] *Law Relating to Children* (Butterworths, 8th Edn 1972), p. 1030.
[5] *Family Law* (Butterworths, 4th Edn 1971), p. 253.
[6] County Court and Juvenile Court Rules, r. 9. High Court Rules, r. 15.
[7] *Re C.S.C.*, [1960] 1 All E.R. 711; [1960] 1 W.L.R. 304.

the decision turned upon the vital fact that the child was taken away by his natural parents. It seems that the issue which the court must decide is whether the applicant or some other person had effective control over the child during the three-month period.[1] "The question seems to be whether the adoptive home is the home and only home of the child and whether the applicants are in all respects in loco parentis to the child during that period."[2]

A similar problem can arise when one of the spouses is absent from the home for a time, through illness or because his work involves travel. An extreme case would be that of a merchant seaman, who might well be absent for considerable periods during the three months. The case-law provides no guidance here; it is suggested that the absence can be disregarded if it was the sort of absence which would be normal for a working spouse.

THE HEARING

The culmination of the adoptive process is the court hearing, which may well be an anti-climax for the adopters at least;[3] the social worker may experience a feeling of relief that no problems have arisen, or that they have been safely overcome. It is only where the court is asked to dispense with consent that the hearing is likely to be critical. In all cases the function of the court is twofold: to be satisfied first that consent has been given, and that the consenting parent understands that an adoption order will permanently deprive him of his parental rights; and second that the order will be for the welfare of the child.[4]

If the hearing is in a county court it will usually only last for a few minutes, the judge having read the papers beforehand. It will generally last a little longer in the juvenile court, as the bench will probably not have seen the papers until the day of the hearing. The applicants must be present at the hearing in the county court and juvenile court, so too must the child if the guardian *ad litem* has reported to the court that the child is able to understand the nature of an adoption order.[5] But where the judge has a very recent report from the guardian *ad litem* which tells him what the child's wishes are the judge may accept that report without speaking to the child himself.[6] The hearing will be in the judge's private rooms, or in the relative privacy of the juvenile

---

[1] *Re B. (infant)*, [1964] Ch. 1; [1963] 3 All E.R. 125.
[2] *A., Petitioners* 1953 S.L.T. (Sh. Ct.) 45; but it should be made clear that in this case the child, who returned home only for weekends and holidays, was nearing the age of majority.
[3] See Iris Goodacre, *Adoption Policy and Practice*, p. 102.
[4] Adoption Act 1958, s. 7.
[5] County Court Rules, r. 13; Juvenile Court Rules, r. 14.
[6] *Re G.* [1963] 2 Q.B. 73; [1963] 1 All E.R. 20.

court.   Personal attendance is not required by the High Court, which can rely on affidavit evidence.

DISPENSING WITH CONSENT

Sometimes a parent will not consent to his[1] child being adopted.   He either gives consent and later withdraws it, or gives consent but seeks to impose special conditions (in which case the court cannot regard it as a valid consent), or never consents to the adoption at all but remains unable or unwilling to care for his child himself.   The court has power to dispense with consent, but only on certain grounds specified in the Act:

(i) *Abandonment, neglect or persistent ill-treatment*

The court may dispense with the consent of a parent who has abandoned, neglected or persistently ill-treated the infant.[2]   These findings all involve culpability on the part of the parent.   Thus abandonment is used in the sense of criminal abandonment which will render the parent liable to prosecution; the mother who handed her child over to prospective adopters, visited her only once and paid nothing towards her maintenance did not abandon her child.[3]   The abandonment must exist at the time of the application and not merely relate to past behaviour which has come to an end.   A single act of ill-treatment does not provide a ground for dispensing with consent, as the section requires persistence.   However, the Houghton Committee proposed that as an alternative to "persistent" ill-treatment there should be added "serious" ill-treatment which made the rehabilitation of the child in the family unlikely.[4]

(ii) *The parent cannot be found*

If a parent cannot be found his consent may be dispensed with.[5] Notice of application to adopt must be served on the parent at his last known address.   Sometimes there will be no address at which service can be attempted, and if this is the position the applicants may need to rely on section 5 (1) (*b*).   The phrase "cannot be found" has been interpreted as meaning "cannot be found by taking all reasonable steps"; consequently the steps will vary according to the circumstances. In one case[6] a letter written to a mother's last known address was returned marked "gone away".   The applicants then tried to trace her through advertisements in the press and through the Post Office.   When the application came before the county court judge the mother had been absent for three years; he dispensed with her consent on the

---

[1] The parent is referred to as "he" although in this context it is almost always the mother's consent which is dispensed with.
[2] Adoption Act 1958, s. 5 (1) (*a*).
[3] *Watson* v. *Nikolaisen*, [1955] 2 Q.B. 286; [1955] 2 All E.R. 427.
[4] *Report*, Recommendation 52, paras. 214–20.
[5] Adoption Act 1958, s. 5 (1) (*b*).
[6] *Re F.* (*R.*) (*an infant*), [1970] 1 Q.B. 385; [1969] 3 All E.R. 1101.

ground that she could not be found. However she reappeared very soon afterwards and appealed against the order out of time. The Court of Appeal granted her leave to appeal and ordered a rehearing because of the particular circumstances. Apparently the applicants knew the address of the mother's father, yet they had made no enquiries of him as to the whereabouts of his daughter, so that one reasonable step to find the mother had not been taken.

The reader needs to understand the attitude of the court in this case, otherwise the decision will appear unduly harsh to the adopters and over-protective of the mother. If the statute provides a ground for dispensing with a parent's consent then either it exists at the time of the hearing or it does not. If, however the court concludes that the ground exists on misleading evidence then it will make an order relying on false assumptions. If this comes to light soon after the hearing the court can either disregard the error and refuse leave to appeal out of time or it can remit the case for a fresh hearing. The Court of Appeal chose the latter course in this case because the consequences of an adoption order are so serious. It could not at this stage have dispensed with the mother's consent relying on an alternative ground, as such a procedure would not give the mother time to prepare her case in the light of any allegations made against her.

(iii) *The parent is incapable of giving consent*

If a parent is incapable of giving his consent it may be dispensed with.[1] This will cover the position of the parent who is so mentally ill as to be unable to understand the nature of what he is doing. This ground has been used to enable applicants to adopt a political refugee, as the parents could not be made aware of the occasion for consenting and would not be permitted freely to give consent if they were so aware.[2]

(iv) *Persistent failure to discharge parental obligations*

If a parent or guardian has persistently failed without reasonable cause to discharge his obligations to the child his consent may be dispensed with.[3] The court will not lightly find such a failure, which "must be of such gravity, so complete, so convincingly proved, that there can be no advantage to the child in keeping continuous contact with the natural parent, who has so abrogated his duties that he for his part should be deprived of his own child against his wishes".[4] The parent has to have

---

[1] Adoption Act 1958, s. 5 (1) (*b*).
[2] *Re R.*, [1966] 3 All E.R. 613. It was also held that the parents could not be found for the purposes of section 5 (1) (*b*) as there were no practical means of communicating with them.
[3] Adoption Act 1958, s. 5 (2).
[4] *Re D. (minors)*, [1973] 3 All E.R. 1001, at p. 1005.

shown "some callous or self-indulgent indifference with regard to the welfare of the child".[1]

In particular the failure must be "persistent", which the courts interpret as meaning "permanent". A parent who without reasonable cause has never seen or paid maintenance for his child, who has "washed his hands of" the child, may find that his consent is dispensed with.[2] But a less complete failure will not justify the court's intervention. In one case, *Re D. (minors)*,[3]

> two children were born in 1964 and 1965. The father left the mother in August 1969, and did not provide for the children (though he sent some presents and clothes) thereafter. He saw the children on 8 or 10 occasions between the separation and the date of the divorce granted to the mother in September 1970. In October 1971, after the mother's remarriage, the father asked to see the children but the mother refused him all access.

The Divisional Court of the Family Division held, in July 1973, that it was impossible on these facts to find that the father had persistently failed to discharge his obligations; his consent to the child's adoption was needed and would not be dispensed with.

(v) *Consent is unreasonably withheld*

If a parent is being unreasonable in opposing his child's adoption the court may dispense with his consent.[4] If as a result of his own conduct the child has been in the care of the adopters for a long period while he vacillates between giving and withdrawing his consent, his eventual withholding of consent may be an act of unreasonable disregard of his child's interests. The fact that an adoption order would appear to be for the welfare of a child does not of itself mean that a parent's refusal to consent to his child's adoption is unreasonable. In adoption, unlike custody applications, the welfare of the child is not the first and paramount consideration. The court must be satisfied that a reasonable parent would give consent. [5]

The House of Lords has firmly rejected the contention that unreasonableness, like a persistent failure to discharge parental obligations, involves a finding that the parent is culpable, blameworthy or prone to self-indulgent indifference.[6] Lord Hailsham, L.C. held that unreasonableness can include, where carried to excess, sentimentality,

---

[1] *Re M. (an infant)* (1965), 109 Sol. Jo. 574, approved in *Re D. (minors), supra.*
[2] *Re B. (an infant)*, [1968] Ch. 204; [1967] 3 All E.R. 629. See also *Re P.*, [1962] 3 All E.R. 769; [1962] 1 W.L.R. 1296.
[3] [1973] Fam. 209; [1973] 3 All E.R. 1001. See also *Re H. (minors)* (1974), *Times*, Nov. 26th.
[4] Adoption Act 1958, s. 5 (1) (b).
[5] *O'Connor v. A. and B.*, [1971] 2 All E.R. 1230; [1971] 1 W.L.R. 1227.
[6] *Re W.*, [1971] A.C. 682; [1971] 2 All E.R. 49.

romanticism, bigotry, wild prejudice, caprice, fatuousness, or excessive lack of common sense.[1] The following passage from a judgment of Lord Denning, M.R. has been approved in many cases and Lord Hailsham said that it may now be considered authoritative:

"... in considering whether she is reasonable or unreasonable we must take into account the welfare of the child. A reasonable mother surely gives great weight to what is better for the child. Her anguish of mind is quite understandable; but still it may be unreasonable for her to withhold consent. We must look and see whether it is reasonable or unreasonable according to what a reasonable woman in her place would do in all the circumstances of the case."[2]

Child psychiatrists who give evidence in disputed adoption cases all emphasise the risks involved in transferring young children from the care of one person to another. If a parent withdraws his consent the character of this medical evidence has led the courts to recognise the need for urgency in bringing contested applications before the courts, and to condemn any attempt by one side to spin out the proceedings. The time for which the children had been in the adopters' care was a crucial factor in a sad contested case heard in the High Court.[3] A father placed his two children for adoption through an adoption agency. At the time he was a widower but soon afterwards he remarried. He concealed this marriage from the secretary of the adoption society, saying he intended to marry but declined to let his "future" wife be interviewed, as throughout he asserted that he had the right to have his children back. Meanwhile his children became very attached to the prospective adopters and would not return voluntarily to their father. After a lot of delays the application came before the court nearly five years after the children were placed. The court found that the father, by his own deception in not disclosing his marriage to the adoption agency, was largely to blame for the situation which had arisen and that he was now being unreasonable in withholding his consent.

An unreported case in 1971[4] provides an unusual example of "unreasonableness". The mother signed a consent form, and it was arranged for her signature to be witnessed by a Commissioner of Oaths. It should have been realised that he was not an acceptable witness for this purpose; the consent was invalid. The mother sturdily refused to help the bureaucrats to get themselves out of the mess, and washed her hands of the whole matter. She would not sign any more

---

[1] *Ibid.*, p. 56.
[2] *Re L.* (1962), 106 Sol. Jo. 611. The Houghton Committee recommended the enactment of a statutory formula, directing the court to give first consideration to the effect of the parent's decision on the long-term welfare of the child: *Report*, Recommendation 51, paras. 205–18.
[3] *Re W.*, [1965] 3 All E.R. 231; [1965] 1 W.L.R. 1259.
[4] See (1971), 135 J.P. 298.

forms. Applying an objective standard of what was unreasonable, the court was able to dispense with her consent.

An application to dispense with a parent's consent is obviously of the utmost importance to her. The Rules of Court ensure that she has notice of the nature of the application and, in the High Court where she will not necessarily be present in person, of the grounds on which the application is made.[1] It is in this sort of case too that the court may well consider suggesting to the parties that they obtain legal advice and representation.[2]

THE ORDER

When it makes an adoption order, the court may impose any terms and conditions it thinks fit,[3] but there is no provision for enforcing these conditions and in practice they are very seldom imposed. If the court has doubts about the advisability of making an adoption order it may make an interim order for period not exceeding two years. During this probationary period it may order that the child be supervised by a suitable person, often the guardian *ad litem*; it may also make orders regarding the child's maintenance and education.[4]

An interim order may be made for a short period, making temporary provision for the care of the child during an adjournment of the application, and a date may be given for a further hearing. If no date is given, as will be the case where the period is prolonged, the court officers have a duty to fix a date for a rehearing; in the High Court this must be done not less than two months,[5] in the other courts not less than one month before the end of the period.[6]

In other cases the application is simply adjourned *sine die* (i.e. indefinitely). In some cases the child remains with the prospective adopters, and remains a protected child subject to welfare supervision; in other cases the adjournment is tantamount to a rejection of the application and the child is returned to its mother or taken into care. This seems an unsatisfactory outcome from all points of view.

In the rare cases in which the court rejects the application, the question arises what is to happen to the child. Where the placement was not effected by an agency, the child remains with the applicants unless the natural mother claims it back, but in an agency case the child must be returned to the agency within seven days.[7] The court

---

[1] High Court Rules, r. 12 (3).
[2] *Re M. (an infant)*, [1973] Q.B. 108; [1972] 3 All E.R. 321.
[3] Adoption Act 1958, s. 7 (3).
[4] *Ibid.*, s. 8. See further *S.* v. *Huddersfield B.C.*, [1974] 3 All E.R. 296.
[5] High Court Rules, r. 20.
[6] County Court Rules, r. 19; Juvenile Court Rules, r. 18.
[7] Adoption Act 1958, s. 35 (3). On the whole question of cases in which the court cannot make a final order, see Houghton Committee *Report*, paras. 307–11.

has no power to extend that period, or approve alternative arrangements.

SPECIAL CASES

Mention must be made of two types of special case; in both the adopters have overseas connections, and both raise complex legal problems on which professional advice is very desirable.

The first type of case concerns adopters who are domiciled in Great Britain, that is their permanent home is here, but are ordinarily resident abroad. The usual case involves an Englishman serving abroad in the forces or with an international company or organisation. The Adoption Act[1] makes it possible for such applicants to adopt in England under rather less stringent conditions than normally apply. The provisions are very difficult to interpret but the principal relaxation is that the period of continuous care and possession is satisfied if the applicants and the child live together in Great Britain for one of the three months, and the child is in the care and possession of one of the applicants for the whole three-month period, not necessarily in Great Britain.[2] It is obviously desirable that the guardian *ad litem* should be appointed in time for him to see the adopters and child living together as a family unit, but the Act does not guarantee that this will be possible. In this type of case, application can only be made to the High Court or a county court.

These courts also have exclusive jurisdiction in the second type of case, where applicants domiciled outside Great Britain wish to take a child to their home country for adoption under the laws of that country. The difficulty they face is the statutory prohibition on taking a child abroad "with a view to the adoption" of the child, which has been interpreted as including all cases in which adoption is contemplated, whether immediately or at a later stage.[3] The court can give permission for the child's removal by making what is called, not altogether accurately,[4] a provisional adoption order. The full procedure for a normal adoption order must be complied with, despite the fact that no change of status is made by the order. Indeed the rules are tightened, for six months' notice must be given to the local authority (so that the welfare supervision will continue for at least that period) and the child must have been in the continuous care and possession of the applicants for at least six months before the making of the order.[5]

If it proves impossible to meet these requirements there are two other possibilities which the prospective adopters could explore. One is to

---

[1] Adoption Act 1958, s. 12.
[2] *Re W. (an infant)*, [1962] Ch. 918; [1962] 2 All E.R. 875; *Re M. (a minor)*, [1973] 1 All E.R. 852, at p. 855.
[3] *Re M. (a minor)*, [1973] Fam. 66; [1973] 1 All E.R. 852.
[4] See *Re M. (an infant)*, [1965] Ch. 203, at p. 210.
[5] Adoption Act 1958, s. 53.

seek appointment as the child's guardian, where that is possible; a guardian, like a natural parent, is free to take a child abroad whenever he wishes. The other possibility is for the child to be received into the care of the local authority which can then seek the permission of the Home Office for the child's emigration; the parents' consent will be needed.[1]

---

[1] Children Act 1948, ss. 1, 17.   See generally *Re M. (a minor)*, [1973] Fam. 66; [1973] 1 All E.R. 852.

Chapter 9

THE SICK AND THE HANDICAPPED

Those social workers concerned with the sick and handicapped have never had to cope with close statutory control in the same way as did the staff of the former children's departments or of adoption agencies. There is of course a great deal of legislation governing the National Health Service and the provision of the various kinds of hospital and domiciliary care. Similarly in the area of "welfare rights", the sick, those injured in industrial accidents, pregnant women and the disabled all feature prominently. The "professional law of social workers", with which this book is primarily concerned, is very much the area of law concerned with potential conflict between social work agencies and the interests of the client. Happily these conflicts are less prominent in the welfare of the sick and handicapped, where there may be a different sort of conflict between, say, the patient and his social worker adviser and those responsible for the provision of benefits and facilities.

With this last point in mind some mention is made below of the Chronically Sick and Disabled Persons Act 1970, but the emphasis in this chapter must be on the law governing the position of the mentally disordered, a group very much at the mercy of others and presenting special legal problems.

THE MENTALLY DISORDERED

There is little need to spell out the manifold problems presented by mental illness. Like any other illness, it may lose a man his livelihood; like a prison sentence, it may deprive him of his liberty, with unhappy consequences for his family. The very nature of his illness may handicap him in the normal business of communicating with others, taking decisions and managing daily affairs; and the patient and his family may have to cope with guilt, fear and misunderstanding. Legal provisions are of course powerless in the face of such problems. Here, as elsewhere, the point must be made that the law can only provide a framework within which help and treatment can be given, a framework designed to give adequate protection to the rights of those handicapped by illness. As we shall see, the legal rules present an unusually sharp illustration of the differing approaches and objectives of lawyers and administrators.

"TO DEFINE TRUE MADNESS"

There is a preliminary but fundamental problem. What is mental disorder? How can we distinguish those who are mentally disordered from other deviants? Are the labels indicative of true facts or are they the product of the reaction of the majority group in society? One writer, Szasz, commenting on a statement that mental health law is concerned with patients' rights, describes that as "a brazen falsehood", for "the primary concern of any mental hygiene law is to empower physicians to imprison innocent citizens and impose ostensibly medical interventions on them against their will".[1] These are extreme statements, though they accord with some general sociological theories and they point to some undoubted truths. There is a tendency for laymen to declare they can tell when someone is mentally ill; and in the present state of the law this attitude, as we shall see, has a strange validity. The layman's stance is the more tenable when the medical men disagree, as they certainly do in this area. In particular, one major type of mental disorder, psychopathy, is the subject of great controversy, and it is in that part of the subject that there is the greatest risk of the deviant being identified as mentally ill. This finds a statutory echo in the Mental Health Act 1959 which provides

> "Nothing in this section shall be construed as implying that a person may be dealt with under this Act as suffering from mental disorder . . . by reason only of promiscuity or other immoral conduct."[2]

It is not entirely clear what this means—is immorality limited to sexual immorality?—and in any event it is an extraordinary provision, which can only be explained as a recognition on the part of the legislature of the real danger of wholly unjustified labelling. For most purposes, the legal classification of mental disorder is that contained in section 4 of the Mental Health Act 1959. This in turn is based upon, but does not follow exactly, the recommendations of the Percy Commission which reported in 1957.[3] The Commission proposed a threefold

---

[1] T. S. Szasz, *The Manufacture of Madness*, p. 278. See also his book, *The Myth of Mental Illness*, and a critique by Reiss, 128 American Journal of Psychiatry 108 (1972).

[2] Mental Health Act 1959, s. 4 (5).

[3] Royal Commission on the Law relating to Mental Illness and Mental Deficiency 1954–1957; *Report* published as Cmnd. 169. See generally N. Walker and S. McCabe, *Crime and Insanity in England*, vol. 2, chap. 4.

classification which was avowedly an administrative classification rather than a diagnostic one. The three groups were the mentally sub-normal, the mentally ill, and those suffering from psychopathic conditions.[1] This is reflected in the Act which declares that mental disorder, which is the proper generic term, includes.

"mental illness, arrested or incomplete development of mind, psychopathic disorder, and any other disorder or disability of mind".[2]

This is a very open-ended definition. The final phrase makes this plain. That phrase will include disorders caused by certain forms of physical injury but could include much more. For most purposes, however, it is only by other categories which are important; at a number of points in the process of admitting patients one or other of those categories has to be specified. But this still leaves us with an area of uncertainty, for "mental illness" itself is undefined. The Percy Commission made the unhelpful comment, "We use this term in its usual present sense, including those who become mentally infirm in old age."[3] The matter eventually came before the Court of Appeal in a case, *W.* v. *L.* (*mental health patient*),[4] which illustrates rather well a number of sources of difficulty.

Mr L, then a newly married man of twenty-one, fell down and knocked his head during Christmas 1971. Immediately afterwards he placed a knife at his wife's throat, then put the family's cat in a gas oven and turned the gas on. His wife rescued the cat on this occasion but he cut its throat two months later after causing it great suffering by getting it to inhale ammonia. Later in 1972 after two incidents in which he hanged or strangled dogs he spent a week in a mental hospital as a voluntary patient. By this time his wife was pregnant and Mr L was eventually detained under compulsory powers after threatening to push his wife down the stairs to get rid of the baby. When the case got to court there had been further developments. The husband was at home and was taking pills prescribed in hospital. His wife was anxious to keep him at home, and said that she could make sure he took the pills and could cope with him. The child had been born, but was in the care of the local authority on a temporary basis with the wife's agreement. The medical experts felt that the husband needed hospital treatment. The social services department was also anxious to see the husband safely in hospital; the fear was that the mother might take the baby home and that the baby would be maltreated by the husband. The legal position was that the objections of the husband and wife to hospital treatment could be overruled[5] if, but only if, the husband was

---

[1] See *Report*, paras. 187 *et seq.*
[2] Mental Health Act 1959, s. 4 (1).
[3] *Report*, para. 189.
[4] [1973] 3 All E.R. 884; [1973] 3 W.L.R. 859.
[5] I.e. by the appointment of an "acting nearest relative". This aspect of *W.* v. *L.* is discussed at pp. 144-5, below.

"mentally ill" within the meaning of the Act. A social workers' meeting had decided that he was sick; a group of clinical experts failed to agree; but in the end a distinguished consultant certified that Mr L was mentally ill, and it was this finding that was challenged in court.

A number of comments can be made on this statement of the facts. Mr L had clearly committed a number of criminal offences, of cruelty to animals and of assault. Here, as so often is the case, the same facts could provide a basis for either criminal proceedings or direct action under the Mental Health Act. Secondly, the facts illustrate the number of conflicting interests involved: the medical needs of Mr L (as seen by the doctors), the need to keep the family together (stressed by Mrs L), the need to safeguard the future of the child (of concern to the local authority), and Mr L's understandable wish to stay out of hospital and to continue to earn his living. Thirdly, it is intriguing to see that a social workers' meeting, presumably within the social services department, should seek to resolve the medical question as to whether Mr L was "mentally ill" or, as they thought, a psychopath.

The Court of Appeal upheld the view of the consultant that Mr L was mentally ill. Lawton, L.J. answered the question how he should construe the words "mental illness"?

> ". . . ordinary words of the English language should be construed in the way that ordinary sensible people would construe them. . . . What would the ordinary sensible person have said about the patient's condition in this case if he had been informed of his behaviour to the dogs, the cat and his wife? In my judgment such a person would have said, 'Well, the fellow is obviously mentally ill'. . . . It is that application of the sensible person's assessment of the condition, plus the medical indication (abnormalities revealed by EEG tests), which . . . brought the case within the classification of mental illness."[1]

The other members of the court were virtually silent on this point, but the lay view of mental illness does receive judicial blessing in the passage quoted. This is a disturbing situation, and the reader will have noted that one group of ordinary sensible persons—the social workers presumably come within that description!—reached a conclusion quite opposed to that attributed to such persons by the judge.

SUBNORMALITY

The second main category of mental disorder, "arrested or incomplete development of mind", is divided into "severe subnormality", where the patient is incapable of living an independent life or of guarding himself against serious exploitation, and "subnormality", a less serious condition which nevertheless requires or is susceptible to medical treatment or other special care or training of the patient.[2] Although the Percy Commission described their proposed category

---

[1] [1973] 3 All E.R. 884 at p. 890.
[2] Mental Health Act 1959, s. 4 (2), (3).

of severely sub-normals in terms of persons with a mental age below $7\frac{1}{2}$ to 9, or an intelligence quotient below 50 to 60, they stressed that intelligence was not the sole criterion,[1] in particular a person may be educationally sub-normal[2] without being sub-normal for mental health purposes.

PSYCHOPATHY

The most controversial category is "psychopathic disorder", defined as being "a persistent disorder or disability of mind (whether or not including subnormality of intelligence) which results in abnormally aggressive or seriously irresponsible conduct on the part of the patient, and requires or is susceptible to medical treatment".[3] The causes of psychopathy are highly controversial, as is the question whether it will respond to treatment; the Act does not require proof that the condition will respond to medical treatment, only that it "requires or is susceptible to" it, and treatment includes nursing or care and training under medical supervision.[4] Most psychiatrists agree at least that psychopathy exists, but they describe it in a bewildering variety of ways. Some witnesses before the Percy Commission emphasised a lack of social conscience: one described psychopaths as patients "whose daily behaviour shows a want of social responsibility and of consideration for others, of prudence and foresight and of ability to act in their own best interests. Their persistent anti-social mode of conduct may include inefficiency and lack of interest in any form of occupation: pathological lying, swindling and slandering; alchoholism and drug addiction: sexual offences, and violent actions with little motivation and an entire absence of self-restraint".[5] It will be remembered that all agreed that Mr L was a psychopath: "persistence" in that case was based on relatively few acts, but spread out over a considerable period. Another description of a psychopath, which does not place the same emphasis on lack of conscience, was written for the benefit of general medical practitioners:

> "Psychopaths are most easily recognised by their characteristic drifting erratic way of life, which can be summarised . . . as showing the three multiples—multiple jobs, multiple mates, multiple digs; the four troubles—trouble at school, trouble with the law, trouble with money, trouble with long-term friends; and the two others, lies and charm."[6]

Not an immediately attractive pen-picture, one which, as most social workers will recognise, fits a surprisingly large group of people.

---

[1] *Report*, paras. 192–6; in their proposals many who would be classed as "sub-normals" under the Act would have been grouped with psychopaths.
[2] See further p. 155.
[3] Mental Health Act 1959, s. 4 (4).
[4] *Ibid.*, s. 147 (1).
[5] *Report*, para. 169.
[6] P. D. Maddocks, [1972] Post-graduate Journal of General Practice, 413.

Walker and McCabe, having examined the history and current use of the term "psychopath", have concluded that it serves a "pseudo-diagnostic" function: a psychiatrist may be unable to say with confidence that a patient is suffering from any particular illness, or that he is sub-normal—and yet be quite confident that he is mentally disordered. "Psychopathic" is a convenient label offered by the legislation and accepted with relief by the psychiatrist.[1]

TREATMENT: THE LEGAL ISSUES

Some 90 per cent of all patients receiving hospital in-patient treatment for mental disorder are admitted informally as voluntary patients, and are free to discharge themselves at will. There are few legal rules dealing specifically with their treatment. Their illness may, of course, have legal consequences, affecting for example their legal capacity to marry or enter into binding contracts. It is not possible to discuss the relevant rules here,[2] except to note the existence of a body called the Court of Protection. This court, which functions in some ways more like an administrative agency, is technically "an office" of the Supreme Court, and has powers to control the administration of the property and affairs of mentally disordered persons.[3]

Legal considerations are much more important when compulsory admission to hospital is involved. The lawyer sees this as deprivation of liberty, and his training will immediately put in his mind the need for safeguards against unnecessary detention. There should be a court or tribunal to act as monitor of administrative decisions. The adversary procedure of the courts requires that there be someone with the power to act for the patient, to enter objections and present his case. Detention should only be allowed subject to careful and frequent review, so that liberty is restored as soon as possible.

From the medical and administrative point of view, the scene looks rather different. No doubt legal safeguards have their place, but they must not operate to delay the giving of necessary care and treatment. Certainly a court hearing before admission to hospital would lead to wholly unacceptable delay and stigma. If some person, such as a near relative of the patient, is given rights of objection in the patient's supposed interest, there must be procedures for overriding these objections if the relative is misguided and insists on applying folk-lore rather than medical judgment. When release is being considered, it is better to be cautious, to be sure that the time is really ripe.

---

[1] Walker and McCabe, *op. cit.*, chaps. 9–10 and especially at p. 235.
[2] For a general review, see G. H. L. Fridman, "Mental Incompetency" (1963), 79 L.Q.R. 502, (1964), 80 L.Q.R. 84.
[3] The standard work on the subject is Heywood and Massey, *Court of Protection Practice* (9th Edn 1971).

A legally trained commentator questions this paternalistic attitude. "It may be for instance perfectly true that an attractive subnormal girl is likely to become pregnant if released. But is detention permissible for the purpose only of protecting her from an unwanted pregnancy?"[1] The same sort of conflict of interests was revealed in *Re V.E.*[2] The patient had suffered brain damage as a result of tubercular meningitis. This caused a personality disorder: she became an uncontrolled alcoholic and drugtaker, neglected personal hygiene, wandered in the streets as a serious hazard to traffic, and was prone to miss the insulin injections essential for the treatment of a diabetic condition. She had no relatives or friends who could look after her, and there was no suitable accommodation for her other than the hospital. Despite all this, the Divisional Court of the Queen's Bench Division held that she must be discharged, for she was a psychopath aged forty, and there is no legal power to use compulsory admission procedures in the case of psychopaths aged over twenty-one, except those available to the criminal courts in the case o persons charged with offences.[3]

The Mental Health Act 1959, which contains the legal rules on this subject, is long and complicated, largely because of the need to accommodate these conflicting legal and medical interests. The reader should decide for himself whether the correct balance has been struck.

COMPULSORY ADMISSION TO HOSPITAL

The decision to admit a patient is for the hospital authorities and staff. They act upon an application for admission, and the legal rules relating to compulsory admission procedures are largely concerned with the contents of the application, and the grounds on which it can be made. The application itself, duly completed, is authority for the detention of the patient and his conveyance to hospital.

The persons most likely to be concerned with the admission of a patient, apart from the doctors and hospital authorities, are the mental welfare officer and the "nearest relative". The mental welfare officer, appointed by the local authority social services department, is under a legal duty to make an application for the admission of a patient in a proper case, having regard to the wishes of the patient's relatives—the relatives may see the need for hospital treatment but be reluctant to sign the forms themselves—and other relevant circumstances.[4] The

---

[1] J. C. Wood, "Mental Health Review Tribunals" (1970), Medicine, Science and the Law, 89.

[2] [1973] Q.B. 452; [1972] 3 All E.R. 373.

[3] See Mental Health Act 1959, ss. 26 (2) (*a*), 60 (1) (*a*); and p. 147-9, below.

[4] Mental Health Act 1959, s. 31 (1). "Hospital" includes a mental nursing home; there are elaborate provisions in Part III of the Act, and in Regulations, for the registration and inspection of nursing homes.

phrase "other relevant circumstances" is beloved of the draftsmen of Acts of Parliament; they do not have to say what it means, and no-one can accuse them of having forgotten any salient point. In this context the relevant circumstances will obviously include the possibility of care in the community or as an informal in-patient; the general attitude of the family and neighbours; the care which they can give and will give to the patient. Clearly the wishes of the patient's relatives are not the *only* relevant circumstances. If the mental welfare officer thinks the case is not a proper one for the use of compulsory procedures he should so advise those concerned.

When the admission procedure is put in action by the patient's general practitioner, as will often be the case, the mental welfare officer may find that he is expected to act in an entirely ministerial role, simply signing the appropriate forms and arranging for the patient's removal to hospital. The Act puts upon the welfare officer, in this situation, the responsibility of making the application[1]; he clearly has a discretion and there may be circumstances where he should refuse to make the application. Obviously much depends on the knowledge and experience of the parties, both generally and in relation to the circumstances of the particular patient.[2]

The "nearest relative" is the person whom the lawyer would perceive as representing the interests of the patient. This may not always be realistic, for some relatives are anxious that a difficult person should be put away in an institution. There are complicated rules for determining who is the nearest relative. The Act lists nine categories: husband or wife (including persons living together as "common-law" spouses, but excluding spouses permanently separated, or deserted); son or daughter; father; mother; brother or sister; grandparent; grandchild; uncle or aunt; and nephew or niece. Except in the case of spouses and parents, anyone aged under eighteen is excluded, as is anyone living outside the United Kingdom. The general rule is that the categories are looked at in the given order of priority, and the eldest person in any category, regardless of sex, is the nearest relative.[3]

It can easily happen that the patient is closest to, or even living with, a relative who is not the nearest relative under these rules. The nearest relative can transfer his powers under the Act to someone else, and this is the sort of case in which he might be advised to do so.[4] Where parental rights in respect of a child are vested in the local authority, those rights include the powers of the nearest relative.[5] In certain

---

[1] Mental Health Act 1959, s. 54.
[2] See the Percy *Report*, para. 404.
[3] Mental Health Act 1959, s. 49; Guardianship Act 1973, s. 1 (8).
[4] See Mental Health (Hospital and Guardianship) Regulations 1960 (S.I. 1960 No. 1241), reg. 25.
[5] Mental Health Act 1959, s. 50; this applies to children subject to a care order under the Children and Young Persons Act 1969 and to other children in whose case parental rights have been assumed under s. 2 of the Children Act 1948.

cases, where for example there is no nearest relative, or he is himself mentally disordered, the county court can appoint an acting nearest relative; a mental welfare officer can apply to the court for such an appointment, and the local authority may be appointed to act.[1]

ADMISSION FOR OBSERVATION

A compulsory admission for observation authorises the detention of the patient for up to twenty-eight days. An application must be made by the nearest relative or a mental welfare officer and it must be supported by written recommendations from two doctors.[2] Special forms are prescribed. The Act provides that an application can only be made if the patient is stated to be suffering from such mental disorder that his detention for observation is warranted for at least a limited period, and that he ought to be detained in the interests of his own health or safety or with a view to the protection of other persons. The prescribed forms require the doctors to state that informal admission is inappropriate,[3] but it is not necessary to specify the type of mental disorder from which the patient is suffering.

Once admitted for observation, the patient can only be discharged by the responsible medical officer or the hospital authorities.[4] There is no provision for judicial review or other special safeguards; there is no time for any elaborate procedures, and short-term detention for observation scarcely warrants them.

EMERGENCY ADMISSION FOR OBSERVATION

In an emergency, a patient can be admitted for observation without all the normal requirements being met. The application may be made by a mental welfare officer or any relative (not just the nearest relative) of the patient; only one medical recommendation is needed, given if practicable by a doctor acquainted with the patient, normally his general practitioner. If a second recommendation is later obtained the admission is treated as a full admission for observation; so long as it remains an emergency one it only authorises the detention of the patient for seventy-two hours.[5]

The case must be one of "urgent necessity", and compliance with the usual procedure must be thought likely to "involve undesirable delay".[6] These are of course imprecise terms, but it is clearly intended that this emergency procedure should be wholly exceptional. The convenience

---

[1] Mental Health Act 1959, s. 52.
[2] There are elaborate provisions as to who those doctors should be: see below, and Mental Health Act 1959, s. 28.
[3] *Ibid.*, ss. 25, 27; Mental Health (Hospital and Guardianship) Regulations 1960 (S.I. 1960 No. 1241), Forms 1, 3A, 3B.
[4] Mental Health Act 1959, s. 47.
[5] *Ibid.*, s. 29. A similar procedure exists for persons who are already informal patients: see *ibid.*, s. 30.
[6] *Ibid.*, s. 29 (1), (2).

of doctors, social workers or relatives is not a sufficient justification for its use; the complaint is sometimes heard that mental welfare officers, especially if relatively inexperienced, are over-eager to use the emergency procedure.

ADMISSION FOR TREATMENT

Admission for treatment is a very serious step. The patient can be detained for up to one year in the first instance, with one extension of one year, and then any number of further periods of two years.[1] The safeguards are correspondingly more elaborate.

The application must be made either by the nearest relative or by a mental welfare officer, but the nearest relative is in a special position. An officer contemplating making an application must consult the nearest relative unless that proves impracticable; so long as the person who appears to be the nearest relative is consulted the legal requirement is satisfied, and the application will not be invalid should it be discovered that an honest mistake has been made, and that some other person is actually a nearer relative. If the nearest relative objects to the making of an application, the officer cannot proceed.[2] In this situation we have the classic conflict between the interests of the patient as seen by the doctors and social workers and the rights of the patient represented by the nearest relative's objections. The only way this conflict can be resolved is by the courts. If agreement cannot be reached, the mental welfare officer may seek to have the local authority or some other person appointed by the county court as acting nearest relative on the ground that the actual nearest relative is objecting unreasonably.[3]

It was an application of this sort which was before the court in *W*. v. *L*. (*mental health patient*), the facts of which have already been given. The social services department took the view that Mrs L was acting unreasonably in opposing the compulsory admission of her husband for treatment. He needed treatment, there was a risk to the baby, and resistance to admission procedures was unreasonable. As the Court of Appeal recognised, there was another side to the picture, the wife's: "She says she knows her husband better than anyone else does; she will see that he takes his tablets; she is quite satisfied that neither she nor the baby will be in danger. So if you look at it from her own point of view, she may not be unreasonable. The court held that the question of "reasonableness' had to be looked at objectively, and not just from the relative's point of view; the question to be answered was what would a reasonable relative in her position do, and the court's answer on those facts was: assent to the making of an application for admission.[4]

---

[1] Mental Health Act 1959, s. 43.
[2] *Ibid.*, s. 27 (2).
[3] *Ibid.*, s. 52 (3) (*c*).
[4] [1973] 3 All E.R. 884 at p. 889.

The application must be supported by two medical statements but these have to be more detailed and specific than is the case on an admission for observation. In particular they must specify the type of mental disorder, using the statutory classification,[1] from which the patient is suffering. If the diagnosis is of psychopathic disorder or subnormality, the application can only proceed if the patient is under twenty-one, and older patients in these categories can only be received as informal patients. As we have seen from the cases of *Re V.E.* and *W.* v. *L.* this restriction can cause difficulty in the case of psychopaths; the Percy Commission was in error in grouping them with sub-normals. In the latter case, Lawton, L.J., commenting on the fact that dangerous psychopaths over twenty-one can only be dealt with if they commit an offence, had this to say:

> "The doctor who has made the diagnosis and who on reasonable grounds expects violence and harm to others to result can only await what he thinks will happen, no doubt in a state of agonised expectation. This seems to me a clear case of the law shutting the stable door after the dangerous animal has escaped."[2]

In other cases, there is no age-limit. In all, the statements must declare the disorder warrants the detention of the patient for medical treatment and that detention is necessary in the interests of the patient's health or safety or for the protection of others.[3]

MEDICAL RECOMMENDATIONS

Even in the case of admission for treatment there is no judicial review before the decision to admit is taken; the correctness of the decision depends almost entirely on the doctors who make the medical recommendations. There are stringent rules about the time which may elapse between the examinations of the patient, and between an examination and a report based upon it; about the doctor's qualifications (one must be an approved doctor, that is be recognised[4] as having special experience in the field of mental disorder; the other should preferably have known the patient for some time); and, in particular, as to the relationship between the two doctors concerned.[5] There must be nothing which might suggest collusion. The doctors must not be partners, or in the relationship of employer and employee, or related by blood or marriage. The rules can be quite troublesome: if, for example, one doctor is the sister-in-law of someone employed as an

---

[1] I.e. mental illness, severe subnormality, subnormality or psychopathic disorder. An admission for treatment cannot be based upon the residual category of "any other disorder or disability of mind": see Mental Health Act 1959, s. 26 (2).

[2] [1973] 3 All E.R. 884 at p. 890.

[3] Mental Health Act 1959, s. 26.

[4] Under the National Health Service Reorganisation Act 1973, the recognition of approved doctors is a function of the Secretary of State delegated to Regional and Area Health Authorities.

[5] Mental Health Act 1959, ss. 27 (3), 28.

assistant by the other doctor, the application is defective.[1] It is
clearly important to ensure that each doctor knows the name of the
doctor who has prepared or will prepare the second recommendation,
so that any such relationship will come to light.

Disasters sometime happen, and they can sometimes be put right.
The Act contains what lawyers call a "slip" rule; errors in the forms
can generally speaking be corrected within fourteen days of admission.[2]

DISCHARGE

There are five principal sets of circumstances in which the authority
to detain a patient who has been admitted for treatment comes to an
end. The two most obvious are where the authority expires with the
passing of time (for example, it is not extended after the expiry of the
first year) and where the responsible medical officer or the hospital
authorities order the patient's discharge.[3]

The patient's discharge can also be ordered by his nearest relative.[4]
We have seen that the nearest relative's powers represent an important
safeguard for the patient, but that in some cases they can be overriden.
So it is here. If the hospital doctors report that a patient is likely, if
discharged, to act in a manner dangerous to himself or others, the
nearest relative cannot obtain his discharge; though he can, as we shall
see, apply to a Mental Health Review Tribunal.[5] Also if the nearest
relative exercises his discharge powers, or is thought likely to do so,
without due regard for the welfare of the patient or the interests of the
public, an application can be made to the county court for an order
appointing an acting nearest relative in his place.[6]

The patient cannot discharge himself, but can obtain his discharge
indirectly. The more regular method is an application to a Mental
Health Review Tribunal; his enquiry about such an application may
itself lead to a review of the case, and perhaps his discharge before a
Tribunal hearing is arranged.[7] The other "back-door" method is to
abscond. If the patient remains at liberty for a certain period there is
no longer any power to return him to hospital. There is of course
nothing to stop a fresh application for admission being made in suitable
cases, but it must be based on new medical recommendations based on
fresh examinations of the patient. For most groups of patient, the
period of liberty needed to earn this "discharge by operation of law" is
twenty-eight days, but in the case of sub-normal and psychopathic
patients aged over twenty-one the period is extended to six months.

---

[1] Mental Health Act 1959, s. 28 (3).
[2] *Ibid.*, s. 32.
[3] *Ibid.*, ss. 43, 47 (2).
[4] *Ibid.*, s. 47 (2).
[5] *Ibid.*, s. 48; and see pp. 150–2, below.
[6] *Ibid.*, s. 52 (3) (*d*). The displaced nearest relative retains limited powers of application to the Mental Health Review Tribunal: *ibid.*, s. 52 (6).
[7] See pp. 150–2, below.

The Percy Commission offered as a reason for this extension the fact that "it might take more than twenty-eight days to find such a patient", the real point being that, as we have seen, it is impossible to begin again with fresh applications in such cases, as the patients are over the age-limit applying to admissions for treatment.[1]

GUARDIANSHIP

Part of the philosophy of the Mental Health is reliance on care in the community rather than in the hospital wherever possible. Guardianship is a possible means of providing a framework for that care. After a procedure similar to that prescribed for a compulsory admission for treatment, a patient may be subjected to guardianship. The guardian may be the local authority or a private person; he has the same powers in relation to the patient as a parent has in relation to a child under fourteen and is under a duty to endeavour "to make arrangements for the occupation, training or employment of the patient and for his recreation and general welfare and (to) ensure that everything practicable is done for the promotion of his physical and mental health".[2] Guardianship appears to be very little used.

ADMISSION TO HOSPITAL OR GUARDIANSHIP UNDER A COURT ORDER

The criminal courts have powers to order various forms of treatment of persons found to be mentally disordered, and to order that such a person be placed under guardianship (though this latter is very seldom used in practice).[3]

HOSPITAL ORDERS

The Crown Court or a magistrates' court may deal with a convicted offender by making a hospital order. In many ways this corresponds to compulsory admission for treatment. The court must receive, orally

---

[1] Mental Health Act 1959, s. 40 (3); Percy *Report*, paras. 478–82. See also Woolf (1966), 6 B.J. Crim. 59, and (for offences of assisting and harbouring patients without leave) s. 129 of the Act.
[2] Mental Health (Hospital and Guardianship) Regulations 1960 (S.I. 1960 No. 1241), reg. 6 (1); see generally Mental Health Act 1959, ss. 33–4.
[3] See generally Walker and McCabe, *op. cit.*, and Rollin, *The Mentally Abnormal Offender and the Law*. The whole subject is under examination by a Government committee established in 1972 under the chairmanship of Lord Butler. Guardianship orders are not further considered here; nor are the special verdict of insanity under the McNaughten Rules, the notion of diminished responsibility in homicide cases, or the special procedures for those found incapable of instructing lawyers to conduct their defence. The numbers affected are tiny, but the rules, of considerable theoretical interest, are fully discussed in textbooks on criminal law or procedure.

or in writing, evidence from two doctors, at least one being an approved doctor, that the accused is suffering from a mental disorder of one of the four types defined in the Mental Health Act, and must record its findings that the accused is so suffering. The court must also be satisfied that hospital treatment is warranted, and decide "having regard to all the circumstances including the nature of the offence and the character and antecedents of the offender, and to the other available methods of dealing with him, that the most suitable method of disposing of the case is by means of a hospital order".[1]

Magistrates' courts sometimes make use of their power to make a hospital order in cases where the defendant is mentally ill or severely sub-normal, without formally recording a conviction.[2] This avoidance of stigma may well help the patient make a positive response to treatment, but the power is little known and the policy behind it is unclear. In practice it seems to be used in cases in which the offence is very trivial or the defendant is so disordered that he is incapable of making a real defence.[3]

The court has a rather difficult sentencing decision. It must decide whether treatment or punishment is to have priority. Even if the accused needs medical attention, the court may feel obliged to pass a prison sentence (which could lead to the patient's transfer to a hospital under the Home Secretary's powers),[4] but if treatment considerations predominate a hospital order is the appropriate decision.[5]

A hospital order can only be made if a hospital place is available, or will become available within twenty-eight days; any waiting period is spent in a "place of safety".[6] In practice hospital doctors can exert another form of control on the court's decisions. The courts almost always accept recommendations made by medical witnesses, and there is some reason to suppose that medical pessimism concerning the treatment of psychopaths in particular has kept down the number of hospital orders made.

Once a hospital order has been made and the patient admitted he is in much the same position as a patient admitted for treatment under the usual compulsory procedure. An important exception is that the nearest relative cannot discharge him; but application can be made to a Mental Health Review Tribunal, and the patient can use the "back-door", that is to obtain his discharge by absconding and remaining at liberty.[7]

---

[1] Mental Health (Hospital and Guardianship) Regulations 1960 s. 60 (1); see gener ally ss. 60–2 and Walker and McCabe, *op. cit.*, chaps. 4 and 5.
[2] Mental Health Act 1959, s. 60 (2).
[3] See Walker and McCabe, *op. cit.*, pp. 104–7.
[4] Under Mental Health Act 1959, s. 72.
[5] *R. v. Morris*, [1961] 2 Q.B. 237; [1961] 2 All E.R. 672. See Thomas, *Principles of Sentencing*, pp. 266–70.
[6] Mental Health Act 1959, ss. 60 (3), 63.
[7] *Ibid.*, s. 63.

RESTRICTION ORDERS

The Crown Court has power to make a special order restricting the discharge of a patient subject to a hospital order; a magistrates' court can commit an offender to the Crown Court with a view to this power being used. A restriction order may only be used if it is considered necessary for the protection of the public; and the court must consider *oral* evidence from at least one of the doctors who have reported on the accused's condition. The order may be for a stated period or for an unlimited time.[1]

While a restriction order is in force the patient can only be discharged with the consent of the Home Secretary. The powers of the hospital authorities, the nearest relative and the Mental Health Review Tribunal are all excluded, and the "back-door" is closed. In practice the Review Tribunal may well be asked for advice before an order for discharge is made; and the discharge order may contain conditions, including one of supervision by a probation or mental welfare officer.[2]

The use of restriction orders has received encouragement from the Appeal Court,[3] but there are problems in their use. The order assumes reasonably secure conditions which are not in practice readily to be found outside the three "special hospitals" of Broadmoor, Rampton and Moss Side. Only about one-half of patients subject to restriction orders are accommodated in those hospitals.

PROBATION ORDERS

Provided the offender consents, a probation order may be made which includes a condition that the probationer receives medical treatment for his mental condition. The treatment cannot be ordered for more than three years, the maximum duration of the probation order, and may be as an informal resident patient or as an out-patient. The court must receive evidence from an approved doctor that the offender's mental condition requires and may be susceptible to treatment but that it does not warrant the making of a hospital order.[4]

This type of probation order presents special problems for the social workers involved. Obviously medical considerations have first priority, and it is expressly provided that where the probationer is an out-patient, the probation officer should carry out only such supervision as is necessary for the discharge or amendment of the order.[5] But the probationer is an informal patient, free to discharge himself from hospital at any time. If he does so, he is in breach of probation,

---

[1] *Ibid.*, s. 65.
[2] *Ibid.*, ss. 65, 66.
[3] *R.* v. *Gardiner*, [1967] 1 All E.R. 895; [1967] 1 W.L.R. 464; see Walker and McCabe, *op. cit.*, pp. 94 *et seq.*
[4] Powers of Criminal Courts Act 1973, s. 3. For the, limited, use made of these powers see Grunhut, *Probation and Mental Treatment.*
[5] Powers of Criminal Courts Act 1973, s. 3 (4).

and the probation officer must decide what steps to take. The need for careful and sensitive liaison is evident.[1]

MENTAL HEALTH REVIEW TRIBUNALS

Several references have already been made to Mental Health Review Tribunals. Although admission to hospital is now a medical rather than a legal decision, the Tribunals provide the safeguard of an independent forum for the review of decisions affecting the liberty of the patient. The patient can apply to the Tribunal within six months of his compulsory admission for treatment or to guardianship (including admission under a hospital order, unless a restriction order has been made, and admission to hospital after having been under guardianship) and of each occasion on which the period of detention or guardianship is renewed.[2] In addition the patient or his nearest relative can apply to the Tribunal within twenty-eight days of the making of certain decisions which reclassify the patient, or, by declaring that a psychopathic or sub-normal offender would be likely if released to behave in a manner dangerous to himself or others, reduce the chances of discharge.[3] The nearest relative of a patient detained under a court order, and a nearest relative displaced by order of the county court, both have the right of making annual applications.[4]

Each tribunal consists of at least three members, a lawyer who is President, a medical member who examines the patient and his medical records in advance of the tribunal's meeting, and a lay member selected for his experience of administration or the social services.[5] Legal or other representation, in practice often supplied by the National Council for Civil Liberties, is permitted, but there is no legal aid. A mental welfare officer could appear as the patient's representative, but this seldom happens. The rules of procedure[6] allow for both formal and informal hearings, but are so generally drawn that there is in practice little distinction between the two procedures.

The Tribunals have limited powers and their working has been criticised on a number of grounds. The Tribunals can only consider whether a patient should be discharged or reclassified.[7] They cannot

---

[1] See A. C. West, "Medical Treatment as a condition of Probation" (1971), 11 B.J. Crim. 371.

[2] Mental Health Act 1959, ss. 31 (4), 34 (5), 41 (5), 43 (6) and 63 (4).

[3] *Ibid.*, ss. 38 (2), 44 (3) and 48 (3).

[4] *Ibid.*, ss. 52 (6) and 63 (4).

[5] *Ibid.*, s. 3 and Sched. 1. For a full and critical examination of the work of Tribunals, see C. Greenland, *Mental Illness and Civil Liberty*. See also J. C. Wood, "Mental Health Review Tribunals" (1970), Medicine, Science and the Law 86.

[6] Mental Health Review Tribunals Rules 1960 (S.I. 1960 No. 1139).

[7] Mental Health Act 1959, s. 123. In some cases reclassification as a sub-normal or psychopathic patient may lead to automatic discharge: see *Re V.E.*, [1973] Q.B. 452; [1972] 3 All E.R. 373, settling a controversy summarised in Greenland, *Mental Illness and Civil Liberty* (1970), pp. 81–3.

interfere in matters affecting his treatment, such as his placement in a secure ward or the chances of home leave, cannot order his transfer to another hospital, and, if the patient is to be discharged, cannot impose conditions as to after-care. A Tribunal must direct that a patient be discharged if they are satisfied that he is not suffering from one of the categories of mental disorder listed in the Act (even if they believe his continued detention would be in his own or society's best interests); or if they find that the patient's continued detention is not warranted in the interests of his health or safety or the protection of others (even if they are satisfied that he is mentally disordered).[1] Clearly the Tribunal has little discretion, and must sometimes reach decisions which conflict sharply with the judgment of the medical staff concerned.

The Tribunal is concerned with the facts as they exist at the time of the hearing. It is not really concerned with the state of affairs at the time of the original admission, except as part of the case-history. In particular this means that the Tribunal cannot consider any legal defects in the original application for admission. The historic remedy of *habeas corpus* is available in the courts for persons wrongly detained; it will be seldom used, for procedural defects can always be remedied by the making of a fresh application. The hospital staff and welfare officers are protected from claims for damages by discontented patients; an act done under the Mental Health Act provisions cannot be the subject of a court action unless there is evidence of bad faith, and the court itself grants leave for procedings to be taken.[2]

A major criticism of the workings of the Tribunals concerns the information on which they have to rely. The medical information should be readily available from the hospital staff and records and the examination by the medical member, though commentators have been dissatisfied even here.[3] Equally important is information about the circumstances in which the patient would find himself if he were discharged. The hospital authorities are obliged to supply a report on the facilities available for the care of the patient on discharge,[4] but this can be narrowly interpreted; the information is not always readily available from the patient himself, who will always be interviewed by the Tribunal, or from any representative who attends. Ideally there should be a full home circumstances report prepared by a mental welfare officer or other social worker, and the Tribunal has the power to adjourn to enable more information to be gathered. An experienced commentator has suggested that the Tribunal is best helped by a report which discusses the strength and stability of the home, the attitudes of those at home and of the local community to the patient (including the opportunities for training and recreation), and the possibility of work.[5]

---

[1] Mental Health Act 1959, s. 123 (1).   [2] *Ibid.*, s. 141.
[3] Greenland, *op. cit.*, pp. 63–5, 73–5.
[4] Mental Health Review Tribunal Rules, 1960 (S.I. 1960 No. 1139), r. 6, Sched. 2.
[5] J. C. Wood, *loc. cit.*, at p. 88.

A great deal must depend on the quality of the reports which the Tribunal receives. All that was said above about reports to court applies, with the added point that a tribunal hearing is not a fully adversary proceeding; the patient is often in a weak position when it comes to contesting statements which tell against him, and in some circumstances may not see parts of the reports, which may be withheld if the Tribunal considers that the disclosure of some information could be harmful to the patient. Especial care should be taken in preparing reports based, as they must often be, on case-notes compiled over a period of time: do the examples chosen reflect the *current* position? Are they balanced, or selected because of their vividness? In reporting apathy, or aggression, or homosexuality, is enough consideration given to the nature of institutional life?

Legal safeguards are of no value unless they are used. There is no certainty that the nearest relative will want to apply for the patient's discharge, so it is vital that the patient is himself properly informed of his rights of application and given advice and encouragement in completing the official forms.

IN AN EMERGENCY

The most common emergency situation concerning the mentally disordered involves the sudden onset or reccurence of serious mental disturbance, perhaps making the patient behave in a bizarre or violent fashion or reducing him to incoherence. If this condition warrants it, he can be admitted to hospital for observation under the emergency procedure already described.[1] This will meet the case of the patient taken ill at home, or work, or amongst friends, but even in these cases there may be practical problems well illustrated by the facts of *Townley* v. *Rushworth*.[2] The defendant's wife, as nearest relative, signed an application for his emergency admission. The form was taken to their doctor who, before completing it, went to the defendant's house with the defendant's brother-in-law and two policemen. When the doctor entered the defendant ordered him out and after a scuffle one of the policemen intervened and the defendant punched him, breaking his nose. The forms were eventually completed but, for reasons which are not at all clear, the defendant was charged with the criminal offence of assault occasioning actual bodily harm. The Divisional Court held that the magistrates, who convicted him, should have proceeded on the footing that as the forms were not completed at the time of entry all four men were trespassers which entitled the defendant to use some force in ejecting them. The procedural lesson is clear enough, though

---

[1] See pp. 143–4.
[2] (1963), 107 Sol. Jo. 1004.

the patient may well have proved just as difficult if the forms were in perfect order.

IN A PUBLIC PLACE

It sometimes happens that a man will be found in a confused or deranged state either in the street or in some yard or building to which the public have access. He cannot be left where he is; he must be taken to some place of safety to see what attention he needs, and perhaps to arrange for his admission to hospital for observation. He may respond voluntarily to an offer of help; if he does not or cannot, legal powers must be invoked to detain him. A police constable—and no-one else—has power to take a person found in a public place and who appears to be suffering from mental disorder and to be in immediate need of care or control, to a "place of safety", which usually means a police station. A hospital is also within the legal definition of "place of safety", but in some parts of the country the hospitals will not admit patients brought in by constables; the patient will be kept in the police station until other help can be summoned. The patient can be kept there for seventy-two hours, and the Mental Health Act spells out very clearly the purposes of the detention: "of enabling him to be examined by a medical practitioner and to be interviewed by a mental welfare officer and of making any necessary arrangements for his treatment or care".[1]

A policeman finding someone in these circumstances may well arrest him in the mistaken belief that he is drunk or under the influence of drugs. The arrest is perfectly lawful; if it later becomes clear that the detained man is mentally disordered, the usual procedure for admission to hospital can be put into operation.

ON PRIVATE PREMISES

There are further difficulties if the patient is not in any public place but on private premises. He may be being neglected or ill-treated, out of malice, fear or ignorance; or he may live alone, an elderly person or a recluse, and become incapable of looking after himself. But no-one can lawfully walk into another's house without his consent. Even the normally acceptable practice of walking up his front path or steps to ring the doorbell can be made unlawful by a suitably hostile notice. In one case, Diplock, L.J. said that a notice on a front gate, "No Admittance to Police Officers", would prevent the police from calling to make enquiries.[2] A sign, "No Doctors or Social Workers" is perhaps even less likely, but it would be effective. In any case, if the doorbell is rung and there is no response, no progress has been made.

---

[1] Mental Health Act 1959, s. 136. For studies of the use made of these powers, see Walker and McCabe, *op. cit.*, Appendix A, especially pp. 255–61, and M. D. Eilenberg and P. B. Whatmore, 'Police Admissions to a Mental Observation Ward' (1962), 2 Medicine Science and the Law 96.

[2] *Robson* v. *Hallett*, [1967] 2 Q.B. 939; [1967] 2 All E.R. 407.

The Mental Health Act gives a mental welfare officer a power of entry and inspection. Provided he is armed with a suitable identifying document and produces it on demand, the welfare officer may enter and inspect any premises (other than a hospital) where a mentally disordered patient is living if he has reasonable cause to believe that the patient is not under proper care.[1] Anyone refusing the officer entry or obstructing him will be guilty of an offence,[2] but in practice even a warning as to possible prosecution may not gain admittance, and the power does not extend to the use of force. Nor does it help where the officer is merely trying to discover whether or not there is anyone on the premises who is mentally disordered; and it certainly does not authorise him to take a patient away.

If it is felt that greater powers are needed, the mental welfare officer should obtain a warrant from a magistrate, stating his suspicions on oath. If granted, the warrant will authorise the police to enter the premises, using force if need be, and to remove a patient to a place of safety. The police must go accompanied by a mental welfare officer and a doctor. Up to seventy-two hours' detention in the place of safety is allowed;[3] prompt admission for observation normally follows.

ESCAPED PATIENTS

This phrase covers hospital in-patients who are absent without leave, including those over-staying leave of absence, and also mentally disordered persons who escape from a place of safety or while being taken to or between hospitals or other places in which they may lawfully be detained.

The legislation is very complicated but the general principle is that an escaped person may be apprehended by a police constable, a mental welfare officer, an officer on the staff of the hospital from which he is absent, and others from whose custody he may have escaped. The principal limitation on these powers is that they expire once the authority under which the patient was originally detained expires; so, a patient detained as being "mentally ill" in the strict sense of that term may not be retaken after twenty-eight days of freedom from hospital, and a patient escaping from detention in a place of safety has to be recaptured within the seventy-two-hour period.[4]

PROPERTY EMERGENCIES

A mentally disordered person may behave very irresponsibly as regards his own property. He may, for example, try to give all his property away, leaving his wife and family destitute. If the patient is

---

[1] Mental Health Act 1956, s. 22.
[2] *Ibid.*, s. 130.
[3] *Ibid.*, s. 135 (1), (3), (4).
[4] *Ibid.*, ss. 40, 135 (2), 139, 140.

admitted to hospital the local authority social services department has power to take steps to safeguard his property.[1]   In other cases, and where it is necessary to receive money or take decisions as to transactions concerning property, legal authorisation must be sought from the Court of Protection.   This court has an emergency procedure which can be invoked by a relative, the mental welfare officer, or any other concerned person; it is very rapid and leads to the granting of interim authority to act.[2]

CHILDREN

In principle the Mental Health Act 1959 applies to all mentally disordered patients whatever their age.   The only special rule applying to the young is that an application by a patient to the Mental Health Review Tribunal cannot be made before the patient's sixteenth birthday.   In practice young children will be informal patients.

It was formerly the practice to classify certain children suffering from a disability as ineducable, as "children unsuitable for education at school".   This practice was ended by the Education (Handicapped Children) Act 1970.   Such children will be classified as "requiring special educational treatment" under the Education Act 1944[3] but will remain within the educational system, whether in hospital, special schools or training centres.   The same principle applies to children with other forms of handicap such as autism or other forms of early childhood psychosis.[4]

THE HANDICAPPED

There is a large body of legal rules dealing with the special problems of the mentally disordered, and some of it has been examined in this chapter.   There is no equivalent corpus of law affecting patients suffering from other forms of illness or disability.   The general law applies to most situations: for example a medical examination of a patient, or surgical operation, or dental treatment, may constitute an assault unless the patient gives his consent or (probably) the patient is unable to give his consent (due to unconsciousness or other incapacity) and the treatment is necessary to save his life.   If the patient is under

---

[1] National Assistance Act 1948, s. 48; Local Government Act 1972, Sched. 23, para. 2 (10).
[2] Mental Health Act 1959, s. 104.   See Heywood and Massey, *Court of Protection Practice* (9th Edn), especially at p. 43.
[3] Education Act 1944, s. 33.
[4] See Chronically Sick and Disabled Persons Act 1970, ss. 25 (deaf-blind), 26 (autism etc.) and 27 (acute dyslexia).

sixteen,[1] any necessary consent must be given on his behalf by his parent or guardian.[2]

The general responsibility of local authorities for the welfare of the handicapped derives from the National Assistance Act 1948. That Act provides that:

> "A local authority may, with the approval of the Secretary of State, and to such extent as he may direct in relation to persons ordinarily resident in the area of the local authority shall, make arrangements for promoting the welfare of . . . persons who are blind, deaf or dumb, and other persons who are substantially and permanently handicapped by illness, injury or congenital deformity or such other disabilities as may be prescribed. . . ."[3]

and this covers the provision of workshops, hostels and the maintenance of a register of disabled persons.

Many local authorities took a rather limited view of their responsibilities under this section and the resulting concern led to the passing of the Chronically Sick and Disabled Persons Act 1970. This Act was hailed as "a charter for the disabled", and there was widespread disappointment when its immediate practical effects were limited.[4] Much of the Act could only produce indirect benefits: no fewer than eight of the Act's twenty-eight substantive provisions are designed to ensure the representation of the interests of the disabled on various governmental or advisory committees; a further six sections require housing authorities and those concerned with public buildings, universities and schools to "have regard to" the special needs of the chronically sick and disabled, or to make provision as to access, parking or sanitary conveniences "so far as it is in the circumstances both practicable and reasonable" for the disabled. This form of statutory exhortation, though thoroughly desirable, does not guarantee results.

At the time the Act was passed, there was much attention given to the smallness of the number of registered disabled. Section 1 of the Act imposes a duty on all local authorities with responsibilities under section 29 of the National Assistance Act 1948 (already set out) to inform themselves of the number of persons to whom that section applies, but this falls far short of the compulsory registration of disabled persons which some advocated, though many disabled persons would strongly resent.

The main provisions of the Act which should prove of direct assistance to those in need are those dealing with vehicles, and with welfare services generally. The Act enabled the regulations governing road traffic to be relaxed to meet special needs; for example it enabled small

---

[1] Family Law Reform Act 1969, s. 8.
[2] See p. 50.
[3] S. 29, as amended by the Local Government Act 1972.
[4] There have been a number of Parliamentary debates reflecting this disappointment. One of the most informative is reported in 831 *Parliamentary Debate (Commons)*, col. 913.

electrically-driven cars provided for some child victims of the "thali-domide" disaster to be used legally on the pavement. Of wider interest was the provision for special badges for display on cars used by disabled drivers (or, in some cases, disabled passengers) and there are now exemptions in favour of cars with such badges from some of the parking regulations in towns.[1]

The most important single provision in the Act is section 2. This makes it mandatory for the local authorities with responsibilities under the National Assistance Act to provide certain facilities to persons ordinarily resident in their area in cases of need. It converts the powers existing under the earlier legislation into specific duties; a disabled or handicapped person needing these facilities can demand them as of right. The list of matters covered by the section includes

the provision of practical assistance in the persons's home;
assistance with adaptations to the home (such as ramps, widened doorways);
provision of telephone equipment, wireless and television, library books and similar recreational facilities;
provision of lectures, games, outings;
travelling to such services;
holidays in special holiday homes or elsewhere;
provision of meals in the home or elsewhere.

Some of these facilities, such as "meals-on-wheels" services, will usually be provided by the authority, but the section also covers some facilities provided by other bodies. For example, a charitable body may arrange holidays for the severely disabled or may organise modified athletics competitions for those in wheelchairs; the section would apply to participation in and travel to these facilities. What is required depends on the circumstances of the particular client: a very severely disabled person may use a Possum, an advanced machine controlled by small movements of the head or arm and operating a number of devices such as a typewriter, a television set, an alarm device, and so on; the section will cover the cost of installing special equipment enabling a telephone to be operated via the Possum.

The Chronically Sick and Disabled Persons Act applies to the sick and disabled of all ages, children, those of working age, and the elderly, and those whose handicaps are the result of some mental disorder as well as those of a purely physical nature.

---

[1] Chronically Sick and Disabled Persons Act 1970. The regulations governing the issue of badges are the Disabled Persons (Badges for Motor Vehicles) Regulations 1971 (S.I. 1971 No. 1492, amended by S.I. 1972 No. 906).

ENVOI

The preceding chapters have concentrated on those areas of law which regulate active intervention by social workers, in which there is at least a potential conflict between the social worker and the client or others concerned. This is the essential professional legal equipment of the practising social worker; without it, "he is like a bricklayer who cannot use a plumbline".[1]

Almost all social workers will find that they are turned to for advice on many other matters which have a legal content. Accidents at work, redundancy, marital problems, social security claims, housing rights—all can be raised at any time. In some of these areas individual social workers will acquire considerable expertise, and most will pick up a smattering of information; though all are outside the scope of this book.

If one of these legal problems is raised what can the social worker best do to help? There are of course legal textbooks and articles; and useful guides such as CANS, the compendious Citizens' Advice Notes. In some areas legal advice is available within the local authority establishment. There are particular types of problem on which special agencies have expertise—official or unofficial Housing Advice centres, or consumers' groups. Some urban areas have legal advice centres, and some have lawyers and social workers working side by side, an arrangement which has much to commend it for the enquirer may not realise the legal implications of his problem' or, alternatively, may not have explored the informal means of resolving his problem which the social worker may be able to identify.

In many situations the best service the social worker can give is to encourage the enquirer to make use of the official Legal Aid and Advice services. These official schemes have made limited impact in the past, but since the passing of the Legal Advice and Assistance Act 1972, now consolidated with other relevant provisions in the Legal Aid Act 1974, great attempts have been made to publicise the availability of legal services; sedate and forbidding solicitors' offices even flaunt a gaudy magenta window-sticker advertising their operation of the schemes.

---

[1] C.C.E.T.S.W., *Legal Studies in Social Work Education*, para. 4.11.

The most useful of the schemes in the present context is the "Green Form scheme" for legal advice and (limited) assistance. Under this scheme legal advice and help with letters and so on can be given, in some cases free of charge. The means limits are constantly changing but those in force from September 1974 were a maximum of £250 of disposable capital, and on the income side a maximum (for a married man with two young children) of about £24 a week for entirely free help and £38 for advice and assistance at a reduced charge. The scheme is administered by the participating solicitors with minimal formalities.

It is only in relatively rare cases that actual litigation is involved, but this will sometimes be necessary—for a divorce, or a contested adoption for example. Again legal aid is available under the Civil Legal Aid scheme. The procedure is more complicated but again the initial approach is to a solicitor. Taking the standard case used above, free aid will be available if weekly income is below £26, and a reduction in charges if the maximum of £55 is not reached. There are, inevitably, complex rules for calculating disposable income and capital.

In criminal cases, legal aid is also available but this time it is administered through the courts. The court staff and the police have the necessary forms. Some areas operate a "duty solicitor" scheme, offering legal advice facilities to defendants awaiting their first appearance in court.

There may be occasions on which the client asks the social worker to help him present his case to a court or tribunal. Subject always to agency policy, there is usually little difficulty if the hearing is before a tribunal. Parties appearing before tribunals are commonly allowed by the relevant rules of procedure to be accompanied by "a friend" who can act as spokesman. So, for example, a person involved in a matter before a Supplementary Benefit Appeal Tribunal is entitled to be accompanied by two persons, who may but need not have some sort of professional qualification, and either or both of those persons may conduct the case.[1] Legal representation is possible, but legal aid is not available and solicitors generally lack expertise in the subject-matter handled by most tribunals.

If a court case is involved there are greater difficulties. As a general rule only barristers may take an active part in the conduct of a case in the higher courts, and only barristers or solicitors in the lower courts. The party may always conduct his own case but if he does so he may be at a real disadvantage.

At least in magistrates' courts it is clear that the court may allow other people to conduct the case. It happens frquently that a police officer who is not the complainant and not a lawyer conducts prosecutions, but this is only an illustration of a rule of more general applica-

[1] Supplementary Benefits (Appeal Tribunals) Rules 1971 (S.I. 1971 No. 680), r. 11.

tion,[1] but it is not a rule which the courts are likely to use with much generosity.

To meet the difficulty which some parties felt—they needed help, but did not want, or could not afford, a lawyer—the practice of using "McKenzie men" has grown up. The name is taken from the case of *McKenzie* v. *McKenzie*,[2] in which a petitioner for divorce had conducted his own case in a complex hearing lasting ten days. The Court of Appeal, reversing the trial judge, held that it was in order for him to have sitting beside him an adviser, whether professionally qualified or not, to take notes, quietly make suggestions and generally prompt the party in the conduct of his case. There was authority dating from 1831[3] in support of this practice, but the decision in *McKenzie* v. *McKenzie*, coinciding with the great proliferation of legal advice centres, did much to made the practice fashionable.

It is not entirely clear what are the limits on the McKenzie principle. In the delightfully named case of *Mercy* v. *Persons Unknown*,[4] the Court of Appeal criticised the trial judge for having allowed a London Borough councillor with no legal qualifications to argue a case for a group of squatters. It is not clear whether the objection was to his speaking openly, as opposed to giving quiet advice, or to the appearance as advocates of what one of the Lords Justices described as "persons who might be interested in ventilating matters which were no concern of courts of law". Ultimately the courts must retain a discretion to regulate their own procedure, and the signs are that the McKenzie men fashion will be kept within fairly tight limits.

The best approach seems to be not that social workers should try to take over the lawyers' role, nor vice versa, but that both professions should learn to make better use of one another's special skills with a greater willingness to refer cases to the other profession, and to co-operate where both have a contribution to make. Then English lawyers and social workers may come to deserve those flattering declarations of mutual esteem with which this book began.

---

[1] *O'Toole* v. *Scott*, [1965] A.C. 939; [1965] 2 All E.R. 240; *Simms* v. *Moore*, [1970] 2 Q.B. 327; [1970] 3 All E.R. 1.
[2] [1971] P. 33; [1970] 3 All E.R. 1034.
[3] *Collier* v. *Hicks* (1831), 2 B. & Ad. 663, at p. 669 per Lord Tenterden, C.J.
[4] (1974), *Times*, June 5.

THE CHILDREN BILL

A Government Bill was introduced in December 1974 to give effect to the recommendations of the Houghton Committee on the Adoption of Children and to deal with various other matters affecting the care and protection of children. This appendix indicates the principal contents of the bill, following the order of treatment in the chapters of this book. If the bill becomes law in the form in which it was introduced its main provisions will take effect on 1st January 1976. It must be stressed that the bill is likely to be changed as it goes through the legislative process; and some matters will be covered by regulations and Rules of Court which have yet to be published.

REPORTS TO COURT

The bill will add further to the number of different types of report to court. In the adoption area the court will in some cases appoint an "adoption officer" as well as, or as an alternative to, the guardian *ad litem*. Reports will be submitted directly to the court by the placing agency or, in non-agency cases, by the local authority conducting the welfare supervision. The local authority will also report in cases concerning "custodianship", a new concept explained below. The bill itself does not contain the important procedural details about these reports (e.g. who is to have access to them); these will be in Rules of Court.

The court will also be able to call for reports on an application by parents or others who jointly exercise parental rights or jointly perform parental duties for a court order resolving a dispute between them as to a particular right or duty. The procedural provisions of s. 6 of the Guardianship Act 1973 (see p. 34) will be extended to this new type of case.

TERMINOLOGY IN CHILDREN'S LEGISLATION

The text (pp. 38-9) refers to the confused terminology in this area. The bill proposes that "child" should mean a person under 18 in the bill itself and all future legislation, and substitutes "child" for "infant" in the Adoption Act 1958 and for "minor" in the Guardianship of

Minors Act 1971. New definitions of "parental rights and duties", "legal custody" and "actual custody" are proposed.

REPRESENTATION OF CHILDREN'S INTERESTS

In most court cases involving children, the procedural rules assume that the child's parent or guardian can represent the child's interests as well as his own. In practice there may well be a conflict of interest, and the bill will enable a separate guardian *ad litem* to be appointed for the child in certain cases under the Children and Young Persons Act 1969. The parents may be separately represented, with provision for legal aid.

SECTION 2 RESOLUTIONS

The bill proposes a new section 2 for the Children Act 1948. The new version sets out the existing statutory grounds, including those now contained in section 48 of the Children and Young Persons Act 1963, with minor changes to allow for the existence of custodians as well as guardians. Two new grounds are added:

   (i) that the child has been in local authority care under section 1, or in the care of a voluntary organisation, or partly the one and partly the other, for three years—but the child must be in local authority care at the time of the resolution;

  (ii) that a resolution has been made on one of the grounds numbered (ii) to (vii) in the text (pp. 50–2) in respect of one parent, and the child is, or is likely to become, a member of a household comprising the child, and his other parent—this is designed to deal with the problem referred to at pp. 53–4.

The provisions in the present Act dealing with the procedure for objecting to a resolution are re-drafted and clarified, and an appeal to a Divisional Court is allowed against the order of a juvenile court either confirming or terminating a resolution.

CARE AND SUPERVISION AFTER A CUSTODIANSHIP APPLICATION

Under the scheme proposed by the bill, an application for custodianship could lead to the child being committed to the care of the local authority or placed under supervision; the rules applying in similar cases under the Guardianship of Minors Act 1971 (see pp. 73–4) would be extended to custodianship cases.

CHILDREN IN CARE

The bill would restate the general duty of local authorities in care cases, substituting for the provision set out on p. 75 the following:

In reaching any decision relating to a child in their care, a local authority shall take full account of the need to safeguard and promote the welfare of the child throughout his childhood; and shall so far as practicable ascertain the wishes and feelings of the child regarding the decision and give due consideration to them, having regard to his age and understanding.

The rights of a parent to demand the return of his child under section 1 (3) of the 1948 Act would be curtailed. If the child had been in the care of the local authority for 12 months, it would be an offence for the parent to remove his child unless he either obtained the consent of the authority or gave 28 days' notice of his intentions (which would of course give time for a section 2 resolution to be passed).

CUSTODIANSHIP

The position of foster-parents would be greatly affected by Part II of the bill dealing with custodianship. The courts could give legal custody of a child to any person with whom the child had lived for periods totalling three years (and including the last three months); and, if the application was supported by the person (or local authority) which had legal custody, then to any relative or step-parent with whom the child had lived for the last three months, or other foster-parent with whom the child had lived for periods totalling 12 months (and including the last three months). Once a custodianship application was made by a person with whom the child had lived for three years, it would be an offence for the child to be removed from him (e.g. by the natural parent) without leave of the court.

ADOPTION

The bill would implement almost all the recommendations of the Houghton Committee noted in chapter 8. As they are there dealt with in context, it is unnecessary to repeat them here; but this in no way minimises the importance of the proposed changes.

Some procedural changes are not covered in the bill (e.g. that the detailed duties of a guardian *ad litem* should no longer be prescribed) but may be included in new Rules of Court. The recommendation to extend the concept of guardianship to assist relatives, step-parents and foster-parents has, as noted above, emerged in the bill as "custodianship". Similarly what the Committee called "relinquishment" proceedings will now lead to an order that the child is "free for adoption". One recommendation not implemented is that there should be a definition of "unreasonableness" in relation to the withholding of consent; understandably the draftsman could not improve on that splendidly all-embracing term.

Finally, an important feature of the bill is the new statement of a general duty applying to the courts and adoption agencies alike:

> "In reaching any decision relating to the adoption of a child, a court or adoption agency shall take full account of the need to safeguard and promote the welfare of the child throughout his childhood."

Provision for taking the child's own views into consideration is also made, as in the case of children in care, noted above.

INDEX

PRINTED AND BOUND IN GREAT BRITAIN BY
BUTLER AND TANNER LTD, FROME AND LONDON